J.K. LASSER'S™

WINNING WITH YOUR 401(k)

Look for these and other titles from J.K. Lasser™—Practical Guides for All Your Financial Needs

J.K. Lasser's Pick Winning Stocks by Edward F. Mrkvicka, Jr.

J.K. Lasser's Invest Online by LauraMaery Gold and Dan Post

J.K. Lasser's Year-Round Tax Strategies by David S. De Jong and Ann Gray Jakabcin

J.K. Lasser's Taxes Made Easy for Your Home-Based Business by Gary W. Carter

J.K. Lasser's Finance and Tax for Your Family Business by Barbara Weltman

J.K. Lasser's Pick Winning Mutual Funds by Jerry Tweddell with Jack Pierce

J.K. Lasser's Your Winning Retirement Plan by Henry K. Hebeler

J.K. Lasser's Winning with Your 401(k) by Grace W. Weinstein

J.K. Lasser's Strategic Investing After 50 by Julie Jason

J.K. Lasser's Winning with Your 403(b) by Pam Horowitz

J.K. Lasser's Winning Financial Strategies for Women by Rhonda M. Ecker and Denise Gustin-Piazza

J.K. LASSER'S™

WINNING WITH YOUR 401(k)

Grace W. Weinstein

John Wiley & Sons, Inc.

New York • Chichester • Weinheim • Brisbane • Singapore • Toronto

This book is printed on acid-free paper. ♾

Published by John Wiley & Sons, Inc.
Published simultaneously in Canada.

Library of Congress Cataloging-in-Publication Data:
Weinstein, Grace W.
J.K. Lasser's winning with your 401(k)
p. cm. — (J.K. Lasser—practical guides series)
Includes index.
ISBN 0-471-39773-3 (pbk. : alk. paper)
1. 401(k) plans. 2. Retirement income—United States—Planning. 3. Old age pensions—United States. 4. Individual retirement accounts—United States. 5. Investments—United States. 6. Income tax—United States. 7. Finance, Personal—United States. I. Series.
HD7105.45.U6 W45 2001
332.024'01—dc21

2001026129

Printed in the United States of America.

10 9 8 7 6 5 4 3 2 1

For Steve, always

Acknowledgments

I am indebted to the following for generously sharing their knowledge, research data, and support: CCH, Inc.; the Employee Benefit Research Institute (EBRI); Hewitt Associates; the Investment Company Institute; William M. Mercer, Inc.; the Profit Sharing/401(k) Council of America; T. Rowe Price; Spectrem Group; and the Vanguard Group. Special thanks, too, to Marvin Rotenberg, national director of retirement services for Fleet Bank's Private Clients Group, who provided a technical review of the complex rules regarding distributions from tax-sheltered retirement plans. And a vote of thanks (with love) to my daughter, Janet W. Mercadante of Prudential Securities, a financial adviser who specializes in 401(k) plans.

G.W.W.

Contents

PART 1

New Rules of the Retirement Game

CHAPTER 1

The Ball Is in Your Court

The introduction of the 401(k) plan and the related 403(b) and 457 plans has made a huge difference in the way we save for our retirement years. These defined contribution plans—so called because the amount you can contribute, and not the benefit you will receive, is defined—may be the best thing to come along in decades. These plans let you eliminate some taxes (contributions are pre-tax; they come off the top of your salary) and defer others (earnings are compounded and no income tax is due until the money is withdrawn). You usually get to choose from a wide array of investment vehicles. And you may get to invest some of your employer's money as well as your own, if your company matches contributions. It doesn't get much better in the world of saving for retirement.

And make no mistake: *you must save* for your retirement. No one else cares about your future as much as you do. Even if you still have a traditional employer-paid pension at work, no one else is going to make sure that you have enough income to sustain what may be a very long retirement indeed.

"Retirement is in the midst of a radical redefinition. It's growing longer, getting better." That's the conclusion of a new study by the

National Council on the Aging. But NCOA also asks, "Are Americans financially prepared for 30+ years of vital aging?" If you are prepared, you owe thanks, in large part, to wise management of your 401(k).

Neal Cutler, Director of Survey Research at NCOA, notes: "Retirement used to be defined by what one was no longer doing—not parenting, not working, not actively involved. Increasingly, it will be defined by what one does do—second career, volunteer work, travel, sport activities."

"What one does do," however, may be limited by the amount of money available to fund a desirable retirement lifestyle. Here, too, the NOCA study is optimistic. People tend to worry about having enough retirement income as they near retirement, but their anticipation is generally worse than the reality. More than nine out of ten of the NCOA respondents—including 84 percent of those age 65 years or older—thought not having enough money to live on was a serious problem for people over age 65. By contrast, 36 percent of those over age 65 found that it was a personal problem.

Although 36 percent is a significant portion of the over-65 population, retirees in general have seen their income increase in recent decades. For one thing, the booming bull market lifted the fortunes of retirees along with those of younger investors. But no one should count on an endless bull market. Bridget A. Macaskill, president and CEO of OppenheimerFunds, points out: "Retirement security is a moving target. . . . The low inflation and 25 percent annual stock market returns of recent years are phenomenal in every respect. From a retirement planning perspective, it's a bad idea to count on them."

It's also a bad idea to figure that you won't live very long after you retire. The 2000 Retirement Confidence Survey—cosponsored by the Employee Benefit Research Institute (EBRI), the American Savings Education Council (ASEC), and Mathew Greenwald & Associates—found that many workers may be preparing for an unrealistically short retirement. Eighteen percent expect retirement to last for no more than 10 years, and another 15 percent believe that they will spend 11 to 19 years in retirement. Yet, the report goes on, "Half of men reaching age 65 can expect to be alive at 82, and some will make it to 100 and older, while half of women reaching age 65 can expect to be alive at 86, and some will make it to 100 and older."

Life expectancies are always expressed as averages; many people live considerably longer. Remember, too, that the longer you live, the longer you can expect to live. At age 75, the average life expectancy is 11 years. At age 85, it is still six years. So it's a mistake, in the view of most financial planners, to plan retirement income as if it will not be needed beyond age 85. It's much wiser to plan as if you will live at least to age 90. Today, you can do the planning. You can take charge of your future.

Your Future Is in Your Hands

In a retirement revolution going on around the world, government and corporate retirement programs are giving way to retirement income funded and managed by workers. How well you perform these tasks—how much you contribute and how wisely you invest—will determine how well you will live during your retirement.

This might be called the third era in history, in terms of providing income during retirement.

In the first and longest period, there was no "retirement" as such because most people simply didn't live long enough. The life span was considerably shorter than it is today. In 1900, the average life expectancy at birth was a little more than 47 years. As recently as 1940, the average life expectancy at birth was just 62.9 years. As a result, most people died in the saddle. The relatively few who lived for the Biblical three-score-and-ten years either kept right on working or relied on their own savings—or, more likely, on their families' support.

The second period lasted about 50 years. Social Security, designed to provide a foundation for retirement income, came into being in 1935. And, as the average life span gradually lengthened, private employers began to provide pension plans for their workers. These "defined benefit" plans, funded entirely by the employer, provided a monthly benefit based on a formula that typically included the employee's age, income, and length of service. These traditional pensions worked well in an era when many people spent the bulk of their working life with a single employer.

Today, it's a brave new world. There are still traditional defined benefit pension plans, especially at the largest companies, but far more workers are covered under the new umbrella of defined contribution plans. The best known plan is the 401(k), named after the previously obscure section of the Internal Revenue Code that actuary Theodore Benna reportedly unearthed as he pored over the Code in 1981. 401(k) plans are now found throughout the corporate world.

Defined contribution plans have even become a global phenomenon. The United States is way ahead of the game, but the rest of the industrialized world is rapidly catching up. According to the benefits consulting firm of William M. Mercer, defined contribution arrangements account for 60 percent of all employer-sponsored retirement plans in the United States and are expected to reach 70 percent by 2003. Worldwide, defined contribution plans account for half of retirement plans in developed nations. Although the move from guaranteed pensions to employee-funded savings is a political football—particularly when it comes to handling the transition—Japan, Australia, Canada, and the United Kingdom are all moving in this direction. In the United Kingdom, a new defined contribution arrangement became available to almost everyone on April 1, 2001.

In the United States, meanwhile, defined contribution plans have outdistanced defined benefit plans and are solidly entrenched. In 1984, defined contribution plans held $92 billion in assets, according to the Profit Sharing/401(k) Council of America (PSCA). By 1999, these plans held $1.7 trillion in assets. The number of participants rose in the same period from 7.5 million to 34 million, and from under 40 percent of eligible employees to about 80 percent. The average account balance rose from $12,200 in 1984 to abut $50,000 in 1999, thanks at least in part to the long bull market in stocks. The 401(k) clearly dominates the retirement saving scene, but variations on the theme include 403(b) plans, available to employees of nonprofit entities such as schools and hospitals, and 457 plans, for employees of government agencies and some state university systems.

The defined contribution concept has spread like wildfire, for several reasons. Employers like the idea because employees put up most of the money and, not incidentally, assume the investment risk. (In almost 5 percent of defined contribution plans, according to the most recent PSCA survey, employers still make the investment decisions. As a general rule, however, employees make the decisions and assume the risk.)

Employers pay for administration and may choose to make matching contributions. Employees like being able to put up pre-tax dollars and take the entire account with them if they move. Many, although far from all, enjoy taking charge of the investment decisions. Because defined contribution plans have advantages for both employers and employees, they have made a quantum leap in the past 15 years. In 1984, there were 17,000 401(k) plans in the United States. In 1999, according to the latest PSCA survey, there were 340,000.

Recent growth, by some measures, has been even more spectacular. Assets in 401(k) plans grew an average of 18 percent a year from

1990 to 1999. The Investment Company Institute reports that $385 billion in assets in 1990 grew to an estimated $1.7 trillion at year-end 1999. Much of this money is invested in mutual funds. Combined with funds in other tax-sheltered retirement accounts, such as IRAs, a total of $1.98 trillion was held in mutual funds within retirement plans at year-end 1999. Some of that growth has been fueled by stock market growth. At the same time, this money spurs stock market growth and may be partly responsible for the unprecedented bull market of the 1990s. (It may also be partially responsible for preventing a major downturn, despite the market's enormous volatility. Employees are less likely to cash in investments made within the tax-sheltered umbrella of retirement plans.)

What does this phenomenon mean to you? You gain significant tax advantages by contributing before-tax dollars to a 401(k) plan and allowing the contributions and earnings (along with any employer match) to grow, tax-deferred. In this era of job mobility, there are also significant advantages in having a portable retirement plan. You can take your money with you to a new employer if you change jobs, or roll it over into an Individual Retirement Account (IRA). And there is a decided advantage in investing steadily through automatic payroll deductions (Table 1.1). Studies have shown that, over the long term, steady investing counts more toward returns than the selection of specific investment vehicles. (You'll find more on investing in Chapters 4 through 7.)

There are some potential drawbacks to 401(k) plan participation. One disadvantage is that the investment choices may be limited. This concern has diminished as employers have added choices to the investment menu. The average plan now has 11.5 investment alternatives, up from an average of 9.6 in 1998—but some plans, especially those offered by small employers, may have only three or four choices. Another possible disincentive to saving through a 401(k) plan is that your money is tied up for a long period of time. You can get at it if you really need it (see Chapter 9), but at significant cost.

The biggest drawback may be uncertainty. When a retirement *benefit* is defined, you know exactly how much you will receive. When the *contribution* is defined—as it is in the 401(k) and its related plans—you know how much you are permitted to contribute but you don't know how much you'll eventually receive. Your retirement income will depend on how much you put in during your work years and how well the money is invested. You may have more control over

TABLE 1.1 Why Employees Participate in a 401(k) Plan

REASON	PERCENTAGE OF PARTICIPANTS SURVEYED
Concern about funding retirement	85
Company match*	67
Tax-deferred status of contributions	64
Payroll deduction	55
Ability to make a hardship withdrawal*	23
Ability to take a loan*	19
Advice of friend or family members	15
Advice from fellow employees	10

* Asked of those in plans that offer these features.

401(k) Participants: Characteristics, Contributions, and Account Activity, 2000. Reprinted by permission of Investment Company Institute (www.ici.org).

your future retirement income, but you have no way of predicting what that retirement income will be.

Your best bet is to make the most of your 401(k). Contribute as much as you can, within plan limits, and invest those contributions in a diversified portfolio of investment vehicles that blend with the investments you hold outside your tax-sheltered accounts.

Reading this book, and referring to it as questions arise later, puts you a step ahead. If you participate in a 401(k) plan, you are likely to be better educated and more financially secure than employees who opt out of the plan, according to an Investment Company Institute study of plan participants. And, as certified financial planner Michael K. Stein wrote, in the *Journal of Financial Planning,* people who take an interest in their future are more likely to outlive the average population because they are more apt to eat well, exercise, and seek proper medical care. And, of course, they are more likely to be financially prepared.

Shifting Work Patterns

How much money you will have in retirement also depends on two other factors: (1) how much job hopping you do during your work life and (2) when you retire.

Job hopping can mess up the amount received in a traditional defined benefit pension because the formula is typically based on age, income, and length of service. Many plans key the benefit to the five highest-paid years—often, the last pre-retirement years. If you don't stick around very long, you don't get much of a pension. Stay on the job for 30 years but retire early, and you may still lose out. Before you decide to retire early and take monthly checks from a defined benefit pension plan, look at the plan's provisions. You will definitely lose out by retiring early because you won't have as many years of service. You will probably lose out by not having your salary increases in those additional years factored into your pension formula. And you may lose out—you need to check this with your employer—if the company pension plan reduces pensions by a specified percentage for each year of early retirement, that is, if you leave before the company's "normal" retirement age.

But defined contribution plans are portable, right? Well, yes and no. You are always entitled to your own contributions and the earnings on those contributions. But both the date of an employer match, if any, and how long you must wait before being enrolled in a new employer's 401(k) plan can have a significant impact on the amount of money you'll accumulate toward retirement.

These red flags will be explored in more detail in later chapters, but keep them in mind if you're considering a job change. Let's say you miss out on $4,000 in contributions because you switched jobs, and you must wait a year before you can participate in the new employer's plan. Assuming annual growth of 10 percent, you lose out on almost $70,000 in your retirement nest egg 30 years down the road. This is likely to become less problematic as more employers move to immediate eligibility for plan participation. By year-end 1999, according to PSCA, 40 percent of all companies—and 57 percent of companies with more than 5,000 employees—offered newly hired employees immediate participation in the 401(k) plan. Find out the rules your new employer applies to 401(k) contributions, and try to time a move accordingly.

The age at which you retire also affects how much money you'll have. Keep on working and you can keep on contributing to your 401(k) plan. Retire early, on the other hand, and you'll have to fund more years from lower total accumulations. And, inevitably, inflation will be eating away at the value of the dollars you depend on. Identifying and meeting your retirement income goals will be discussed more fully in Chapter 4.

Many people, these days, seem to want to retire early—prior to age 65. Why 65? It has been pegged as the "normal" retirement age by the Social Security Administration from its inception, but this arbitrary retirement age actually stems from a decision made by German Chancellor Otto von Bismarck when the first government pension program began. Few Germans then reached age 65, so pegging it as the age when retirement benefits would begin was a money-saving measure.

Many things have changed. As we live longer, on average, we retire earlier. It's important to note, however, that there can be a gap between expectation and actuality. Nearly half of today's workers, according to the 2000 Retirement Confidence Survey, expect to retire at age 65 or later (Table 1.2). But most retirees report actual retirement ages younger than 65. Sometimes, early retirement is planned. Sometimes it's a response to circumstances beyond the individual's control, such as ill health or company layoffs.

The average age of retirement was 66 in the late 1950s. It is now 62. At the same time, faced with fiscal pressures, Social Security is gradually extending the "normal" retirement age. The age when full retirement benefits may be obtained remains 65 only for those born by December 31, 1937. It becomes 67 for those born in 1960 and thereafter (see Table 1.4, p. 14). They can still collect reduced benefits starting at age 62, but benefits once reduced stay reduced—a fact that could pose a problem as the years go by.

TABLE 1.2 Expected and Actual Retirement Age: 2000

	EXPECTED (% OF WORKERS)	ACTUAL (% OF RETIREES)
Age 54 or younger	9	14
Ages 55–59	13	19
Age 60	12	6
Ages 61–64	10	31
Age 65	28	10
Age 66 or older	19	13
Never retire	4	NA

Sources: Employee Benefit Research Institute, American Savings Education Council, and Mathew Greenwald & Associates.

In any case, you may want to continue working—at least part-time—throughout your sixties and possibly beyond. Even if you don't need the money—and you may not, if you play your cards right—you may still want the stimulation. A recent survey of baby boomers, the segment of the population born between 1946 and 1964, indicated that more than seven out of 10 expect to work part-time in retirement. In fact, as Table 1.3 shows, earnings make up a key component of retirement income.

But Table 1.3 shows averages, across income levels. The truth is that workers in the lowest income brackets rely on Social Security for 80 percent of their retirement income. The 20 percent of retirees in the highest income brackets—those with annual pre-retirement income of $38,000 or more—receive just 18 percent of their retirement income from Social Security.

Sources of Retirement Income

This book focuses on maximizing your 401(k) benefits, but you need to analyze all of your financial resources to get a complete picture. There are other ways to beef up retirement income—you might, for example, take a reverse mortgage on your house—but the primary sources for most people are: Social Security, continued earnings and personal savings, pensions, and defined contribution plans.

Social Security

As a rule of thumb, you will need 70 to 80 percent of your pre-retirement income for a comfortable retirement. Social Security currently provides a bit less than 40 percent of the pre-retirement

TABLE 1.3 Sources of Income for Americans Age 65 and Older

Social Security retirement benefits	38%
Earnings	21
Asset income	20
Pensions	19
Other (Veterans' benefits, etc.)	2

Source: Social Security Administration.

income of an average worker, defined as someone earning about $35,000 in the year before retirement. Earn more and you'll receive a smaller proportion of your pre-retirement income from Social Security. At $80,400, the maximum earnings on which the Social Security tax (formally called FICA) is levied in 2001, the "replacement ratio" is about 25 percent. In other words, those who earned the maximum will receive no more than 25 percent of the portion of their pre-retirement pay that was subject to the Social Security tax, and nothing at all for their earnings above that level.

Put another way, the average Social Security recipient who retired at 65 in January 2001 currently receives $804 a month in retirement benefits, and the maximum benefit for a 65-year-old worker who retired in January 2001 is $1,536. "It's not a generous system," in the words of former Social Security Commissioner Kenneth S. Apfel, "although two-thirds of today's elderly live on it."

On the plus side, Social Security retirement checks, unlike most pension checks, are adjusted each year for inflation. And, unlike the two-thirds of today's elderly who are living on their Social Security checks, you have the decided benefit of participating in a 401(k) plan at work, thereby significantly boosting your future retirement income.

The not-so-happy news is that many recipients must now pay income tax on their Social Security retirement benefits. Half of the benefits are taxable for single recipients with "provisional income" between $25,000 and $34,000 and for married couples filing jointly with income from $32,000 to $44,000. As much as 85 percent of the benefits are subject to income tax if you earn more than $34,000 as a single person, or $44,000 as a married couple filing jointly. "Provisional income" is defined as modified adjusted gross income plus tax-exempt interest.

The tax rules are complicated (of course), but the most important fact to bear in mind may be that the interest from municipal bonds—a mainstay of many retirees' investment portfolios, and otherwise tax-free—is counted in calculating whether Social Security retirement benefits are taxable. Investment strategies appropriate for various life stages, including retirement, are discussed in Chapter 7.

In addition, if you plan to continue working after you retire—whether for the income or for the sheer pleasure of doing something you enjoy—you may be penalized. Fortunately, at the start of 2000, the earlier "earnings test" for Social Security recipients age 65 and over was repealed. Once you reach 65, there is no limit on how much you can earn; you will still receive full Social Security retirement benefits. But Social Security recipients between ages 62 and 64 still lose $1 in benefits for every $2 earned over a threshold that increases each year (in 2001 the amount is $10,680). If you decide to retire early but plan to keep on working—perhaps part-time, perhaps switching job fields—you may want to delay receiving Social Security retirement benefits until you reach age 65. Your benefits will be larger and you won't have to give any of them back because you are earning money.

How much will you receive? The Social Security Administration has begun mailing annual statements of estimated benefits to all workers, age 25 and over, who are not currently receiving benefits. You should receive your personalized statement each year, about three months before your birthday. The statement includes a summary of how much you can expect to receive at your normal retirement age as well as at earlier or later retirement dates. It also shows how much monthly disability income to expect if you should become severely disabled and unable to work, and how much your survivors would receive if you should die.

The statement is based on your current taxable earnings and assumes that those earnings will remain steady. For a tailor-made statement reflecting other retirement ages and earnings assumptions, call Social Security toll-free at 1-800-772-1213 or go online to www.ssa.gov/mystatement. You can submit a request online for a personalized statement but, until privacy issues are resolved, you'll receive the answer through the regular mail.

But can you expect to receive anything at all? Given the recent publicity about the dire financial straits of the Social Security system, many baby boomers are cynical about their future chances of receiving Social Security income. I think they *can* count on Social Security—any politician who might support its complete elimination would be in deep trouble—but in a somewhat different format than the one we know today.

Some change is necessary. The Social Security "trust fund" (a legal fiction; it is a pay-as-you-go system and no money is actually set aside) will run out of money, according to current estimates, by 2037. While today there is a surplus of income over outgo, an aging population, with fewer workers per retiree, is expected to produce revenues covering only about 72 percent of projected benefits. Suggested solutions include raising the payroll tax that funds Social Security, reducing benefits, or privatizing the system.

Another suggestion for reducing the shortfall is to tax all Social Security benefits for every recipient above a specified income level. This would make Social Security more like a welfare system instead of the entitlement it was designed to be. Still another way to reduce benefits is to further extend the age at which full benefits are paid. As shown in Table 1.4, that age is currently scheduled to become 67. Some proposals would push it to 70. A later "normal" retirement age will produce smaller benefits for people who choose to retire early.

Proposals to "privatize" the system or to place varying amounts in the stock market—whether invested by an individual or by the federal government—have been under discussion but do not appear likely candidates for implementation in the near future. Justifiable concern centers on subjecting essential retirement income to the inherent volatility of the stock market. A few years of a bull market, even an extended bull market, are not a guarantee of future returns. An extended downturn in share prices could have a serious impact on retirement income.

As you plan ahead for retirement, count on Social Security as a foundation of your retirement security. But develop your own retirement savings as well. Center them around your employer-sponsored

TABLE 1.4 Eligibility for Full Social Security Retirement Benefits

IF YOU WERE BORN IN:	YOU MAY RECEIVE FULL BENEFITS AFTER AGE:
1937 or before	65
1938	65 and 2 months
1939	65 and 4 months
1940	65 and 6 months
1941	65 and 8 months
1942	65 and 10 months
1943–1954	66
1955	66 and 2 months
1956	66 and 4 months
1957	66 and 6 months
1958	66 and 8 months
1959	66 and 10 months
1960 and thereafter	67

retirement plan and your personal savings, to make up what will probably be a very large shortfall.

Continued Earnings and Personal Savings

"Retirement" is associated with "leisure," but, for many retirees, it also means ongoing employment, either full-time or part-time. Of all the retirees surveyed in a Retirement Confidence Survey, 25 percent reported working full-time and 22 percent part-time. Three-quarters of those working said, they enjoyed work and wanted to stay involved. But 30 percent also wanted money to buy "extras," 21 percent needed money to make ends meet, and 25 percent were eager to retain job-related health insurance or other benefits. Whatever the reason, you may be wise to keep working. "Inactivity is one of the greatest threats to the physical and mental health of older people," says Dr. Robert Butler, president of the International Longevity Center-USA.

Whether or not you plan to work after retirement, you'll want a personal savings program alongside your tax-sheltered retirement contributions—to pay for college for your kids, or to buy a house, or to pay for a trip around the world, as well as to supplement your retirement income.

There are various tax-sheltered and taxable ways to invest. When you've maxed out your contributions to tax-sheltered retirement plans at work, take a look at the tax-sheltered retirement plans available to individuals, detailed in Chapter 3. Then start a taxable savings program as well. Chapters 6 and 7 discuss blending your tax-sheltered and taxable portfolios and allocating your assets among specific investment vehicles.

Pensions

Traditional defined benefit pension plans appear to be dinosaurs; their number dropped by more than half from 1987 to 1997. But they are still offered by many large U.S. corporations, often in tandem with defined contribution plans. These pension plans offer monthly checks based on salary and length of service. Most pension benefits are fixed once they start, although some are indexed to inflation.

Traditional pensions are governed by federal regulations that stipulate how benefits must be paid. If you are married, for example, your pension must be paid in the form of a joint-and-survivor annuity guaranteeing lifetime benefits to your surviving spouse. The only way you can elect a (typically larger) pension based on your individual life expectancy is if you and your spouse both sign a waiver provided by your employer. (Additional discussion of distribution options can be found in Chapter 11.)

Traditional pensions also have a distinct advantage over defined contribution plans: most of them are insured. (Defined benefit plans offered by church groups, governments, or professional service firms with fewer than 26 employees are not covered.) If a company terminates its pension plan because it no longer has the financial resources to support the plan, the Pension Benefit Guaranty Corporation (PBGC) steps in.

If your plan is terminated, you won't earn any additional benefits. But the PBGC will provide a pension based on the plan's provisions, the form of your benefit, and your age. That pension is clearly better than nothing, but it may be less than you would have received if your employer's plan had continued. The maximum amount that PBGC guarantees changes each year. For the year 2001, the maximum guaranteed amount is $3,392.05 per month ($40,704.60 per year) for a worker retiring at age 65. There is no cost-of-living adjustment; once established, a PBGC pension is fixed. And the guarantee is lower for someone who retires early or whose pension includes survivor benefits.

For more information on guaranteed defined benefit pensions (including a Pension Search Program that can help you connect with a missing pension from a former job), go online to www.pbgc.gov or write to PBGC, 1200 K Street NW, Suite 930, Washington, DC 20005-4026. If you are writing about a missing pension—after first trying to contact the plan administrator or the company where you earned the pension—include as much information as possible. At a minimum, include your name, address, daytime telephone number, Social Security number and date of birth, and the name and address of the employer. If possible, include the dates of employment, the name of the pension plan, the nine-digit Employer Identification Number, and the three-digit Plan Number.

If you are covered by a traditional pension plan, find out how much you can expect to receive under that plan and then develop your other retirement savings toward your income needs. A worksheet in Chapter 4 will help you identify how much income you will need in retirement.

But be prepared for change. To their dismay, many employees are finding that amendments to their plan can reduce a pension benefit

Ceilings on Monthly Guarantees from PBGC

YEAR PLAN TERMINATED	MONTHLY LIMIT AT AGE 65	MONTHLY LIMIT AT AGE 62	MONTHLY LIMIT AT AGE 60	MONTHLY LIMIT AT AGE 55
2001	$3,392.05	$2,679.72	$2,204.83	$1,526.42
2000	3,221.59	2,545.06	2,094.03	1,449.72
1999	3,051.14	2.410.40	1,983.24	1,373.01
1998	2,880.68	2,275.74	1,872.44	1,296.31
1997	2,761.36	2,181.47	1,794.88	1,242.61
1996	2,642.05	2,087.22	1,717.33	1,188.92
1995	2,573.86	2,033.35	1,673.01	1,158.24
1990	2,164.77	1,710.17	1,407.10	974.15
1985	1,687.50	1,333.13	1,096.88	759.38
1980	1,159.09	915.68	753.41	521.59

Source: Pension Benefit Guaranty Corporation (www.pbgc.gov/ygptabl.htm).

they thought was fixed. The *Wall Street Journal* reported, in July 2000, that many large companies are cutting pension benefits to improve their bottom line—in other words, favoring shareholders over employees.

Defined benefit pensions, as noted above, are typically based on salary and length of service. But the formula usually includes a "multiplier," set by the employer, which can be changed. Let's say you have 30 years of service and your average annual salary was $70,000 for the last three years. If the multiplier is 1.5 percent, your annual pension at age 65 (30 × $70,000 × 1.5 percent) will be $31,500. If the multiplier is reduced to 1.2 percent, your pension becomes $25,200.

The other elements of the formula can also be changed. Instead of counting all of your income—including bonuses—toward the pension calculation, the company may change the formula to reflect only your base pay. Instead of basing the pension on average salary in the last three years of employment—typically the highest-paid years—the plan may reflect average salary over 5 or 10 years or over your entire job tenure. Including your lower paid years in the calculation reduces the amount of the pension.

Some big companies are replacing traditional defined benefit pension plans with new hybrid plans that may produce lower annual pensions for some workers. Cash balance plans are among these hybrids.

CASH BALANCE PLANS

Cash balance plans, a new kid on the retirement block, look like defined contribution (DC) plans because the accumulated benefit is described as a "cash balance" in terminology that resembles an individual account balance under a DC plan. But cash balance plans are actually defined benefit plans; the benefit is calculated as a percentage of compensation plus annual interest credits at a rate set by the employer. The rate is typically the same as or similar to the yield on 30-year Treasury bonds. If the plan's investments earn less, the employer makes up the difference. If the investments earn more, the company keeps the excess. Despite surface similarity, cash balance plans are fundamentally different from defined contribution plans. The investment risk rests with the employer, but so do the profits.

In contrast to traditional pensions, however, cash balance plans usually provide higher benefits to young mobile workers. If you're going to change jobs frequently during your career, a cash balance plan will probably provide you with higher retirement benefits. And because cash balance plans are portable, you can take the money with you if you change jobs.

The flip side of the coin, however, is that conversions to cash balance plans from traditional pension plans often hurt older workers who have devoted their working lives to one company. Employees who leave at the time of conversion can get their full pension but, if they're older, they may find it tough to find another job. Older workers who stay may find pension benefits stuck on a plateau for a number of years after the new plan is put in place, thanks to built-in "wear-away" provisions, before increases take effect. Following a lot of negative publicity about the impact on older workers, the Internal Revenue Service began a study of cash balance plans and wear-away features. Its report, when issued, may be a catalyst for change.

New cash balance plans don't hurt anyone because all employees start off on equal footing. But, according to a report by Aon Consulting, employers rarely design and install a cash balance plan from scratch. Instead, they convert existing pension plans by adding cash balance features. Benefits build steadily instead of increasing sharply in the last few years before retirement, and, unless a transition or "grandfather" arrangement preserves their benefits, this is where older workers get hurt. Some companies try to cushion the blow by beefing up matching contributions to 401(k) plans. Others give slightly larger annual pay credits to older workers, based on age. And some allow workers over a specified age or within a few years of retirement to choose between the old plan and the new.

Considerable negative publicity has made corporations conscious of the need to make long-time employees whole through some adequate transition measure. If your company is adopting a cash balance plan, ask for a detailed comparison of benefits under the old plan and the new plan. And, if you're on the far side of age 40, find out what transition features will be in place.

Defined Contribution Plans

With Social Security in trouble and defined benefit pension plans biting the dust, your best hope for comfortable retirement income lies in defined contribution (DC) plans. Although the primary focus of this book is the 401(k) plan, because it is by far the most popular, DC plans actually come in several flavors:

- The 401(k) plan allows corporate employees to contribute pretax dollars. Many employers also match a portion of employee contributions—typically, up to a specified limit.
- The 403(b) plan, available most often to employees of nonprofit institutions such as schools and hospitals, follows the 401(k) model in being funded by employee contributions with an employer match permitted.
- The 457 plan is for government workers. It is funded by employees, with annual contribution limits below those of 401(k) and 403(b) plans—although a measure introduced in Congress in 2000 and again in 2001 would—if passed and signed by the president—equalize contribution levels at the higher amount.
- Savings and thrift plans permit employees to contribute a percentage of earnings to an individual account. Employers may provide matching contributions—either a fixed percentage of employee contributions or a varying percentage based on length of employee service, the amount of employee contributions, and other factors. These plans are designed for long-term savings, but may permit pre-retirement loans or withdrawals.

- Profit-sharing plans are funded by voluntary employer contributions and permit eligible employees to share in company profits. Most plans are deferred arrangements; the money is held in employee accounts until the employee retires, becomes disabled, or dies. Some profit-sharing plans are cash plans; employer contributions are paid directly to employees as cash or company stock. Distributions under cash plans are immediately taxable as ordinary income.
- Money purchase pension plans are funded by fixed employer contributions, typically calculated as a percentage of employee earnings and allocated to employee accounts. Employers may also make profit-sharing contributions to these plans, if they choose to do so, but employees do not have to contribute.
- Employee stock ownership plans (ESOPs) use employer contributions to buy shares of company stock, which are then distributed to employees.
- Stock bonus plans take contributions from the employer alone, or from both the employer and employees, and invest the money in a trust fund that then invests in various securities.

These plans have many features in common, but one is really significant: As a participant, you can defer income tax on your contributions and your earnings until the money is withdrawn.

At the heart of your retirement savings program is your 401(k) plan. To make the most of this golden opportunity to build a retirement nest egg, contribute as much as you possibly can, up to the limits set by your plan. Select your investments wisely, monitor their performance, and pay attention to legislative and regulatory changes.

Coming attractions, to be addressed throughout this book, include:

- Higher limits on contributions and "catch-up" contributions to let older workers boost their retirement savings.
- Increased portability so that moving from the corporate world to a job in the nonprofit sector, or vice versa, won't mean locking prior retirement benefits in place.
- Elimination of waiting periods so that you can participate in a 401(k) plan as soon as you take a job.
- Automatic enrollment so you won't even have to make a choice about participating in your 401(k).

- Liberalized vesting requirements, so that employer contributions will belong to you in three years instead of five.
- More investment choices, so that you can adequately diversify your retirement portfolio.
- More self-directed brokerage accounts, so that you can choose from an investment menu that encompasses virtually every individual security and mutual fund on the market.
- More investment education and advice. Employers currently offer education but shy away from advice, except through impartial third-party providers. A bill recently introduced in Congress would permit employers to provide full access to investment advice.

CHAPTER 2

Understanding Your 401(k)

Pension is often used as a one-size-fits-all word that describes retirement plans. As described in Chapter 1, however, a pension is a defined benefit arrangement that typically is funded by the employer and provides employees with fixed monthly checks during retirement. A 401(k) plan is not a pension; it is a defined contribution (DC) arrangement. How much you will receive in retirement from a 401(k) depends on how much you contribute, how much (if at all) your employer kicks in, the investment decisions you make, and how well those investments perform.

At the end of the road, instead of a pension's fixed monthly checks, you will probably receive a lump sum that you can use to buy an annuity (which will provide fixed monthly payments) or roll over into an Individual Retirement Account (for continued tax-deferred growth). Other options for dealing with 401(k) money when you change jobs or retire are described in Chapter 11.

The 401(k) is one of several defined contribution arrangements, as outlined in Chapter 1. Of the others, the 403(b) plan deserves a closer look.

403(b) Plans

These retirement savings plans, for employees of nonprofit institutions such as hospitals and colleges, are also known as annuities. And therein lies the rub. Although the legal and tax structure of 403(b) plans closely resembles that of 401(k) plans, investment choices are often severely limited. Although times are changing—a big step forward was a 1973 law permitting the direct purchase of mutual funds within 403(b) plans—many plans are still, almost 30 years later, largely invested in annuities sold by insurance companies. A full discussion of annuities can be found in Chapter 3.

Although variable annuities offer mutual funds within the annuity wrapper, annuities are still, by and large, conservative investments. In addition (with the notable exception of those offered by the Teachers Insurance Annuity Association-College Retirement Equities Fund (TIAA-CREF) a major provider of 403(b) plans), they often have both sizable fees and surrender penalties. The fee differential over the typical 401(k) plan—as much as 1 percent—stems from insurance company "mortality and expense" (M&E) charges on annuities. M&E charges of 0.75 to 1.25 percent are meant to cover the cost of guaranteeing a death benefit at least equal to the employee's contributions. But this is a dubious benefit. You should expect a variable annuity to be worth more than you put into it, not less, by the time you die.

Where mutual funds are an investment option, some employers offer plan participants a preselected menu of funds. Others open the doors for outside vendors to offer funds directly to plan participants. The second approach can mean a bewildering choice. As reported on 403.mpower.com, the Los Angeles Unified School District lists more than 100 providers, each with its own array of investment programs.

Although investment choices may be limited—participants are never allowed to purchase individual stocks—the 403(b) plan can be an essential part of retirement savings. Yet many eligible employees don't participate at all. They skip the tax-advantaged opportunity of contributing up to $10,500 a year (the limit for 2001) and thereby harm their own future retirement security.

If you are eligible to participate in a 403(b) plan:

- Evaluate the available investment options and associated fees. If they are reasonable—you may want to seek advice from an independent financial planner (see Chapter 13)—sign up and contribute as much as you can.

- If you are limited to a variable annuity and happy with that choice, stay away from the fixed-income alternative within the annuity wrapper. With it, you'll pay high fees for an investment with no potential for growth. Worse yet, money in an insurer's fixed accounts is part of the company's assets and subject to creditor claims if the company should get into financial hot water.
- If you are unable to make the maximum allowable contribution in some years, consider making "catch-up" contributions when you become eligible to do so. Under this provision, unique to 403(b) plans, participants may make up earlier missed contributions when they have remained with the same employer for at least 15 years. The maximum catch-up contribution is $3,000 a year over a five-year period.
- Join forces with other employees, and lobby for an improved plan—one with solid investment choices and low fees. Since 1997, nonprofit organizations have been allowed to establish 401(k) plans as well as the traditional 403(b) plans. Perhaps you can spur a switch to this more flexible retirement plan.

For most people—with the exception of government employees and people who work for nonprofit organizations—the focal point of retirement savings is the 401(k) plan.

401(k) Plans

A 401(k) plan can be designed as a profit-sharing arrangement with an employer match based on profits. But the more common arrangement is a salary reduction plan in which employee contributions come off the top of salary, thereby reducing taxable compensation (FICA taxes for Social Security and Medicare must still be paid). Contribute $3,000 to a 401(k) and, if you're in the 28 percent federal income tax bracket, you save an immediate $840. If your salary is subject to state income tax, you save even more.

It pays to pay attention. Knowing the 401(k) rules can help you maximize your retirement savings.

Eligibility

Taking a new job? Whether it's a first job or a midcareer switch, be sure to ask how soon you can participate in your company's 401(k) plan. A delay will make a big difference in your retirement nest egg.

Companies can legally exclude employees under age 21 and employees with less than one year of service. This makes sense because job mobility among short-term employees tends to be high, and companies don't want to incur enrollment costs for folks who won't stick around. But things are changing. In a competitive environment where good employees are in short supply, more and more companies are allowing employees to begin contributing their own money to a 401(k) as soon as they start working, so that no time is lost in saving for retirement. However, although they can contribute their own money the new hires may not be eligible for company matching contributions until they have been on the job for a year.

According to a 1999 survey by the Profit Sharing/401(k) Council of America (PSCA), at least two out of five companies let new employees participate in the 401(k) plan within their first three months. This is a dramatic increase from the 32 percent of companies doing so in 1998. But be sure you understand the rules. "Immediate eligibility" can be defined in different ways. For some employers, it's the first day on the job. For others, it's the end of the first pay period, or the first day of the first or second full month at work.

At a growing number of companies, you won't even have to elect to participate in the plan; enrollment will be automatic unless you opt out. At least 50 large corporations have initiated automatic enrollment plans; many more are expected to follow suit in the light of recent favorable IRS rulings. Although contributions must legally be elective in order to qualify for tax deferral, the Internal Revenue Service has ruled that automatic contributions may be considered a tacit election so long as two conditions are met. The employee (1) must receive adequate notice of the automatic enrollment and (2) can elect to receive cash or contribute a different amount instead. Early in 2000, the IRS extended this ruling to apply to current employees as well as newly hired employees.

These IRS rulings apply to 403(b) and 457 plans as well as to 401(k) plans. David L. Wray, president of PSCA, expects automatic enrollment to take hold so rapidly that more than half of all plans will use it within the next five years.

Automatic participation typically comes with a contribution rate of 3 percent (more on contribution rates later in this chapter) so as to not unduly burden participants but still provide some meaningful savings toward retirement. If you don't sign up for your company's 401(k) plan and it has an automatic enrollment feature, you may find that your pay is automatically reduced by 3 percent and the "missing" amount has been contributed to the 401(k) on your behalf. Again, you must be given adequate notice and a reasonable period to change the election. You can elect to make a larger contribution to the 401(k) (probably the better choice) or to receive cash in your paycheck instead.

With automatic enrollment, too, the contributions are typically invested in company-selected funds until the participant decides where to invest. Most often, company choices are conservative. No employer wants to risk a lawsuit by placing employee contributions in risky vehicles. Among the companies recently surveyed by PSCA, the most popular choices included stable value, money market, balanced, and lifestyle funds. (These are described in more detail in Chapter 5.) Two-thirds of the surveyed companies also provided matching contributions—most often, 50 cents on the dollar.

Under another version of automatic enrollment, employees must elect to participate—often via a simple check-off form—and the company then suggests a contribution amount and appropriate levels of investment. This approach may protect the employer against liability if preselected investments should go sour.

Automatic enrollment has dramatically increased employee participation in 401(k) plans, thereby boosting retirement savings and eliminating the participation gap between high earners and low earners. The down side is that the process may give employees a false sense of security. A recent joint study by the benefits consulting firm of Hewitt Associates, Harvard University, and the Wharton School of the University of Pennsylvania suggests that too many employees who join through automatic enrollment remain at the low contribution rate and conservative investment options offered by the plan. By doing so, they cheat themselves out of significant retirement savings.

If you're in this boat, don't accept your employer's default elections as suggestions for appropriate

TIP

Reluctant to tie up money in a long-term investment? You may be able to have your cake and eat it too. If you need your money before you reach age 59½, you may be able to get at it, without penalty, if you:

1. **Leave your job and are at least age 55.**
2. **Take regular annual withdrawals for at least five years or until you reach age 59½, whichever is later.**
3. **Keep the cash representing your own contributions and roll the earnings on those contributions into an Individual Retirement Account, where they can continue to grow tax-deferred.**
4. **Take your withdrawal in the form of company stock. There will be no 10 percent tax penalty because gains haven't been realized. You can sell the stock after it's out of the plan.**

These options are described in more detail in Chapter 11.

contribution rates or investment options. Make your own decisions based on how much you need to save to reach your retirement goals and how much risk you are willing to assume. Give some serious thought to your savings objectives, familiarize yourself with the investment options and strategies described in Chapters 4 through 7, and take charge of your future.

Why are companies so eager to enroll participants? In part, there's a genuine concern about boosting retirement savings. Americans are notoriously poor savers, and too many workers—especially younger ones—never get around to participating in 401(k) plans when they are offered. As John Rother of AARP (formerly known as the American Association of Retired Persons) told a conference sponsored by the Employee Benefit Research Institute in April 2000, "We do have to recognize the fundamental fact that not everybody is economically prudent with regard to their own future. In fact, there are an alarming number of grasshoppers in our society, people who are basically in a live-for-today mode."

As noted above, companies are also seeking qualified workers and adding perks such as instant eligibility and automatic enrollment as sweeteners. But there's another reason: antidiscrimination laws limit the amount highly paid employees can contribute unless a large number of rank-and-file employees sign up. About one-third of the companies surveyed by Hewitt Associates anticipated limiting the percentage of contributions that highly compensated employees could contribute, in order to pass the nondiscrimination test.

(Bear in mind that the Hewitt study, like most studies by benefits consultants, focused on larger companies. In Hewitt's comprehensive 1999 survey of 401(k) trends, 41 percent of the employers had from 1,000 to 4,999 employees. At the extreme ends of the spectrum, 23 percent had more than 15,000 employees, and 9 percent had under 1,000 employees. If you work for a very small company, nondiscrimination rules may have a stronger impact. Other aspects—such as investment options—may be more limited.)

The rules say that contributions by highly compensated employees, as a group, cannot exceed by more than 2 percent the contributions by other employees, as a group. In addition to the 2 percent spread cap, contributions by highly compensated employees may not be more than twice the percentage of contributions by the other employees. These rules hit hard in small companies. In an example provided by Clifton Linton of mPower [visit www.401kafe.com, a valuable site for checking out 401(k) news], a company has 10 employees, three of whom are considered highly compensated. If the other seven, as a group, contribute 5 percent of their pay to the retirement plan and the three who are highly compensated contribute 8 percent, the company would fail its nondiscrimination test.

If a company flunks its nondiscrimination test, it must take corrective action or the entire plan may be disqualified. The most popular correction entails sending refunds of excess contributions to the highly paid workers. The refunds are taxable income and, because they often arrive after employees have filed their income tax returns for the prior year, the income may have to be reported by filing an amended return. To avoid this unpopular situation, some employers simply limit the contributions that may be made by highly compensated employees. Or, to sidestep annual testing, employers can find a "safe harbor" by making nonelective contributions. Easing regulatory compliance in this manner is particularly attractive to small employers.

"Safe harbor" provisions require the employer to do one of two things: (1) contribute 3 percent of compensation for *all* eligible employees, regardless of whether they choose to participate in the plan, or (2) match employee contributions dollar-for-dollar up to 3 percent of pay, and an additional 50 cents on the dollar for the next 2 percent of pay. These contributions must be fully vested. Safe harbor plans can exclude employees who are under age 21 and have less than one year of service. According to ScudderKemper Investments, these employees can be eligible to make and receive contributions but do not need to receive the additional safe harbor contributions.

By increasing the number of lower-paid participants, executives can contribute more toward their own retirement. Participation rates in plans with automatic enrollment are significantly higher than in 401(k) plans in general.

Enticing more employees to participate may smack of enlightened self-interest in the executive suite. But self-interest, in this instance, is good for everyone. Whatever the reasons on the company's side, you stand to benefit if you participate in the 401(k) and contribute as much as you can, up to the

NOTE

Who is highly compensated?
Uncle Sam has a precise definition for highly compensated employees. The group includes anyone who:

- **Owns 5 percent or more of the company, regardless of salary.**
- **Is in the top-paid 20 percent of the company's employees, regardless of salary.**
- **Earns more than $85,000, adjusted for inflation.**

Companies must run nondiscrimination tests each year, so the status of a particular employee may change from year to year.

allowable limits. Don't fall into the trap of thinking that small contributions don't add up to much. According to David Wray of PSCA, "An extra one percent can easily provide an extra $100,000 at retirement for low-paid workers." For an employee earning $25,000 a year, this means putting away an additional $4.80 a week. This modest sum should be manageable for almost every employee. Yet, with modest pay increases of 3.5 percent a year and investments earning 8 percent a year, a 25-year-old employee following this 1 percent rule could have an extra $100,000 at retirement.

Contributions

There are two sets of government limits on contributions to defined contribution plans. First, Uncle Sam says that you and your employer, together, may contribute up to the lesser of $30,000 or 25 percent of your salary (to a maximum of $170,000 in 2001) to all the DC plans for which you are eligible: 401(k), thrift/savings, profit sharing, money purchase, and ESOP.

Until a couple of years ago, the 25 percent limitation was on net pay: salary minus your contribution to the plan. In 1998, the law was changed. The ceiling is now 25 percent of gross pay. This seemingly minor difference is actually quite significant. In an example provided by the accounting firm of Ernst & Young, the maximum combined employee-employer contribution for someone earning $40,000 at a company that matches, dollar-for-dollar up to 5 percent of salary, rises from $8,400 to $10,000 under the gross-pay formula. Building tax-deferred growth on an additional $1,600 a year for 30 years at an assumed steady 8 percent return—even without pay increases or other increases in contributions—would produce an additional $181,248 in your retirement nest egg!

Second, you are allowed to contribute 20 percent of your salary or a maximum of $10,500 (in 2001), whichever is less, to your 401(k) plan. The ceiling is adjusted each year for inflation, although indexing changes are limited to $500 increments and therefore do not take place every year.

Federal regulations set outside limits. Your company plan may not be as generous as Uncle Sam permits. Instead of 20 percent of pay, many plans limit annual contributions by employees to a maximum of 10 percent or 15 percent of pay. More than seven out of ten plans set maximum employee contribution rates of 10 percent to 16 percent. According to Hewitt Associates, 41 percent of these plans go with a 15 percent ceiling. Lower limits translate into smaller retirement savings. Within your plan's limits, you should contribute as much as you can.

What if you feel that you must make a choice between paying off your mortgage and saving for retirement? Both are admirable financial goals. For most people, the best bet is paying the mortgage off over its full term and contributing as much as possible to a 401(k) to boost retirement savings. But, as with any rule, there are exceptions. If you don't itemize deductions on your income tax return and hence don't get the full benefit of mortgage interest, you might want to pay off the mortgage. Or, if your mortgage carries an interest rate much higher than you could reasonably expect to earn on your 401(k) investments, you may want to pay down the mortgage. But don't forget that the accumulated interest and dividends within your 401(k) are tax-deferred, which boosts the effective yield. Again, in almost every circumstance, it pays to build the 401(k).

But what if you think you could earn a better rate of return outside the 401(k) plan? What if your investment choices within the plan are limited? Would it then make sense to invest in a taxable account instead? Generally not. In an example provided by Maria Crawford Scott, editor of the *AAII Journal*, contributing $3,000 of a $45,000 annual salary to a 401(k) immediately reduces your tax bill by $840, assuming you are in the 28 percent federal income tax bracket. Investing $3,000 every year for 20 years, at an annual rate of 8 percent, produces a total of $148,269. You'll owe income tax when you withdraw the money; at 28 percent, if you withdraw all of the money in a lump sum, you will owe $41,515 in taxes, leaving a balance of $106,754.

Let's say you invest in a taxable account instead. Because you have to pay taxes on the $3,000, you have only $2,160 to invest. In addition, because you must pay income tax each year on the earnings, an 8 percent return becomes an effective after-tax return of 5.76 percent. After 20 years, you would have $81,897, or $24,857 less than you would have in the 401(k). Unless you can earn far more in a taxable account, you clearly come out ahead by deferring the tax bill as long as possible.

Highly compensated employees face a different dilemma. Under the federal government's nondiscrimination rules, a complex formula governs how much the top echelon may put aside for retirement in a DC plan. If the rank and file fail to participate, executives must contribute less to their own plans—sometimes much less than the $10,500 annual ceiling—under federal rules. In a worst-case scenario, "excess" contributions will have to be refunded, and tax will be due on the refund.

You may not face that problem but, unless you carefully calibrate the pace of your own contributions throughout the year, you may still run into a situation where you forfeit part of your employer's match. This pitfall can trip up employees who contribute the maximum permitted from each paycheck and hit the legal ceiling on employee contributions before year-end. Let's say your plan permits contributions up to 10 percent of pay, and your employer is matching dollar for dollar on contributions up to 5 percent of pay. If you earn $120,000 a year, 10 percent of pay will bring you to the $10,500 limit on employee contributions by mid-November, closing out employer matching contributions for the last six weeks of the year.

To avoid this problem, do some calculations early in the year, then spread your contributions evenly over the twelve months, even if it means contributing a bit less than the maximum allowed. But watch out for two more possible pitfalls:

1. If your employer makes a match to bonus payments, your calculations will be more complicated.
2. If you earn more than $170,000, you will hit the legal ceiling for 401(k) contributions. In these situations, you may want to consult an independent financial adviser. (Advisers are discussed in Chapter 13.)

WHAT HAPPENS TO YOUR CONTRIBUTIONS?

When you decide to participate in a 401(k) and elect a percentage of your salary to contribute (within the allowed limits set by law and by your plan), the money is contributed through payroll deduction—taken off the top before you receive your paycheck. These are pre-tax dollars, so the contribution is not subject to income tax. However, it is still subject to your share of the combined Social Security and Medicare tax (FICA) of 7.65 percent. Earnings up to $80,400 are subject to Social Security tax in 2001; there is no ceiling on earnings subject to the Medicare portion of the tax.

But you can't assume that the money has been invested just because it has been taken out of your paycheck. Following some

Repeated pension reform efforts in Congress, if enacted, would raise the ceiling on contributions to defined contribution plans. If a bill introduced in 2000 and again in 2001 is signed into law, two significant restrictions on employee contributions would be lifted:

1. **The annual dollar limit on elective salary deferral through a 401(k) plan—$10,500 in 2001—would increase in $1,000 increments each year until reaching $15,000 in 2005.**
2. **"Catch-up" provisions would enable anyone age 50 or older to make additional contributions starting at 10 percent of the dollar limit in 2001 and increasing to 40 percent in 2004 and thereafter. With this provision, someone who is 50 or older could contribute as much as $21,000 in 2005 ($15,000, under the limit described above, and another $6,000 as a 40 percent catch-up).**

well-publicized instances of employers "borrowing" employee contributions for their own use, the government stepped in. Federal law now requires contributions to be deposited no later than the fifteenth business day after the end of the calendar month in which the contributions are withheld. (Employers can apply for a 10-day extension.) This allows considerable leeway. Some employers always wait until the last possible moment. Others deposit the money immediately. Meanwhile, until the money is invested, it is supposed to be segregated and protected.

If there is a delay in investing contributions, the employer collects any interest earned. The sums are probably not substantial for any individual employee's account. Taken together, however, the employer may earn a tidy sum. Nonetheless, few employers deliberately delay investing the money for the sake of the earned interest. Large companies can afford the extra paperwork entailed in coordinating payroll deductions and immediate deposits. Smaller companies may simply not have the ability to do so.

Once your money has been invested in your choice of investment vehicles, you may want to change your investment mix from time to time. Although David Wray of PSCA says that "80 percent of employees probably never make a change," you should rebalance your investments at least once a year. (We'll come back to investment choices in Chapters 4 through 7.) What will make your life easier, however, is the increasing use of technology to enhance communication, administration, and investment transactions.

The biggest shift is toward use of the Internet. Well over half of companies offering defined contribution plans are now using the Internet in some way. Even without this Web-based technology, however, the almost universal use of touch tone telephones means that you can easily check up on your investments and make changes. Although at least three-quarters of companies allow daily transactions, Wray points out that you may not be able to trade as often as you like. There is often a "modifier" in place. For example, an employee may be able to buy or sell an investment on any day, but only once within a quarter. These restrictions have been put in place because a handful of employees were making such frequent transactions that they were running up considerable costs for the plan, costs that were shared by all employees.

After-Tax Contributions

If you can afford to contribute to your 401(k) beyond the limits set on pre-tax contributions, you may want to consider making after-tax contributions—if your plan permits. Not all plans do. According to the 1999 Hewitt survey, 43 percent of company plans allow after-tax contributions that are not matched by the employer, and 27 percent of company plans offer after-tax contributions with a match. (See the following section for more on matching contributions.) Both percentages have decreased since 1997.

After-tax contributions, with or without a match, have some advantages: After-tax contributions to your 401(k) account get the same tax break offered to pre-tax contributions; that is, the money grows tax-deferred. In addition, you can withdraw your after-tax contributions at any time, without penalty or tax, because you've already paid the tax on this money. Earnings on your contributions, however, will be subject to tax when withdrawn—and to a 10 percent tax penalty if you are under age 59½ on the date of withdrawal.

Matching Funds

The notion of an employer match has become well entrenched in the 401(k) world. According to research by the Spectrem Group, 95 percent of companies with more than 1,000 employees make a match. Among smaller companies offering 401(k) plans, at least three-quarters make a match—including those with fewer than 100 employees. (If you work for a very small company, one with a handful of employees, you'll be lucky to have a 401(k) plan at all. Chapter 3 provides some information on plans available to small employers.)

Matching funds, where they exist, range from as little as 10 cents to more than a dollar for each dollar of employee contributions. A sampling of major corporations surveyed by *Money* magazine in the fall of 2000 showed Philip Morris with no match, Bristol-Myers Squibb with a 75 percent match on up to 6 percent of pay, and Texaco with a 200 percent match on up to 3 percent of pay. The most common match is 50 cents on the dollar, up to 6 percent of pay. The 6 percent limitation on the employer match is common even where total employee contributions are 10 percent or 15 percent.

Most employer matches follow this kind of per-dollar formula. Almost three-quarters of all plans surveyed by Hewitt Associates in 1999 provided a fixed match. But there are variations. An employer might, for example, base the formula on a percentage of compensation instead of a per-dollar amount. Or it might make discretionary contributions based on profit sharing, as 15 percent of surveyed employers do. This is one of the details that you need to find out about your company's plan. But don't be surprised if plan documents leave matching contributions to the discretion of the plan sponsor even though you know the match percentage is fixed. Employers often use discretionary language in legal documents so that they are not locked in, even if, in practice, they regularly make fixed matching contributions.

Another variation lies in what compensation counts toward a match. Some employers include bonuses in the 401(k) formula for matching contributions; others do not. Some penalize younger workers by basing matching contributions on age, salary, or length of time on the job. Both of these variations steer a larger match to higher-paid workers.

Some employers also limit employee investment choices by making the match payable in employer stock. Cash is preferable. You can then choose the investment vehicles that suit your needs and also—not incidentally—ensure a diversified portfolio that is not dependent on the fortunes of your employer. However, a match in employer stock is better than no match at all. [Chapter 11 describes what happens to employer stock in your 401(k) when you retire or leave your job.]

From an employee's point of view, an employer match is found money. It's an absolutely risk-free guaranteed return on your money. Where else can you earn a sure-fire 25 percent, 50 percent, or 100 percent on your money? If you can't afford to contribute the maximum to your 401(k) plan, you should make every effort to contribute the amount necessary to receive the full employer match. This is typically, as noted, 6 percent of salary. You may be allowed to contribute more, but the employer contribution stops at 6 percent.

Playing Close to the Vest

Your own contributions to your 401(k) plan are always yours. They are "portable," in the jargon of the pension world; you can take them along if you leave your job and move to greener pastures. If you do leave and join another company, several options may be available for your 401(k) money. You may be able to simply leave the money in place (if your current plan permits you to do so), put it directly into your new employer's plan (if you are allowed to do so without a waiting period), transfer the money to a rollover IRA to preserve its tax-deferred growth, or take the cash. (All of these options are discussed in detail in Chapter 11.) For now, let me just deliver this message: *Whatever you do, don't take the cash.* Doing so subjects you to immediate taxes and tax penalties. Worse yet, it puts an irreparable dent in your retirement savings.

Your employer's contributions are another matter. They belong to you only after you become "vested" in the plan. Some benevolent employers vest participants right away, but most require a waiting period—although you generally become vested at the normal retirement age at your company, even if you haven't otherwise met the plan's vesting schedule.

Uncle Sam requires companies to adhere to one of two vesting schedules: (1) immediate vesting after a wait of no more than five years, or (2) gradual vesting over a period of no more than seven years (Table 2.1). ("Multiemployer" plans, such as those offered under union contracts, were allowed to have slower vesting schedules through the end of 1998; now they must conform to standard vesting rules.) Immediate ("cliff") vesting is more common.

Pension reform legislation introduced in 2000 and again in 2001 would reduce the maximum vesting period under cliff vesting from five years to three years. The quicker vesting is designed to help workers who move from job to job—and, especially, women who are in and out of the workforce meeting family obligations.

TABLE 2.1 Methods of Vesting

YEARS ON THE JOB	PERCENT VESTED
"Cliff" (Immediate) Vesting:	
0 to 5	0
5 or more	100
"Graded" (Gradual) Vesting:	
0–3 years	0
3–4 years	20
4–5 years	40
5–6 years	60
6–7 years	80
7 and more	100

Note, however, that a different vesting schedule applies to so-called "top-heavy" plans. A 401(k) plan is "top-heavy" if the account balances of key employees, as a group, exceed 60 percent of the entire account balance in the plan. Being top-heavy does not make a plan discriminatory, but it does put limits on participation by the highly compensated. If the key employees who create the top-heavy situation choose to participate in the plan, the sponsor must make a 3 percent contribution to the 401(k) for other employees. In addition, in a top-heavy plan, all employees become vested after no more than three years (cliff vesting) or six years (graded vesting).

The above is a significant simplification of complex rules governing top-heavy plans. The rules are so duplicative and burdensome, in fact, that the Clinton administration's ERISA Advisory Council recommended outright repeal. Congressional sponsors of pension reform legislation note that the top-heavy rules discriminate against married couples who work for the same business. Legislation introduced in 2000 would not repeal, but would streamline top-heavy rules to make them fairer and simpler to administer.

What Does It All Cost?

In the bright early days of 401(k) plans, employers picked up much of the associated costs. This is no longer the case. According to research by the Spectrem Group, employers now pay an average of 79 percent of plan costs, so you'll probably be sharing the costs with your company. But you may not know exactly what expenses you're paying, and that information may be hard to get.

Costs count. The Pension and Welfare Benefits Administration, a division of the U.S. Department of Labor, provides an eye-opening example. Let's say you are an employee who is 35 years away from retirement, and the current balance in your 401(k) account is $25,000. Let's also assume that you will never put another penny into the plan. If your account earns an average of 7 percent over the next 35 years, but fees and expenses reduce your average returns by 0.5 percent, your account balance will grow to $227,000 by the time you retire. If fees and expenses are 1.5 percent, however, your account balance will grow to only $163,000. The seemingly minor difference of 1 percent in fees and expenses would reduce your account balance at retirement by 28 percent! So pay attention to plan costs, and ask your employer for more information if it is not immediately available.

[In all fairness, employers are sometimes confused about the true cost of running a defined contribution plan. Because this is so—especially among small employers—the American Council of Life Insurers, the Investment Company Institute, and the American Bankers Association combined their efforts and developed a fee disclosure form to help employers identify and compare the costs of sponsoring a 401(k) plan. The new form, initiated by the U.S. Department of Labor, has a summary page that can easily be used by employers to compare costs. The form can be found on the Department of Labor Web site, www.dol.gov/dol/pwba.]

Costs fall into two basic categories: (1) administration and (2) asset management. There may also be service charges and sales charges associated with buying and selling specific investments, such as loads on mutual funds and commissions on individual securities.

Administrative expenses spring from all the chores associated with operating a plan: enrolling participants, keeping records, mailing statements, hiring accounting and legal services, and so on. One study showed average per-participant administrative fees ranging from $34 a year for plans with 1,000 participants to $42 a year for plans with 200 participants. Another study cited annual per-person administrative costs in the $100 to $200 range. Bear in mind that, generally, your employer is not levying these charges. Most employers use an outside plan provider—a mutual fund family, a bank, an insurance company, or a benefits consulting firm—to do the plan administration. These folks set the fees—although, of course, your employer has a role in the fee structure by selecting the plan provider. (See Chapter 8 for more on the cast of characters involved in running your 401(k) plan.)

One thing is clear. Larger firms benefit from what providers like to call "economy of scale." As a practical matter, if you work for a smaller company, you are less likely to have a 401(k) plan at all; if you do have a plan, it will be more expensive—for your employer and, in all likelihood, for you. In addition, as today's 401(k) plans expand services to include such items as daily valuation of account balances, telephone voice response systems, interactive Web sites, and educational seminars for participants, these costs can be expected to increase.

Administrative costs may be included in the asset management fees that cover the cost of investing (see below). Many times, however, they are a separate item and are then either paid by the employer or charged against the plan's assets. More and more often, they are charged against the plan's assets. They then come out of participants' pockets, either as a flat fee against each participant's account or as an allocation among participants in proportion to the size of their accounts. The latter approach may be more equitable; employees with larger plan balances will then pay more of the plan costs. Either way, definite cost-shifting is going on. In 1995, research by the Spectrem Group showed that 7 percent of companies were shifting administrative costs to participants; by 1997, the number was 24 percent.

In addition to broad-based administrative costs, some plans charge specific fees associated with optional features available to participants. There may be a fee for selecting individual securities through a brokerage "window" (see Chapter 5 for investment choices within 401(k) plans) or for taking a loan from the plan (see Chapter 9 on access to your money). One study found that loan application fees ranged from $3 to $100; $50 was the most common fee. Annual loan maintenance charges ranged from $3 to $75 a year; almost half the charges were in the $10 to $15 range. Remember, some plans don't charge directly for loan origination or maintenance; related costs are buried elsewhere in the fee structure.

Investment fees are typically larger than administrative costs. They are also typically assessed as a percentage of the assets in the plan, which means that they are deducted directly from your investment returns. Your net total return is your return after fees, but the fees themselves are not identified on your account statements. This, as the PWBA points out, makes it tough to isolate the direct cost.

In addition to the investment management fees that are a percentage of assets, you'll pay costs that may be associated with the specific investments you choose to include in your 401(k) account. Mutual funds, for instance, may be "load" or "no-load." The load represents a broker's commission on the sale. Where there is a load, it may be paid up front, when shares of a fund are purchased. More often, today, loads are levied when shares are redeemed within a specified number of years, as a "back-end load" or deferred contingent sales charge.

Note, though, that loads—and investment management fees in general—are subject to negotiation. Many mutual fund companies will eliminate them on funds offered through 401(k) plans if asked to do so by the employer. "If asked" is the key element. Some employers don't ask too many questions; they simply turn plan management over to a provider who assumes the burden. Among employers that do care, large companies can bring more clout to the negotiating table than smaller ones. As with so many other employee benefits, from health insurance to retirement plans, working for a large corporation offers some advantages.

Note, too, that institutional funds—those offered to the largest investors, including the 401(k) plans of major corporations—are less expensive than the retail funds offered to ordinary investors. If you work for a large corporation, it should have access to lower-cost institutional funds and offer them to employees.

Mutual funds also have management or investment advisory fees, expressed as a percentage of the fund's assets. Higher fees are usually associated with actively managed funds seeking to provide higher returns. Funds tracking market indexes are passively managed and typically have lower costs. Some funds also levy so-called 12b-1 fees to cover the costs of marketing the funds to new investors. Chapter 5 contains more detail on investment options.

Ask for a prospectus for each mutual fund. The prospectus will show the fees associated with the specific fund and an "expense ratio" you can use as a measuring rod against other funds with similar objectives. If you do not receive a prospectus—there may not be one, if the fund is available only to plan participants—you will have to rely on plan documents (see Chapter 8) for information. If you cannot find the answers, request them from your plan administrator.

On a plan with 100 participants and $2 million in assets, total per-participant per-year fees ranged, in one study, from $114 to $428. Other studies show annual per-participant costs as high as $860. The important things to remember are: (1) fees vary enormously, depending on the kind of plan provider your employer uses; and (2) you can't do anything to change the fees, other than selecting low-cost individual investment vehicles in your own account—although performance is more important than cost. But you can make it your business to understand the fee structure and the impact it has on your investment returns. When fees are out of line, you might try banding together with other employees and pressuring your employer to make a change. Shifting to a lower-cost provider—a move that may save the employer money, too—may be all that it takes.

The Good, the Bad, and the Ugly

If you are eligible to participate in a 401(k) plan, the conventional wisdom goes, you should leap at the opportunity. For the most part, this is absolutely correct. The 401(k) plan is the single best opportunity most Americans have to put aside tax-sheltered dollars for retirement. There are other strategies—I'll describe some in the next chapter—but the 401(k) tops the list.

Should you ever pass up the opportunity? Probably not, although that doesn't mean that you should never cast a critical eye on your company's plan. Some companies' offerings are far better than others. Some are mediocre, and a handful may be really bad. Here's a checklist of things to look for—and, perhaps, to lobby for if your company's plan is deficient:

- A high ceiling on contributions. Remember, although Uncle Sam lets you contribute as much as $10,500 in 2001, your plan may set a lower limit. Higher is better.
- Matching contributions. The higher the match, the better. You're also better off if you can decide how to invest your employer's contribution as well as your own. A sizable number of plans restrict matching contributions to an investment in company stock. This may make your investment portfolio woefully unbalanced. Worse yet, both your present salary and your future retirement income would depend on the fortunes of a single company. Additional pitfalls may come into play when you retire or leave your job; these will be discussed in Chapter 11.

- Liberal vesting schedules, including immediate vesting in the company's matching contribution.
- Rapid eligibility to participate, so you don't have to miss out on retirement savings for as long as a year before joining the plan.
- A variety of investment choices. The average plan now has eight to ten investment alternatives available to participants. Where there is a "brokerage window" (permitting you to invest in virtually any broker-sold security), the number of investment choices may be overwhelming. More isn't necessarily better if too much choice results in confusion. The ideal arrangement gives plan participants flexible choices among well-balanced investment alternatives: fixed-income, balanced, and a variety of approaches to growth investing through equity funds. Investing within your 401(k) plan will be discussed in more detail in Chapter 5.
- Low cost. High fees eat into your retirement savings in a big way. Some companies pick up most of the cost; others pass more costs on to plan participants. Too many companies pay little or no attention to plan costs when they choose plan providers. They use retail funds when they could use lower-cost institutional funds.
- Access to plan balances and ease of investing. Look for telephone or Internet transaction capability and for the opportunity to adjust your investment mix at least quarterly. More on this in Chapter 4.
- Education about investment alternatives. Many large companies now provide employees with newsletters, seminars, and workshops as well as online advisory services.
- Provision for loans and hardship withdrawals. If you need your money to cover a major emergency can you get it? Access to your money is described in Chapter 9.

CHAPTER 3

Comparing Tax-Sheltered Plans

Defined contribution (DC) plans play the largest role in retirement planning for most workers, but there's more than one way to save for retirement. If your employer does not offer a 401(k) plan, you may be able to use one of the other plans. And even if you participate in a DC plan at work, you may be able to boost your retirement savings by using one of the other plans as well.

Traditional IRAs

The granddaddy of individual retirement savings vehicles is the Individual Retirement Account or IRA. Introduced in 1974 (remember when "All in the Family" was the nation's favorite television show?), the IRA initially permitted workers who had no employer-sponsored pension plan to contribute, and deduct from their income tax, up to 15 percent of compensation or $1,500 each year, whichever was less. In 1976, the annual IRA contribution limit was raised to $1,750, but workers were still eligible only if their employer did not have a retirement plan.

In 1981, the rules changed dramatically. Everyone with earned income, whether or not they participated in a pension plan at work, could contribute (and deduct) up to $2,000 a year. The change was so significant—and the tax shelter so appealing—that IRAs skyrocketed in popularity. The result, perhaps inevitably, was a significant loss of tax revenue for the federal government and—within a very few years—a renewed tightening of eligibility standards.

The Tax Reform Act of 1986 slammed the door on IRA participation. Starting with the 1987 tax year, it restricted deductibility of contributions in terms of both income limits and pension coverage. Married couples filing jointly could deduct IRA contributions only if their annual income was below $40,000 *and* if neither the husband nor the wife was covered by an employer-sponsored retirement plan. If either spouse had a retirement plan at work, neither one could have a tax-deductible IRA. For single taxpayers, the income ceiling on deductible contributions was $25,000. Little wonder that, as Fidelity Investments reported on the twenty-fifth anniversary of the introduction of the IRA, contributions dropped by two-thirds. Without the tax incentive of deductible contributions, people just weren't interested. Nondeductible IRAs (see below for details) do not have the same appeal.

With the Taxpayer Relief Act of 1997 (TRA 97), the tide turned again. Effective in 1998, income ceilings were raised to produce tax-deductible contributions for many more taxpayers. And, equally important, following TRA 97, spouses are no longer linked for the purpose of determining eligibility. One spouse can be covered by a retirement plan at work, and the other, assuming income limitations are met, can have a deductible IRA. At the same time, the Roth IRA was introduced, with its nondeductible contributions but tax-free withdrawals. More details on the Roth IRA are given later in this chapter.

IRA contributions of up to $2,000 a year are deductible at gradually increasing income levels. The full amount is deductible at the lower income level in Table 3.1 but is phased out entirely at the upper income level.

With the new higher limits for deductible IRA contributions, tax publishers CCH Incorporated point out, a single taxpayer earning $30,000 a year is entitled to the full $2,000 deduction. Under the law in effect before 1998, when the deduction for single taxpayers was phased out between $25,000 and $35,000 of adjusted gross income (AGI), the deduction would have been limited to $1,000.

TABLE 3.1 Income Levels for Deductible IRAs

TAX YEARS BEGINNING IN:	SINGLE TAXPAYERS	MARRIED TAXPAYERS FILING JOINTLY
2000	$32,000–$42,000	$52,000–$ 62,000
2001	33,000– 43,000	53,000– 63,000
2002	34,000– 44,000	54,000– 64,000
2003	40,000– 50,000	60,000– 70,000
2004	45,000– 55,000	65,000– 75,000
2005	50,000– 60,000	70,000– 80,000
2006	50,000– 60,000	75,000– 85,000
2007 and thereafter	50,000– 60,000	80,000– 100,000

The new rules for married couples are particularly helpful. Under prior law, if one spouse was covered under an employer-sponsored retirement plan, the other spouse was treated as an active participant as well, which meant being subject to the same phase-out rules for deductible contributions. Under the new law, husband and wives are regarded as separate individuals and are not bound by one spouse's participation in an on-the-job retirement plan. Better yet, the maximum deductible IRA contribution for an individual who is not an active participant, but whose spouse is, is phased out at adjusted gross incomes between $150,000 and $160,000.

This provision is an enormous boon to stay-at-home spouses *and* helps the many workers whose employers do not offer retirement plans. Again, in an example provided by CCH, if you participate in a retirement plan at work and your spouse is not an active participant, your spouse can make a fully deductible $2,000 contribution to an IRA so long as your combined AGI is below $150,000. The total combined annual contribution to an IRA for a married couple is now $4,000.

Under legislation introduced in Congress in 2000 and again in 2001, annual deductible contributions to IRAs would be raised to $5,000. Increased limits, at any level, would be a major help as Americans save for retirement.

It may not seem like much, but $2,000 a year in tax-free growth adds up over time.

NUMBER OF YEARS	TAXABLE INVESTMENT	TAX-FREE IRA
10	$ 26,592	$ 31,291
20	70,406	98,846
30	142,594	244,692

The table assumes that $2,000 is invested each year, at a fixed return of 8 percent.

Here are other things you should know about IRAs:

- Contributions must be based on earned income, which includes wages, salary, bonuses, self-employment income, and alimony or separate maintenance payments that are taxable income. Earned income does not include interest, dividends, pensions, or Social Security benefits.
- Contributions may be made at any time up to the tax-filing deadline for the year (usually April 15, unless this date falls on a weekend), not including extensions. But making your contributions as early in the year as possible earns that many more months of tax-sheltered growth.
- Contributions must stop—and distributions begin—on April 1 of the year following the year in which you reach age 70½. With a 401(k) plan, by contrast, you may continue making contributions and defer distributions if you are still working.
- Annual fees paid to an IRA custodian (mutual fund, brokerage firm, bank, or insurance company) are deductible as itemized miscellaneous deductions—but only if the fees are paid separately. Fees paid out of an IRA account are not deductible. Itemized miscellaneous deductions may be taken to the extent that, as a group, they exceed 2 percent of adjusted gross income. (Other miscellaneous deductions that can be grouped with IRA fees include the cost of safe deposit rental, subscriptions to professional journals, and tax preparation fees.)
- You may move your IRA from one custodian to another, without penalty, so long as the money does not pass through your hands. To do so, arrange for a direct trustee-to-trustee transfer from the first custodian to the second.

- You may not borrow money from an IRA, and you may not use it as security for a loan. However, you may take possession of the money, and use it for any purpose, as long as you do so no more than once a year and as long as you keep it in your possession no more than 60 days.
- You must make investment choices within your IRA (the IRA itself is only a shell to hold tax-sheltered investments) and should choose a custodian offering a wide array of investment alternatives. Although annuities are on the investment menu (see Table 3.2), it generally does not make sense to put a tax-sheltered investment within a tax-sheltered container. You can't shelter the same money twice. (See Chapters 6 and 7 for more on making investment decisions.)

Reluctant to tie money up in an IRA? True, there is a 10 percent tax penalty on amounts withdrawn before you reach age 59½. But the Taxpayer Relief Act of 1997 also expanded the situations in which

TABLE 3.2 Where IRA Money Was Invested in 1999

INVESTMENT	TRADITIONAL IRAS	ROTH IRAS
Bank CDs and money market accounts	28%	14%
Individual stocks	34	28
Individual bonds	11	5
Variable annuities	22	16
Fixed annuities	17	13
Mutual funds	65	75
Stock funds	49	53
Bond funds	18	15
Balanced funds	12	7
Money market	19	13
Other	6	5

The percentages add up to more than 100 percent because IRAs can be invested in more than one investment vehicle.

Source: Reprinted by permission of the Investment Company Institute (www.ici.org).

penalty-free withdrawals may be made from an IRA prior to age 59½. The conditions now include:

- Death or disability.
- Payment of medical expenses exceeding 7.5 percent of adjusted gross income.
- Purchase of health insurance while unemployed.
- Payment for tuition, fees, books, supplies, and equipment (but not room or board) for any member of the IRA owner's family.
- Up to $10,000 toward the purchase of a first home.

In addition, as under prior law, withdrawals are penalty-free if they are made in the form of periodic payments over the life expectancy of the IRA owner or beneficiary. For more detail on distributions from retirement plans, see Chapter 11.

Nondeductible IRAs

If you are not eligible for deductible contributions to a traditional IRA, you may want to consider making nondeductible contributions. Even where contributions may not be deducted, earnings grow tax-deferred until they are withdrawn. This can be particularly valuable when you face many years of work before you plan to retire and tap the money.

But be prepared for massive paperwork headaches, especially if you have both deductible and nondeductible IRAs. If you make a nondeductible contribution, you must file Form 8606 with your federal income tax return each year. You must also hold on to the forms so that, when you reach retirement age and start taking distributions, you can calculate the tax due on the withdrawals. Earnings will be taxed at the time of withdrawal. But your original contributions won't be taxed, if you keep proper records, because they have already been taxed. Without proper documentation, you could wind up paying tax on the same money twice.

What's more, the IRS insists that all your IRAs, deductible and nondeductible, must be lumped together (on paper) and treated as a single account for purposes of calculating withdrawals and the tax due on those withdrawals. You can't deplete one account first and then the other; you must figure proportionate distributions and pay taxes accordingly. (Recent IRS rulings, however, have allowed taxpayers to take distributions from one plan while leaving another intact. Consult a knowledgeable tax adviser before you begin distributions.)

Roth IRAs

At the start of 1998, the Roth IRA (named for its originator, Senator William Roth) was introduced as an intriguing alternative to the traditional IRA. More people are eligible because income limitations on contributions are considerably higher than they are on the traditional IRA. Full $2,000 annual contributions may be made to a Roth IRA at income up to $95,000 for singles and $150,000 for married couples filing jointly. Contributions phase out at income up to $110,000 for singles and $160,000 for married couples. The annual contribution (a maximum of $2,000 for all your IRAs, combined) may be made until the filing date (without extensions) of your federal income tax return for the year.

With the Roth, contributions are never deductible. The attraction comes at the other end. Withdrawals of both contributions and earnings are completely tax-free, as long as the money has been left in place for at least five years from the date of the first contribution to the account *and* one of the following four conditions is met:

- You are over age 59½, or
- You have become disabled, or
- You use the money toward the purchase of a first home, or
- You have died and the money is paid to a beneficiary or your estate.

Even if earnings are subject to tax, the 10 percent tax penalty for withdrawals before age 59½ will be waived if the money is used for medical expenses exceeding 7.5 percent of AGI, medical insurance premiums while you are unemployed, or the cost of higher education. Note, too, that withdrawals from a Roth IRA are deemed to come from contributions first and then from earnings. There is no income tax (or tax penalty) until the total of your withdrawals exceeds the total amount of your contributions.

Other special attractions are built into the Roth IRA:

- It makes no difference whether you are covered by an employer-sponsored retirement plan. If you meet the income limitations, you can contribute to a Roth IRA.
- You are not required to stop making contributions or start taking distributions at any specific age. As noted earlier, you can continue contributing as long as you have earned income, and you can leave the accumulated contributions and earnings in place for your family.
- Although there may be federal estate tax on assets in a Roth IRA, if your total estate exceeds specified amounts (see Table 12.2 in Chapter 12), there is no income tax payable at death as there is with a traditional deductible IRA.

Conversions

Want to jump-start a Roth IRA? You can convert a traditional IRA to a Roth IRA if your adjusted gross income (married or single) is $100,000 or less in the year of the conversion. Some folks with higher income have been able to manage the switch by postponing self-employment income, deferring an anticipated bonus, or investing in growth securities with no current income.

One potential drawback: Income tax is due on the amounts in the traditional IRA at the time of the conversion. For you, therefore, conversion means biting the tax bullet up front—paying the tax now to create a stream of tax-free income later. For your children, it means tax-free income that can be stretched out over their lifetimes.

When the Roth was first introduced in 1998, a temporary tax break allowed taxpayers to spread the income tax over a four-year period. That tax break is gone but, because conversion is not an all-or-nothing proposition, you can create your own tax spread by converting only a portion of a traditional IRA each year.

You may want to convert to a Roth if you will not need the money in retirement, want to pass it on to your heirs, and can pay the tax out of assets other than the IRA. It's generally a poor idea to take money out of the IRA to pay the tax, especially if you are under age 59½ and will owe the 10 percent early withdrawal penalty.

If you are still fairly young, with a small amount accumulated in your traditional IRA and a long time before you retire, a Roth conversion may make abundant sense. At the other end of the spectrum, the Roth can suit some older people with large estates who want to leave IRA assets to children and grandchildren.

Converting to a Roth also provides an opportunity to correct problems with beneficiary designations. With a traditional IRA, the method of distribution is locked in when you reach age 70½. You can change your beneficiary after that date, but not the method of distribution. This can pose a problem if your beneficiary dies first.

Let's say you named your spouse as beneficiary, with payouts based on your joint life expectancy and recalculated each year. Then your spouse died after you had started receiving distributions. Because life expectancy drops to zero at death, your own distributions will be accelerated. (See Chapter 11 for more detail on distributions and alternatives to the recalculation method.)

Convert to a Roth, stop taking distributions (remember, none is required), and you can name a new beneficiary. "You can start the clock ticking again," says Jere Doyle, estate planning manager for Mellon Private Asset Management in Boston. "With a traditional IRA, your hands are tied after 70½, not with a Roth." Because a Roth is tax-free, too, it's better than a traditional IRA when it comes to funding trusts to get assets out of your taxable estate. (This subject—and new rules—is discussed more fully in Chapter 12.)

You can convert to a Roth IRA even if you are already past age 70½ and are taking minimum required distributions from your traditional IRA. Under these circumstances, however, you must first take the required distribution for the year and then make the conversion.

But nothing is ever simple, especially when tax law is involved. A Roth conversion isn't for everyone. In an article in the *AAII Journal*, published by the American Association of Individual Investors, Clark Blackman and Ellen Boling of Deloitte & Touche, pointed to several considerations:

- In some states, Roth IRAs may not enjoy the same protection from creditors as traditional IRAs. Most states have fallen into line on this issue but, if this is a concern, check your state's laws.
- Conversion to a Roth and paying the income tax now may not make economic sense if you will be in a lower tax bracket after retirement. It's impossible to know what tax brackets will be in future years—Congress has a way of tinkering—but you might

owe less tax because your income declines—or because you move to a state with no income tax.

- Although actions under prior tax laws are usually grandfathered when the laws change, some analysts think the tax-free aspect of the Roth is too good to be true and may not last.
- And, perhaps most important, there could be a possible loss of other tax benefits in the year (or years) of conversion because the amount converted, while it doesn't count toward the income ceiling of $100,000 on making the conversion, does increase adjusted gross income. AGI, in turn, affects your tax bill in several ways.

For example, if your AGI exceeds $132,950 in 2001 (the amount is the same for single taxpayers and married couples filing jointly, and is indexed to inflation), you will start to lose some itemized deductions. Medical expenses stay intact. So do casualty and theft losses. But, at the highest income levels, you can lose three cents of every dollar spent on state and local income taxes, real estate taxes, and mortgage interest. The most you can lose is 80 percent of these deductions.

In addition, the personal exemption phases out in 2001 at incomes starting at $132,950 for single taxpayers and $199,450 for married couples filing jointly. Similarly, education tax breaks and child credits phase out at specified income levels. And, to add insult to injury, you may face IRS penalties if converting to a Roth boosts your income for the year and you fail to adjust your tax withholding or to pay estimated taxes to cover the additional tax due.

If additional taxable income from the conversion eliminates or reduces deductions you could otherwise claim, the long-term benefit of conversion could be lost. But the game isn't lost. You can convert to a Roth, and then change your mind.

Undoing a conversion is called "recharacterization." The most frequent reason for reversing a conversion to a Roth IRA is that you underestimated your income for the year. If you find at year-end that you've earned more than $100,000, you weren't entitled to the Roth conversion and your IRA can be disqualified. You can eliminate this potentially serious problem by turning the Roth back into a traditional IRA. You have until the final date for filing your federal income tax return—typically, October 15 of the following year, if you have secured filing extensions—to do the recharacterization.

You can recharacterize for any reason, says Ed Slott, editor of *Ed Slott's IRA Advisor*. Let's say you converted a traditional IRA worth $200,000 and then the stock market went into a major decline. Your IRA may now be worth only $100,000, but you still owe income tax on the $200,000 it was worth at the time of conversion. If you undo the conversion, you can avoid the tax on the larger sum. You won't get the money back that you lost in the stock market, but at least you'll save the tax on the money that's no longer there.

To recharacterize an IRA, either rename the account at the institution holding it now or do a trustee-to-trustee transfer to another institution so that the money doesn't pass through your hands. Bear in mind, though, that the unlimited conversions and recharacterizations originally allowed have been cut back. Now, if you convert a traditional IRA to a Roth IRA and then recharacterize it as a traditional IRA, you cannot convert it back to a Roth IRA until the later of the beginning of the following tax year or 30 days after the recharacterization.

Convert to a Roth in April, recharacterize it in August, and you can't reconvert until the following January. Thirty days would bring you only to September, and the rule says the *later* of 30 days or the beginning of the following year. What happens if you go ahead and reconvert earlier? Your Roth IRA remains valid, but you won't get any tax benefit from the reconversion. In other words, if you reconverted to save taxes on an IRA that had lost monetary value, it won't work. You'll be taxed on the higher amount.

Moreover, says CPA Barry C. Picker, "If you were under age 59½ at the time of the conversion, you get hit for an additional 10 percent penalty tax. Then, to add insult to injury, you are hit with a 6 percent excise tax per year since you are considered to have made an excess contribution to a Roth IRA." The 6 percent excise tax is imposed each year until the excess amount is withdrawn. But, once the money is withdrawn, you are left with an ordinary taxable account. You don't have either the tax-deferred income you would have had with a traditional IRA or the tax-free income of a Roth IRA.

SEP-IRAs, SIMPLE Plans, and Keogh Plans

You are reading this book, so you probably work for a company that offers a defined contribution plan. If you also have self-employment income, however, additional tax-sheltered retirement plans are available to you in the form of SEP-IRAs, SIMPLE IRAs, and Keogh Plans.

SEP-IRAs (the acronym stands for Simplified Employee Plans) resemble garden-variety IRAs except that, well beyond the $2,000 IRA ceiling on contributions, you may contribute up to 15 percent of net self-employment income (gross income less business deductions) to a maximum of $25,500. (The law says $30,000 but currently limits the compensation base for contributions to $170,000. Fifteen percent of $170,000 is $25,500.)

A SEP-IRA is easy to set up at almost any bank, brokerage house, or mutual fund. No annual tax filings are required, and you aren't locked into making a maximum contribution. You can vary your contributions from year to year.

One potential drawback, if your moonlighting business employs anyone but yourself and your spouse: You must make contributions for any employee who is at least age 21 and has worked for you, even part-time, in three of the preceding five years. Those contributions are deposited directly into an IRA for each employee. The employees then make their own investment decisions. Once you've made the contributions, the employees are immediately entitled to them.

SIMPLE Plans (the acronym stands for Savings Incentive Match Plan for Employees) may take the form of either a 401(k) plan or an IRA. In practice, only the IRA is widely available in prototype plans from custodial institutions.

A SIMPLE-IRA is a salary reduction plan that is similar to a 401(k) but is designed for small employers. A 401(k) may be adopted no matter how small or how large the company but, in practice, is cumbersome for the smallest employers. A SIMPLE-IRA is specifically designed for companies with 100 or fewer employees. In fact, you can open a SIMPLE-IRA if you have *no* employees.

With a SIMPLE-IRA, you may contribute every penny of self-employment income—up to a maximum of $6,000. In addition, you must make a dollar-for-dollar matching contribution for each employee earning at least $5,000 a year. You do this in one of two ways, contributing (1) up to a maximum of 3 percent of pay for each employee who chooses to participate in the plan, or (2) a flat 2 percent of pay for each employee, whether or not the employee chooses to participate.

You can make a matching contribution for yourself, as an owner-employee. Under a SIMPLE plan with a 3 percent match, you can put aside a maximum of $12,000 a year toward your own retirement—but only if your compensation is at least $200,000 (3 percent of $200,000 is $6,000). (See Table 3.3.)

TABLE 3.3 Maximum Contributions to a SIMPLE Plan, at 3 Percent

COMPENSATION	SALARY DEFERRAL	MATCHING CONTRIBUTION	TOTAL
$ 50,000	$6,000	$1,500	$ 7,500
75,000	6,000	2,250	8,250
100,000	6,000	3,000	9,000
125,000	6,000	3,750	9,750
150,000	6,000	4,500	10,500
175,000	6,000	5,250	11,250
200,000 and more	6,000	6,000	12,000

Here, too, your contributions are immediately vested in the employees. In contrast to the SEP-IRA, however, there is a two-year waiting period before the money can be transferred—even to another IRA—without severe tax penalties: 25 percent of amounts withdrawn within the first two years of participation.

Keogh Plans are the granddaddy of retirement plans for the self-employed. Named after Representative Eugene Keogh, who introduced the original legislation, Keogh Plans are now given the same treatment as qualified corporate retirement plans. As defined contribution plans, they may be structured as either profit sharing or money purchase or as a combination or paired plan.

Under the profit-sharing arrangement, you are allowed to contribute up to 15 percent (actually, 13.04 percent because the contribution itself is subtracted from income) of your net self-employment income each year, to a maximum of $30,000. As with the SEP-IRA, the actual maximum contribution is currently $25,500 because the annual compensation on which the contribution is based is limited to $170,000. The advantage of the profit-sharing arrangement is that you need not make a contribution at all in years when self-employment income is down.

Under the money purchase arrangement, the annual contribution limits are higher but must be made every year. The maximum permitted is 25 percent (actually, 20 percent) of net self-employment income, up to an annual ceiling of $30,000. With a paired plan, combining profit sharing and money purchase, you can hedge your bets by making the maximum contribution of 20 percent or $30,000 while retaining the option of reducing the contribution in a given year.

Most financial institutions have prototype documents for defined contribution Keogh Plans. In making your choice among institutions, look at investment options and consider fees. Remember, too, that annual fees are deductible as itemized miscellaneous deductions *if paid separately;* they are not deductible if paid out of the account.

An alternative Keogh Plan is the *defined benefit* plan, akin to a corporate pension plan. Most appropriate for older high-income individuals, the defined benefit Keogh lets you establish a target benefit (up to a current mandated ceiling of about $140,000 a year), then put away enough money each year to reach that target. There is no dollar ceiling on contributions so, if you have adequate income from other sources, you may be able to sock away most of your self-employment income toward retirement.

Defined benefit plans are more expensive to establish and maintain. You will have to have an actuary calculate the annual contribution, and you may need an accountant to prepare the annual tax return.

Until recently, a highly paid employee covered under a company retirement plan was limited in how much could be contributed to a separate plan for self-employment income. Effective January 1, 2000, the "rule of one" has been repealed. Under that rule, the most that could be put into any combination of retirement plans was determined by a formula that weighed combined contributions to all of the accounts and prohibited contributions exceeding a specified amount. In effect, anyone who continued working after fully funding one plan was prevented from funding another. No longer; for as long as you have self-employment income, you may pour deductible contributions into a defined contribution or defined benefit Keogh, even if you have a fully funded plan at your salaried job. In fact, you may continue making contributions after age 70½, if you are still working, although you will also have to start taking distributions.

Keogh Plans must obey many of the same rules as IRAs, but there are two substantive differences. First, as noted above, you may continue making contributions to a Keogh Plan after you reach the required beginning date for withdrawals; you may not do so with an IRA. Second, a Keogh Plan must be opened by the end of the calendar year (although contributions in following years can be made up to the date you file your federal income tax return for the year). An IRA can be started up until the tax filing date. To shelter earnings for 2001, you would have to open a Keogh Plan by December 31 of that year, but an IRA could be opened as late as April 15, 2002.

One other point: Traditional and Roth IRAs are strictly individual arrangements but, as noted above, you must include any employees under SEP and SIMPLE plans. Also, you must include employees under a Keogh Plan if they work full time, are at least age 21, and have been employed for at least one year. When employees are covered, a Keogh Plan is just like any other pension plan and must meet guidelines established by federal laws. This requirement can generate considerable paperwork—and potential tax problems—when you are ready to retire and want to close down the plan.

Which self-employment retirement plan is best for you? It depends on how much you earn from self-employment and whether you have employees. When your choice comes down to SEP vs. SIMPLE, Rolf Auster, a professor of taxation at Florida International University, writing in the CCH *Journal of Retirement Planning*, suggests that SIMPLE plans work best for people earning relatively little from self-employment, although they may also work well for high-income professionals who have employees. SEP-IRAs, on the other hand, are more likely to suit high-income professionals with no employees.

The break-even point, in terms of income, is roughly $50,000. Below $50,000, consider a SIMPLE plan. Above $50,000, consider a SEP-IRA or, for maximum contributions—with a bit more fuss, because annual tax returns must be filed once assets in the plan exceed $100,000—a defined contribution or defined benefit Keogh Plan.

Annuities

The last entrant in the retirement-saving game is an annuity, an individually purchased contract designed to provide a stream of income in retirement. Annuities are issued by insurance companies and may be purchased from insurance companies, mutual funds, brokerage firms, banks, and other financial institutions. Because payments from an annuity are often many years in the future—like payments under a life insurance policy—it's important to choose a financially sound issuer who is likely to be in business when you are ready to collect.

Annuities may be immediate or deferred, fixed or variable, purchased with a series of payments or a single sizable payment. Although annuities resemble traditional IRAs in some ways—income builds tax-deferred within an annuity and early withdrawals (before age 59½) are subject to a 10 percent tax penalty—contributions to an annuity are never deductible.

Annuities are complicated financial products. Still, you might consider purchasing an annuity if you want to build more retirement income but have maxed out your contributions to tax-qualified retirement plans on and off the job, including a 401(k), an IRA, and, if you have self-employment income, a SEP-IRA, SIMPLE, or Keogh Plan.

Annuities offer several advantages:

- There is no ceiling on contributions; you may put away as much as you like.
- Contributions are not based on income, so you can make contributions from interest, dividends, or liquidated assets of any kind.
- There is no "required beginning date," so you may leave earnings to grow tax-deferred as long as you like.
- No annual tax filings are required.
- Annuities can provide guaranteed lifetime income.
- Proceeds are paid directly to named beneficiaries after the annuitant's death, without any delay associated with probate.
- If you wish to make a switch, perhaps to earn a more favorable rate of return, you can make a tax-free exchange—called a "1035 exchange," after the applicable section of the Internal Revenue Code—from one annuity to another.

But annuities also have some built-in drawbacks:

- Contributions, as noted above, are never tax-deductible.
- Withdrawals are taxed as ordinary income, just like withdrawals from tax-qualified plans, so you can't take advantage of the lower capital gains tax rate available on other investments.
- Many annuities, although not all, carry hefty fees.
- Many annuities have steep surrender penalties for the first six or seven years, making it very costly to buy an annuity and then change your mind.
- If you die owning an annuity, the proceeds (like those in an IRA) will be subject to income tax and, if your estate is large enough, to estate tax as well. There is no step-up in value at death for assets in an annuity.

An annuity may be *immediate* (starting within a year after you pay the premium) or *deferred* (starting at a later date that you select).

An immediate annuity may suit your needs if you receive a windfall—coming into an inheritance, perhaps, or receiving a lump-sum distribution from a retirement plan—later in life and you want the stream of income to start right away.

Deferred annuities are far more popular because they offer tax-deferred accumulations from the time you pay the premium (or premiums) until you decide to take the money out. That decision is pretty much up to you. Some annuity contracts—and some state laws—specify that payments must start by age 85; others leave the starting date indeterminate. In any case, you will not have to meet the required beginning-date rules of tax-qualified plans like IRAs and 401(k) plans.

Annuities may also be either *fixed* or *variable*.

Fixed annuities, either immediate or deferred, promise a fixed return on your money—although the rate can, and probably will, change after an initial guarantee period. With a fixed annuity, the issuer takes the investment risk. Before buying a fixed annuity, consider:

- The current interest rate—how long it is guaranteed and how often thereafter it can change.
- The minimum interest rate guaranteed in the contract and whether, if rates fall below a specified level (typically, below the current market rate but above the guaranteed minimum rate), you can transfer to another contract without incurring surrender charges.
- The surrender charges for early liquidation. Typically, although there are variations, surrender charges start at 7 percent in the first year and decline to zero by the seventh year.
- Whether there is a front-end "load" or sales commission. Many annuities are sold with loads, but some companies—The Vanguard Group is one example—offer low-cost annuities.
- The ongoing cost of maintaining the annuity at a fixed-dollar amount or as a percentage of the principal.
- Whether you can have access to your money before starting regular withdrawals. Some annuity contracts permit you to withdraw the interest each year without penalty; others permit you to take a specified percentage (usually 10 percent, sometimes 15 percent) of the amount in the annuity without a surrender charge. If you are under age 59½, however, you will owe a 10 percent tax penalty.

- Whether there is a "market value adjustment," an additional charge levied if you surrender the annuity. The charge is designed to shift some of the investment risk to you, on the theory that the issuer could lose money if it had to sell out of investments to pay off your annuity early. Fixed annuities that contain a market value adjustment may offer a slightly higher interest rate as a trade-off, but be sure you understand how much it will cost you if you need your money early.

Variable annuities have an insurance core but peg their returns to the performance of underlying "subaccounts" that you select. The subaccounts resemble mutual funds and may even have the same recognizable names as retail mutual funds, although they are not the same funds. Your choice of investments within a variable annuity may be similar to the choices you have within your 401(k) plan at work.

Variable annuities have outdistanced fixed annuities in popularity in a decade of stellar stock market returns. New money has poured into variable annuities in recent years; $12 billion invested in 1990 rose to $121 billion in 1999. Don't forget, though: with a variable annuity, you make the investment decisions *and* take the investment risk.

Variable annuities, as a combination of insurance and investments, may offer the best of both worlds. Although returns will fluctuate, there is generally a guaranteed death benefit consisting of at least the amount you invested; some annuities lock-in investment gains periodically so that your heirs receive more than the premiums you've paid even if value is down at the time of death. There is an opportunity to select guaranteed lifetime income plus the possibility of growth in the underlying subaccounts. Because annuities are tax-deferred accounts, it's also possible to switch investments among the subaccounts without incurring any tax obligation.

Variable annuities also have some significant disadvantages that deserve careful consideration before you invest. Pay special attention to the cost of purchasing and maintaining a variable annuity—and don't buy one if you don't plan to hold on to it for at least 10 years. At shorter holding periods, mutual funds may make more sense. Although some low-cost products have recently become available, many variable annuities still charge a hefty combination of commissions, administrative costs, and so-called mortality and expense charges covering the cost of guaranteed lifetime income and the guaranteed death benefit. The total can be more than 2 percent a year—and that's on top of management fees (for the subaccounts) comparable to the annual management fees paid on mutual funds.

To attract investors in a highly competitive marketplace, the issuers of variable annuities have added a variety of bells and whistles to their product. Many are not worth the additional cost, which—if you take them all—can bring total administrative costs to 3 percent a year. For example:

- A guarantee against market downturns, which typically offers a choice among: the portfolio value at the time of death; the original amount invested plus 5 percent; or the high point of portfolio value at a specified time. The guarantee typically costs from 0.1 percent to 0.5 percent of the assets in the account. But the market would have to suffer a sharp and sustained downturn before this guarantee would become significant.
- Some policies offer the option of withdrawing money from the annuity to cover the cost of long-term custodial care in a nursing home or at home. If you want coverage for the cost of long-term care, it might be preferable to buy a stand-alone policy designed for this purpose.
- Some companies are offering sign-up bonuses that add 3 to 4 percent of the initial contribution to the value of the account at the time of purchase. Weigh the additional cost (and the possibility of a longer surrender period) before you go for a policy with a sign-up bonus.

One more caveat: Although you can reduce the risk of monetary loss within a variable annuity by choosing a fixed-income fund as one of your subaccounts, the high costs associated with most variable annuities can only be offset by growth within the portfolio. A fixed-income subaccount, if it is part of a variable annuity at all, should be a very small part.

But tax-deferred accumulations can't go on forever. As noted earlier, annuities are subject to both income and estate tax if left to your beneficiaries at death. So, at some point, you should start to take the money out. When you do so, you will have to choose between fixed or variable income. With variable income, your payments may change either upward or downward to reflect actual returns. You also have to make a choice among income options.

Distributions under every arrangement are based on life expectancy. The older you are when the payments start, the more you will receive. The largest distributions are made under an individual life annuity, the smallest under the joint-and-survivor life annuity with period certain.

When you start taking distributions, you have a choice between annuitizing and not annuitizing. To annuitize means, simply, to convert your annuity into a stream of regular payments. The problems with electing annuitization are: (1) you are locked in and can't make a change; (2) you lose access to the cash value; and (3) payments cease when you die, even if death occurs on the day after your first payment. An alternative to annuitization is systematic withdrawal of funds. Following is more detail on income options:

- An individual life annuity, with payments made for as long as you live. This approach offers the largest monthly payment, plus the advantage that you can't outlive your income. Its disadvantage is that whenever you die—the day after the first payment or 30 years later—the annuity is at an end and your heirs get nothing.
- A joint-and-survivor annuity promises lifetime payments to you and your spouse, so long as either of you is still living. A further choice lies in the percentage of income your survivor will receive. There are usually several choices; the most common are: 50 percent and 100 percent of the amount the annuitant receives. Providing your survivor with 100 percent of your benefit means that you will receive less during your lifetime.
- A "term certain" or "period certain" annuity, available on either an individual or a joint-and-survivor payout, promises payments for the period of years that you select. Choose a 10-year term, as an example, and payments are made to you for life but for at least 10 years. If you die before the end of the term, your designated beneficiaries will receive payments for the remainder of the period.
- A life annuity with a period certain feature, available on either an individual or joint-and-survivor annuity, guarantees payments for life and continuing payments to a designated survivor if you die before the end of the guaranteed period.
- Systematic withdrawal of funds, unlike any of the above annuity options, lets you change the amounts as needed and avoid the lock-in of annuitization. Contracts offering the systematic

withdrawal option may offer you a choice among taking fixed dollar amounts, a specific percentage of your accumulated funds, or the total value of your account in equal amounts. In each case, payments would be made on a set schedule—monthly, quarterly, semiannually, or annually. Under many contracts, you would be able to convert the remaining accumulation to a lifetime annuity at any time.

Pay attention to the tax consequences of any distribution decision. Annuities are tax-deferred while they accumulate but taxable when withdrawn. If you die during the accumulation period, your beneficiary will owe income tax on any amount in excess of your original investment. The annuity will also be included in calculating whether your estate is subject to federal estate tax.

When you start to take distributions from your annuity, the interest portion of each periodic payment, if you annuitize, is taxed as ordinary income. The portion of each payment that represents return of principal is not taxed. If you outlive your life expectancy, so that the entire principal is repaid, each succeeding payment is fully taxable. If you take systematic withdrawals, on the other hand, the entire amount of each distribution is taxed as earnings until you have used up all the earnings within your annuity and are tapping principal.

If you die after annuitization and there is a continuing benefit to your survivor under the terms of the contract, the value of the joint-and-survivor annuity that you paid for will be included in your estate. (If your spouse is your beneficiary, however, no estate tax will be due because any amount can pass to a surviving spouse without estate tax.)

Proceeds paid after death from a life insurance policy are free of income tax. But proceeds paid after death from an annuity are taxed as ordinary income and are also included in the taxable estate. However, a beneficiary who files an itemized federal income tax return can take an income tax deduction for any estate tax attributable to an annuity. This deduction, called "income in respect of decedent" is discussed in Chapter 12 as it pertains to IRAs.

PART 2

Managing Your 401(k)

CHAPTER 4

Your Investment Mix

Your employer-sponsored retirement plan is a vehicle to hold tax-sheltered retirement savings. Contributing money to the plan on a regular basis is the single most important thing you can do to ensure retirement income. In fact, according to some studies, making regular contributions may be more critical to investment returns than the specific investments you choose. But you still want to make a careful choice of investments and then reevaluate your choice from time to time to be sure you're on the right track.

Before you even look at the investment menu, however, think about how much you'll need to meet your retirement income goals.

Traditional wisdom holds that you should start retirement with 70 percent to 80 percent of your pre-retirement income. The theory is that you'll need less when you are no longer commuting to work, buying weekday lunches, and purchasing business clothes. But the fact is that you may wind up spending more on entertainment and travel in the early active years of retirement. Later, when you're past age 80 or 85, you may need to cover the increased cost of health care.

Don't underestimate your retirement income needs. And, as you plan, remember inflation. The amount of money that's adequate in the first year of retirement may be far from adequate 10 or 20 years down the road. Let's say you retire with an income of $30,000 a year. If inflation were to run a steady 4 percent over 20 years of your retirement—a bit more than today's 3 percent, but considerably less than the double-digit price jumps of the 1970s—it would take $66,000 to buy, 20 years from now, what $30,000 will buy today. In fact, even a 3 percent rate of inflation will cut the value of a dollar in half in 25 years.

Use Table 4.1 to determine how much money you'll need if inflation is at various levels. For example, if you want to find the equivalent of today's $30,000 in 20 years, at an inflation rate of 4 percent, multiply $30,000 by the factor of 2.2. The result: $66,000. If you want to match $50,000, at an inflation rate of 6 percent, the factor for 20 years is 3.2 and the result is $160,000.

How Much Will You Need?

There is no one-size-fits-all retirement budget. Your budget must meet *your* needs, *your* lifestyle, *your* emotional sense of security. A lot depends on the life you've led until now, and the life you plan to lead in retirement. A lot also depends on how much is "enough." Some folks are content with an annual income of $40,000; others feel they must have at least $200,000 to be comfortable.

Before you even think about money, however, ponder these facts about the retirement years:

- Retirement lasts a long time. The average 65-year-old man can expect to live 16 more years; the average 65-year-old woman,

TABLE 4.1 Inflation Factors

YEARS TO RETIREMENT	RATES OF INFLATION						
	4%	5%	6%	7%	8%	9%	10%
5	1.2	1.3	1.3	1.4	1.5	1.5	1.6
10	1.5	1.6	1.8	2.0	2.2	2.4	2.6
15	1.8	2.2	2.4	2.8	3.2	3.6	4.2
20	2.2	2.6	3.2	3.9	4.7	5.6	6.7
25	2.7	3.4	4.3	5.4	6.8	8.6	10.0

almost 20 years. These are averages, of course, and some people will live considerably longer. Plan your retirement—both financially and emotionally—as if you will live to age 95. It could happen.

- The retirement years are not all alike. In the first decade or more, from age 65 to 75 or 80, many retirees are energetic, healthy, and thoroughly involved in life. Only when health begins to fail—for some, not until age 80 or 85, or even later—does old age really set in. Your retirement budget should take the two stages into account.
- Women live longer than men and, often, have less retirement income. Because women are in and out of the work force as they meet family responsibilities—first to children and then, often, to aging parents—their cumulative lifetime earnings are less. As a result, their pensions and the amount they can save in defined contribution plans are also less.

The best way to start your retirement income calculations, as painful as it may seem, is to analyze your current spending and then project that spending into retirement. You also have to make assumptions about the rate of inflation, how much you'll earn on your investments, and how long you'll live. Other considerations include charitable bequests, how much you'd like to leave to your children, and—perhaps an unpleasant thought, but an important one—how much the surviving spouse will need if you are now part of a married couple. This can be a particularly important calculation if, as a couple, you are relying heavily on one partner's pension and Social Security.

There are many software programs that let you plug in various numbers and possible scenarios, to see what you need. Many are listed in Appendix B, for more information. But a number of informal surveys have found that you may get as many results as there are online calculators. In one recent review by *The Wall Street Journal*—based on an average investor who is 44 years old, earns $55,000 a year, and has $34,000 in an IRA and $41,000 in a 401(k) plan—estimates ranged from "expenses covered, plus $669,714 left over" (from The Motley Fool) to a shortfall of $1,104,504 (from T. Rowe Price). Online calculators can be a useful starting point, in other words, but you may want to check the results from more than one.

Software programs can provide some insight. But the old-fashioned pencil-and-paper combo still works well. You may want to fill out the following worksheet to get a preliminary "guesstimate" of your retirement income needs. Then, with either results from an online calculator or your own calculations, you may want to sit down with a financial adviser and fine-tune your projections. Chapter 13 describes financial advisers.

Worksheet: How Much Will You Need?

	STEP 1 CURRENT EXPENSES	STEP 2 ESTIMATED RETIREMENT EXPENSES
Food:	______	______
Housing:	______	______
Utilities:	______	______
Transportation:	______	______
Clothing:	______	______
Medical:	______	______
Insurance:	______	______
Travel/Recreation:	______	______
Taxes:	______	______
Savings/Investments:	______	______
Gifts/Donations:	______	______
Other:	______	______
Totals	______	______

Step 3: Multiply the total from Step 2 by the appropriate inflation factor from Table 4.1. For example, if you are 10 years from retirement and assume that inflation will continue at a steady 4 percent, you'll use inflation factor 1.5 to learn how much you'll actually need in the first retirement year. After that, project your needs when you are five years into retirement, and for five-year increments thereafter:

First retirement year:	______	______
Five years after retirement:	______	______
Ten years after retirement:	______	______

Retire Early?

A key element in all your retirement calculations is *when* you'll retire. As noted earlier, the "traditional" or "normal" retirement age is 65, but the average for American workers is currently age 62. Retire early, of course, and you will have that many more years in retirement. Can you afford those years?

Several factors must be woven into your calculation:

- You can tap your tax-sheltered retirement money without penalty after you reach age 59½.
- You can take your money, without a tax penalty, as early as age 55 if you leave the job where your plan is based.
- If you take the money between ages 55 and 59½ upon leaving employment, you must take regular payments for at least five years or until you reach age 59½, whichever is *longer.* Start at age 57 and you must take the regular payments until you reach age 62; then, if you like, you can stop withdrawals until you reach the required beginning date: April 1 of the calendar year after you reach age 70½.
- You can avoid a major one-time tax hit on your retirement funds if you make a direct transfer of your 401(k) into a rollover IRA.
- You can start Social Security retirement benefits at age 62, although your benefits will be permanently lower than the benefits you'll receive if you wait until the "normal" retirement age of 65 (or later, for those born after 1937).

More details on the complex laws governing retirement plan distributions can be found in Chapter 11.

The single most significant factor is probably the size of your nest egg. How much is enough? Half a million dollars sounds like a large amount to many folks. If you assume a 10 percent withdrawal rate, $500,000 would produce $50,000 a year while keeping your principal intact. That amount, in tandem with Social Security retirement benefits and any pension you may have, might comfortably fund your retirement lifestyle.

Then again, it might not. Two faulty assumptions are buried in the above calculation. First, it assumes that the amount you start out with will be enough as the years go by. Inherent in this assumption is a belief that inflation is under control and won't be a problem through the 20 or 30 years of your retirement. Although inflation has averaged about 3 percent during the past 75 years and has stayed, pretty consistently, just under 3 percent in the past few years, there have been periods of double-digit inflation in our history. As noted earlier, inflation is insidious; it eats away at buying power while you sleep. So the $500,000 portfolio you're starting out with, at a 10 percent withdrawal rate, would give you $50,000 a year—but that $50,000, at a 4 percent rate of inflation, would lose half its buying power in about 18 years.

The second faulty assumption is that you can't count on a 10 percent return from your portfolio. Although the 1990s saw the longest bull market in history, stock prices do move up and down, sometimes sharply and sometimes in a single day. The "crash" of October 1987 registered a drop of almost 22 percent in the Standard & Poor's 500 Composite Index, the index commonly used to reflect broad market value. Stocks rebounded quickly after that incident; they ended up 2 percent for 1987; 12.4 percent for 1988; and 27.3 percent for 1989. But that isn't always the case. In 1973, the S&P lost 17.4 percent of its value. In 1974, as the bear market continued, the S&P lost another 29.7 percent.

Research by Ibbotson Associates of Chicago shows that common stocks have produced an average return of about 11 percent over the past 75 years, but there were ups and downs along the way. Your personal return depends on the investments you select and, equally important, *when* you invest—in other words, did you start early and invest for the long term? I do *not* advise "timing" the market in an attempt to buy at the absolutely lowest price and sell at the highest. It isn't possible to accurately predict the lows and highs. If it were, professional investors would all be wealthy and enjoying the sun on a Caribbean island. Attempting to time the market is a losing strategy. In fact, as the Investment Company Institute recently pointed out, an investor who stayed in the stock market during the entire 30-year period from 1963 through 1993 would have had an average return of 11.83 percent. Missing the 90 best days of that period in an effort to time the market would have reduced the average return to 3.28 percent.

It's far more sensible to choose your investments wisely, both inside and outside your tax-sheltered retirement plans (see Chapters 5 through 7), and invest for the long term. Then, when retirement rolls around, withdrawing 4 percent to 5 percent of your portfolio each year should keep you ahead of both inflation and market volatility. More investment strategies for the post-retirement years are described in Chapter 7.

Along with inflation, one other factor can be a real drag on portfolio returns: taxes. There's no need to consider the tax consequences of trading within your retirement plans; these tax-sheltered plans are immune from taxes during the accumulation years. But income and capital gains taxes can seriously affect returns in taxable accounts. For strategies to help you allocate assets and minimize the tax bite, see Chapter 6.

Working just a few years beyond retirement eligibility can significantly boost your total balance and your retirement income. If you can hang in there for another two years, your $500,000 balance, invested at a conservative 8 percent, would become $580,000. Stick around for four years and earn 10 percent, and your $500,000 would become $730,000. Both examples assume that you don't augment the starting balance with more contributions. But, of course, you would continue contributing to your 401(k) plan during your working years, boosting your ending balance still more.

When you know how much you'll need, it's time for a serious look at how much you'll have. Add up your anticipated income from all the sources described in Chapter 1: Social Security, defined contribution plans, a traditional defined benefit pension (if you have one), investment income, and continued earnings. If there is a gap between how much you'll need and how much you'll have, now is the time to plug that gap. How? You could delay retirement and continue working, or switch jobs and work full-time instead of part-time, as you might have planned. You might tap the equity in your home. (For more on this strategy, see Chapter 7.) You might invest more aggressively, if you're comfortable doing so. (Assessing your risk tolerance is discussed in Chapter 6.) Or you can make a concerted effort to boost your savings now, in the years remaining before retirement.

How much difference can added savings possibly make as you near retirement? The American Savings Education Council (www.asec.org) points out that by putting aside as little as $50 a week, starting at age 50, and earning an average return of 8 percent, you will add almost $75,000 to your retirement nest egg by age 65. If you can manage to put aside $100 a week, starting at age 50 and earning 8 percent on your investments, you'll have an extra $150,000.

TABLE 4.2 How Much to Save Each Month, to Achieve Retirement Savings Goals

YEARS AVAILABLE FOR SAVING	NEST EGG GOALS $400,000		$600,000		$800,000		$1 MILLION	
	AMOUNTS INVESTED MONTHLY AT INTEREST OF:							
	6%	9%	6%	9%	6%	9%	6%	9%
30 years	$ 258	$ 159	$ 388	$ 238	$ 517	$ 317	$ 646	$ 397
20	636	466	954	699	1,271	932	1,589	1,165
10	2,079	1,793	3,119	2,689	4,159	3,585	5,198	4,481

A single year can make a difference. Postpone the start of your disciplined savings plan for another year—after all, you "need" the $50 a week for the big vacation planned for the year you turn 50—and you'll have $7,605 less at retirement.

Table 4.2 shows that the earlier you start to save, the less you will need to put away at each interval to reach the same goal. In short, start earlier and you'll have much more when you reach the finish line. The amount you save also counts. Start saving $50 a week at age 40 and, given the same average return of 8 percent, you'll have $206,000 in your retirement nest egg. Put aside $100 a week starting at age 40 and you'll have $412,000. What a difference $50 can make!

If saving so much seems impossible, remember two things:

1. You are not starting from zero; this nest egg of additional savings is meant to supplement your Social Security and retirement benefits.
2. The earlier you start, the easier it is to reach your goal.

Understanding Investment Vehicles

There are probably more individual investment vehicles than can be counted, and more are developed every week, but the investment pie can be sliced in several manageable ways:

- Cash, equities, and fixed income.
- Taxable vs. tax-free.

- Growth vs. income.
- Individual purchases vs. mutual funds.

Each slice is worth a closer look.

Cash, equities, and fixed income are ways to categorize the results expected from various investments. Cash—or, more accurately, cash equivalents—represents liquid assets. This might be cash itself but is more likely to be readily available money tucked away in a savings account, money market mutual fund, certificate of deposit, or short-term U.S. Treasury obligation. The money in cash and cash equivalents represents your life raft, the money that is immediately accessible if you lose your job, face an uninsured medical emergency, or total your car. Strictly speaking, cash equivalents are savings, not investments.

Equities are shares of common stock. When you own stock, you are a part owner—albeit a very small part—of the corporation that issued the stock. Your fortunes will rise and fall with the fortunes of the company and will be reflected in the share price and in quarterly dividends.

Regarding price, a share of stock is worth whatever someone is willing to pay for it. Analysts may discuss corporate earnings and the like, but the stock market is very much a creature of supply and demand. One measure that investors use to determine a stock's value is the price-to-earnings ratio, or P/E. The P/E is the price of a share of stock divided by the company's earnings per share. A stock selling for $50 a share and earning $5 a share, as an example, is said to selling at a P/E of 10. This figure is also called the multiple. By any name, it is most useful as a means of comparing similar securities or the same security over time.

The P/E and the yield—reflecting dividends as a percentage of the current share price—are found in daily newspaper tables. Those tables are now, for the most part, expressed in our familiar decimal system instead of the eighths that had prevailed since the U.S. stock market began. Table 4.3 shows a sample stock quotation. The column titles differ slightly from newspaper to newspaper, but most of the same basic information is presented.

Fixed-income investments—typically, bonds—are investments that throw off a predictable stream of income. When you buy a bond, you are lending money to the issuing agency or corporation. In return, you will receive the principal amount at the maturity date, plus interest for the use of the money.

TABLE 4.3 Sample Stock Listing for ExxonMobil Corporation

52-WEEK HIGH	52-WEEK LOW	STOCK	DIV	YIELD %	P/E	SALES 100S	HIGH	LOW	LAST	CHG
90.75	69.98^	ExxonMob	1.76	2.0	25	290,344	91.69	89.74	89.44	+0.31

The ingredients in the table are explained as follows:

- The first two figures, the **52-week high and low,** reflect the stock's highest and lowest values over the preceding year, not including the week preceding this listing.
- The ^ means that last week's high was greater than the 52-week high.
- After the **name of the stock** is the annual **dividend,** expressed in dollars and, in the next column, as a percentage of the current share price.
- The **P/E ratio** is the number of times by which the latest 12-month earnings figure for the company must be multiplied to obtain the current stock price.
- **Sales 100s** refers to the volume of reported sales.
- Stock prices are stated in dollar amounts. In this table, the **high, low,** and **last** figures refer to the stock's prices for the week. The **change** is the difference between the last reported price and the previous closing price.

There may be other symbols in the tables. A small **s** means that the stock has split and the price has been adjusted accordingly. An **x** in front of the sales volume figure means that the stock is selling ex-dividend so that a dividend declared during this period will be paid to the seller and not to the buyer. The symbols are generally explained in a boxed area that accompanies the tables.

You are an "owner" when you buy stock, and you could be called a "loaner" when you invest in bonds. Bonds have maturity dates; stocks do not. When you buy an *individual* bond (more on mutual funds later), you know exactly when you will get your money back. You also know when to expect interest payments because the interest is usually paid at regular intervals during the life of the bond. An exception is a "zero coupon" bond, which is sold at a significant discount from its face (par) value and returns the entire face value at maturity.

Bonds can be purchased with a variety of maturity dates to meet your specific needs. The definitions vary slightly among bond analysts, but bonds are generally grouped in three categories: short-term bonds typically mature in two years or less, intermediate-term bonds mature in two to 10 years, and long-term bonds mature in more than 10 years. You may want to peg bond maturity dates to your need for the money, but bear in mind that long-term bonds carry more risk because of the inverse relationship between interest rates and bond prices. When interest rates drop after a bond is issued, the price will rise so that the bond sells at a premium. When interest rates rise, the price will decline so that the bond sells at a discount. The ups and downs are meant to make an older bond salable when new bonds are issued in a different interest-rate climate.

The result: The longer the period before the bond matures, the more likely you'll get whipsawed by fluctuating interest rates. You'll get your money back if you hold to maturity, but you stand a real chance of losing money if you need your money early and must sell.

When bonds are issued by corporations, the interest is taxable. When they are issued by states and municipalities, the interest is often (not always) tax-free. The interest may be taxable if you buy "munis" issued by a state other than the one in which you live. And the interest may be subject to the alternative minimum tax (AMT) if the bonds are so-called *private activity bonds* issued by a government agency to pay for a specific purpose such as an airport or an industrial development.

Taxable vs. tax-free is another investment decision you must make. Tax-free bonds appeal to many investors. But don't be misled. "Tax-frees" make sense only if, in your income tax bracket, the effective yield will be higher than you could get on a taxable investment. To see which investment is most appropriate for you, always calculate the after-tax yield: Divide the tax-free rate by the "reciprocal" of your tax bracket. The reciprocal is the number you get by subtracting your tax bracket from 100. If you are in the 28 percent tax bracket, for example, the reciprocal is 72, so you would divide the yield on a tax-free bond by 72 to find the tax-equivalent yield. If the tax-free bond is paying 6 percent, 6 divided by 72 gives you 8.3 percent. You would have to receive 8.3 percent from a taxable bond to match the yield of the tax-free bond. If you live in a high-tax state, adding state income taxes into the equation may produce a different result. For an easier method, see Table 4.4.

TABLE 4.4 Tax-Exempt Yields and Their Taxable Equivalents

	TAXABLE EQUIVALENT YIELD (%) AT FEDERAL INCOME TAX RATES OF:				
TAX-EXEMPT YIELD	15%	28%	31%	36%	39.6%
3.5%	4.12	4.86	5.07	5.47	5.79
4.0	4.71	5.56	5.80	6.25	6.62
4.5	5.29	6.25	6.52	7.03	7.45
5.0	5.88	6.94	7.25	7.81	8.28
5.5	6.47	7.64	7.97	8.59	9.11
6.0	7.06	8.33	8.70	9.38	9.93
6.5	7.65	9.03	9.42	10.16	10.76
7.0	8.24	9.72	10.14	10.94	11.59

When you are considering whether you should invest on a taxable or tax-free basis, keep these four points in mind:

1. There is a third category besides taxable and tax-free: tax-deferred. All of your tax-sheltered retirement plans—401(k), 403(b), IRA, Keogh, and so on—let your investments compound free of tax during the accumulation years. They are taxed (at ordinary income tax rates) upon withdrawal.
2. There is little point in placing a tax-free investment (such as a municipal bond) or a tax-deferred investment (such as an annuity) inside a tax-sheltered retirement plan. You can't shelter the same income twice. Worse yet, because all withdrawals from retirement plans are taxed as ordinary income, you may be converting nontaxable interest into taxable income.
3. Zero-coupon bonds sell at a significant discount from face (par) value because, with these bonds, there is no stream of income. But—and it's a big but—the interest you don't receive is taxed as if it did make its way into your pocket. The only way to avoid the tax on this phantom income is to invest in zero-coupon bonds within a tax-sheltered account.
4. Some investments are partially taxable and partially tax-free. Interest on U.S. Treasury obligations, discussed more fully in Chapter 6, is subject to federal income tax but not to state or local tax. If you live in a high-tax state, Treasuries may be a welcome addition to your investment portfolio.

Income vs. growth is another way of dividing the investment pie. Growth generally refers to equities, where the value of an investment can grow (although it is never guaranteed to do so) if the company prospers. But growth comes in many colors. The shares of conservative "blue-chip" companies, the giants of American industry, may not hold as much potential for growth as the shares of high-tech start-up companies. But, as we'll see in more detail in Chapter 6, the potential for greater rewards goes hand in hand with greater risk.

Bonds are characterized as income investments because, although it is possible to make or lose money if you sell an individual bond before maturity, bonds offer a steady stream of income and the return of principal if they are held until maturity. At one time, bonds were considered the safest possible investment—the best investment for widows and orphans. No longer. Bonds are not risk-free investments, as we'll see in Chapter 6.

Individual purchases vs. mutual funds may be one of the most important decisions you make. When you buy an individual stock or bond, you are tying your investment results to the performance of the issuing company or agency. This can work well if you can diversify your portfolio by buying a variety of stocks and bonds, thereby avoiding the risk that comes with putting all your eggs in one investment basket. When you buy a mutual fund, by contrast, you are pooling your money with that of other investors and buying pieces of a great many securities, thereby achieving automatic diversification.

There are pros and cons to each approach; you may, in fact, want to buy both individual securities and mutual funds to round out your portfolio. Here are some facts about mutual funds that may help your decision. (Information about individual securities will be found later in this chapter.) Mutual funds offer:

- Professional management.
- A wide choice of investment objectives, from aggressive growth to fixed income.
- A choice between taxable and tax-free funds.
- Built-in diversification; you buy a larger number of securities than might be possible if you remained a solo investor.
- The opportunity to readily switch investments within a fund "family," although switching (unless you are doing so in a tax-sheltered account) is a taxable event.

- A choice between receiving dividends and interest in cash, or reinvesting them to purchase more shares of the mutual fund.
- The flexibility inherent in being able to make small purchases and to sell your shares at any time.
- A trade-off in costs between the annual management fees of the fund and the transaction costs associated with buying and selling individual securities.

It's also important to understand the costs associated with buying shares in mutual funds. No-load funds, which you can purchase directly without going through an intermediary, generally do not have a load (commission) although some "low-load" funds carry a sales charge of up to 3 percent. Load funds, purchased through a stockbroker or financial planner, often carry front-end loads (you pay when you buy the shares). These can legally run as much as 8.5 percent but typically range between 3 and 5.5 percent. Instead of a front-end load, some funds have back-end loads (also called contingent deferred sales charges), which are paid when you sell your shares. Back-end loads may start at 5 or 6 percent and then decline to zero over six or seven years. Some broker-sold funds offer you a choice of an up-front load or a back-end load in different share classes.

Many funds, both load and no-load, also charge 12(b)1 fees (named for the regulatory section that authorized their use) to cover marketing costs. These fees of up to 1 percent are imposed indefinitely (you pay during every year that you own the shares), and can therefore be more of a drain on performance than a front-end load. The total cost of owning a mutual fund, called the *expense ratio*, is set forth in a fee table that is clearly displayed in every mutual fund prospectus. Always review the fee table. Before deciding which way to buy, do the arithmetic and try to decide how long you're likely to hold the shares.

Performance seems to be unrelated to whether a fund carries a load or not. Clearly, more of your money goes to work for you when there is no load. On the other hand, if you want advice as to which funds are most appropriate for you, you may want to work with a trusted financial adviser.

The fee table in a mutual fund prospectus has two sections. As shown in Table 4.5, the first section groups the sales commissions and transaction fees imposed when you buy, sell, or exchange shares. The second section lists the operating expenses—the ongoing fees you will pay every year while you own shares in the fund. As part of

TABLE 4.5 Fee Table (Example)

Shareholder transaction expenses	
Maximum sales charge on purchase (as a percentage of the offering price)	4.5%
Maximum deferred sales charge	None
Maximum sales charge on reinvested dividends	None
Redemption fee	None
Exchange fee	None
Annual account maintenance fee	None
Annual fund operating expenses	
Management fee	0.47%
Distribution [12(b)1 fee]	0.21
Other expenses	0.36
Total operating expenses (expense ratio)	1.04

The following example illustrates the hypothetical expenses that you would incur over various periods if you invest $10,000 in this fund. This example assumes that the fund's annual return is 5 percent and that your shareholder transaction expenses and the fund's annual operating expenses remain the same over the years. The results apply whether or not you redeem your investments at the end of each period:

1 YEAR	3 YEARS	5 YEARS	10 YEARS
$552	$771	$1,013	$1,730

Reprinted by permission of the Investment Company Institute (www.ici.org).

the fee table, there is also an example showing how much, in dollars, it will cost to own shares in this fund for specified periods of time.

Buying individual securities lets you:

- Time the sale of a security for capital gains tax purposes. With a mutual fund, by contrast, you are likely to receive taxable capital gains distributions even if you have not sold any shares. The funds must pass through their own gains to shareholders each year.
- Buy bonds pegged to the specific maturity dates when you will need the money—perhaps to pay a college tuition bill or launch

your retirement. Bond mutual funds continually reinvest and do not have maturity dates.

- Do your own research—or rely on a trusted financial adviser—to select appropriate investments.
- Diversify your portfolio among individual issues—if you have enough money to adequately diversify among a variety of securities.

When you buy and sell individual securities, you generally pay a commission. The amount may be very low at some online brokerage services, at a mid-level if you trade with a discount broker, or on the high side if you use a full-service broker. As with investing in mutual funds, your costs depend on whether you want the research and recommendations of a financial adviser or are prepared to go it alone.

However, there is a way to buy individual securities at virtually no cost: sign up for direct purchase and dividend reinvestment. More than 1,000 corporations sell shares directly to investors, typically at minimum fees. If you own even a single share of stock—purchased directly or through a stockbroker—you can enroll in the dividend reinvestment plans (DRPs) offered by many companies. When you enroll in a DRP, dividends are automatically applied toward the purchase of more shares instead of being sent to you as cash payments. With many DRPs, you also have the option of making cash payments to purchase additional shares.

One cautionary note: Although DRPs are a terrific way to invest regularly with small amounts, you must be scrupulous in keeping track of purchases, stock splits, and stock dividends. You'll be purchasing shares, including fractional shares, at various times and at various prices. When you sell, you'll have to establish the "cost basis" of each share for tax purposes. If you fail to keep accurate records, you'll face a nightmare of tax reporting when you sell. Note, too, that dividends are taxable income, whether you take them in cash or use them to buy more shares. You will pay tax each year while you own the shares; keep track so that you don't pay tax again on the same income when you sell.

Understanding Market Indexes

It's impossible to follow the financial news these days without hearing about the ups and downs of various market indexes. The indexes, from the ubiquitous Dow Jones Industrial Average ("the Dow") to the less-well-known Wilshire 5000, are a kind of shorthand for performance. They are convenient for financial news commentators, but may mean little in terms of evaluating your own portfolio's performance.

Nonetheless, it's useful to understand just what the major indexes represent—not all the indexes, because a great many are being created to track very narrow market segments, but the handful that may have some bearing on your own investments.

The Dow or DJIA is the granddaddy of all the stock market indexes. It originated with Charles H. Dow's average of railroad stocks in 1884 but, today, it may mean less than some of the more recent indexes. Although it is the most prominently cited index, it measures just 30 large stocks selected by the editors of *The Wall Street Journal*. Even though the 30 represent the largest companies and account for about 20 percent of the $8 trillion-plus market value of all U.S. stocks, many analysts consider the Dow unrepresentative of the market as a whole, especially today, when so much of the action takes place in newer technology and "dot-com" stocks.

A major problem with the Dow—beyond the fact that it includes so few companies—is that it is a price-weighted index. Initially, as the folks at Dow Jones & Company describe it, price-weighting was a simple calculation: Add up the share prices and divide by the number of stocks. Today, the calculation is more complicated because it is adjusted for stock dividends, stock splits, and mergers, but higher-priced stocks still exert disproportionate influence.

Changes in the Dow are measured in points—"the Dow is up 150"—and as a percentage. As the Dow reaches new heights, however, a larger swing in points is a smaller percentage of the whole. Between new highs, of course, the Dow can and does go down. On October 19, 1987, the Dow closed at 1735, down 508 points or 22.61 percent. Yet a drop of almost 618 points on April 14, 2000, when the market closed at 10,305, was a percentage decline of just 5.66.

It's hard to believe these days, after a decade of growth and readings in the 10,000 to 11,000-point range, but the Dow first reached, 1,000 in 1972 and 3,000 in 1991. Thousand-point gains now seem to arrive more often. Yet the Dow, with its narrow composition, is not a particularly good performance indicator for individual portfolios.

The Standard & Poor's 500 Composite Index (the "S&P 500") represents about 85 percent of total market capitalization and therefore presents a picture of market trends that is both broader and more accurate than the Dow. The S&P 500 is market-weighted rather than price-weighted. Stock prices are multiplied by the number of shares, so a price move by one stock influences the index in proportion to its importance. If you're going to follow just one index, the S&P 500 is a good bet. Another good choice is the Wilshire 5000. It is not as widely reported as the S&P 500, but this index reflects the returns of the entire U.S. stock market and is a reasonable benchmark to use for measuring the domestic equities in your portfolio. The Wilshire 4500 tracks all of the stocks that are not in the S&P 500.

The Nasdaq Composite Index has garnered a lot of attention in recent years because it tracks technology and dot-com stocks. The Nasdaq started out as a place to trade securities that were not listed on the major stock exchanges. As some of those start-up ventures became industry giants—think of Microsoft—the Nasdaq gained more importance. Unless your investment portfolio is concentrated in Nasdaq stocks, however, contrary to accepted principles of diversification, tracking this index won't tell you much about how your investments are doing.

For serious investors, one index is not enough. If you invest in a mix of market categories, here are some additional choices:

- The Russell 2000 for small-capitalization companies.
- The Russell 3000 and the Schwab 1000 for large companies.
- The Morgan Stanley EAFE (Europe, Australia, and Far East) Index reflects trends in the markets of the major industrialized nations outside the United States.
- The Lehman Brothers Aggregate Bond Index tracks taxable bonds.
- The Lehman Brothers Municipal Bond Index tracks municipal bonds.

Indexes are useful, but they are only a guide. They don't mean anything unless you follow the ones that most closely reflect your holdings during the time you own them. Even then, as you develop and monitor your investment portfolio, focus on your own realistic target for returns.

On the Education Front

All this is bewildering, so you might expect to receive some advice from your plan sponsor or administrator. More and more education is becoming available to plan participants, but most sponsors still shy away from actual investment advice because they are fearful of being held responsible if a recommended investment performs poorly. According to the accounting firm of Ernst & Young, fewer than 15 percent of plan sponsors currently provide investment advice and recommendations.

However, legislation introduced in Congress in mid-2000 would change this picture. In the words of Representative John Boehner, a sponsor of the Retirement Security Advice Act: "Employers would be permitted to provide their employees with access to investment advice from registered investment advisers, provided there is full disclosure concerning any potential conflicts."

Conflicts can arise if the firm giving the advice recommends products it sells. Mutual funds and other financial institutions that typically fill the role of plan administrators and record keepers are natural advice givers, so there is a clear possibility of conflict. The new legislation, if enacted, would let financial institutions recommend products even if selling those products would produce fees. The only requirement would be full disclosure of the compensation arrangement.

Meanwhile, on the education-but-not-advice front, according to a survey conducted in 2000 by the Profit Sharing/401(k) Council of America, 92 percent of plans provide educational materials in print, 44 percent make information available online, and 23 to 27 percent make use of modeling software and videos. Education is usually provided through group employee meetings or seminars, but most plans also provide materials for individual study.

Although advice is only slowly taking hold, one of the biggest developments in recent years is the emergence of so-called third-party players—independent companies that offer actual investment advice to participants in particular plans or, in some cases, to all comers. Many operate online. You enter relevant information and the software makes targeted recommendations.

There are more than a dozen such companies. Among the best known are Morningstar, Standard & Poor's 401(k) Advisor, Financial Engines, and mPower.

Morningstar is making its ClearFuture online retirement planning service available through plan sponsors. In one example of how it works, a mutual fund company, MFS Investment Management, is making two versions of the Morningstar program available to plan sponsors. The first option, Guidance (offered free of charge), provides participants with online educational materials and research, plus personalized asset allocation suggestions. The second option, Advice (offered for a nominal fee), gives participants a specific list of recommended investments and allocations. With either version, an online link will permit immediate implementation of investment choices.

A company called mPower runs a site at www.401kafe.com that provides very useful information to anyone who logs on. There is no charge, and no specific investment advice is given, but the site provides educational information. In a special section, Ted Benna, widely known as the father of the 401(k) plan, answers questions submitted by individuals.

As the amount of money in individual 401(k) accounts grows—the average account is now close to $50,000—there is likely to be increasing interest in tendering advice (and thereby, perhaps, receiving your investment dollars) on the part of financial institutions. In many cases, however, if advice is provided through your plan sponsor, expect to pay an annual fee—and take the advice with a grain of salt. Advisers who work through the plan sponsor may be limited to discussing the investment options available through your company's plan, which may not be the best options available in each category.

Analyzing the Information

In addition to education (and sometimes, advice) from your plan sponsor or an independent firm hired by the sponsor or the record keeper, lots of investment information is available in the world at large. Perhaps too much is available. It's possible to be overwhelmed and become unable to judge the accuracy of what you read, hear, and see.

Financial news is featured in many newspapers, magazines, and newsletters and is covered in radio and television newscasts. Much of the day-to-day news is superficial: How much is "the market" up or down today? But some magazines and newsletters focus on personal finance and/or investment information. While it's possible to glean useful material from these publications, be wary of making investment decisions based solely on their recommendations.

If you're serious about your investments, you should scan publications such as *The Wall Street Journal*, *Barron's*, *Financial Times*, and *Forbes*. They'll tell you about the economic climate, profile some industry trends, and project the outlook for specific companies.

After you narrow down your investment possibilities based on your own objectives, tolerance for risk, and investment horizon, you can begin to evaluate specific companies and mutual funds. Chapters 5 through 7 provide more information about how to invest inside and outside your tax-sheltered retirement plans.

CHAPTER 5

One from Column A, Two from Column B

When the first 401(k) plan was introduced in 1981, there were usually two investment choices: (1) a guaranteed investment contract and (2) either company stock or a growth mutual fund. There wasn't much need for more choice; the average employee had only a couple of thousand dollars to invest. Expansion of investment choice became important as the money invested became more significant. Ted Benna, who is generally credited with creating the 401(k) plan, has noted on the 401kafe Web site that "Investing is now the dominant issue because 401(k) balances are the largest source of investing for most workers."

A few years ago, investment choices in most 401(k) plans were fairly limited. Today, it's a different story. More than half of all employer-sponsored retirement plans, up from just over 30 percent of plans in 1997, now offer an average of 10 mutual funds. Some plans offer as many as 15 to 20 choices. The average number of funds available for participants' contributions, according to the Profit Sharing/401(k) Council of America, is now 11.5. And, as you'll see later in this chapter, a small but growing number of employers have added "self-directed accounts," which permit participants to access hundreds of mutual funds and virtually any individual security on the market.

The big change came a few years ago, when companies were told by regulators that they could get off the liability hook by offering at least three investment alternatives, thereby giving employees the opportunity to control the amount of risk they wished to assume. The three investment alternatives must have different risk-and-return characteristics; it isn't enough to offer three different growth funds. Employees must receive sufficient information to make the choice, and they must be allowed to switch among the investments at reasonable intervals.

These "404(c)" requirements, named for the relevant section of the Internal Revenue Code, opened the floodgates to what appears to be an ever-increasing menu of investment choices. Employers like the arrangement because they can shed the responsibility for making investment choices for employees—and the resulting potential for lawsuits when investments go sour. Employees are happy because they have wider investment choice (although most employees stick with plain-vanilla investments and rarely make a change in their portfolio).

More choice doesn't always make life easier. And frequent trading within a retirement account can be a disaster—especially if commissions are charged for each transaction, thereby diminishing the tax-deferred money that is intended for retirement.

If your retirement savings are to do well, you must make wise selections from your plan sponsor's investment menu, diversifying your portfolio and readjusting it as necessary (but no more than once a year or so) to keep the allocation in place. The first task is to understand the investment alternatives. It isn't easy. Sometimes, mutual funds that have different names and declare different objectives contain many of the same individual securities. As a result, you may not have quite as much choice as appears on the surface, and you may not be as diversified as expected if you buy shares of different funds holding the same securities.

The funds you're most likely to see on your plan's investment menu are: actively managed domestic equity funds (offered by almost 86 percent of all plans), actively managed international equity funds (73 percent of plans), balanced stock/bond funds (73 percent of plans), and indexed domestic equity funds (68 percent of plans).

But many plans offer additional choices, ranging from stable value options to employer stock. It's worth a closer look at what each investment option entails, so that you can mesh it with your overall investment objectives and strategy. This chapter focuses on the investments within your retirement plan; Chapter 6 looks at the big picture—how to seamlessly mesh all your investments inside and outside your retirement plan. This chapter, together with Chapters 6 and 7, will provide an overview of investing both before and after retirement.

Stable Value Options

Not long ago, many risk-averse employees stuck to fixed-income investments in their defined contribution plans. Although fixed-income options range from money market mutual funds to long-term bond funds, the most widely available option—and, for quite a while, the most popular employee choice—was Guaranteed Investment Contracts, familiarly called GICs.

Today, fortunately, most employees realize that they won't build adequate retirement income by sticking to fixed-income investments. In PSCA's 1999 survey, stable value options made up just 7.5 percent of all retirement plan assets. Today, too, GICs have been largely supplanted by other investments in the stable value family: money market mutual funds, short-term bond funds, and an asset class labeled stable value funds.

GICs are still offered by many plans, so participants should understand their advantages and disadvantages. The critical fact is that, despite the word "Guaranteed" in the title, the underlying principal is never guaranteed. Most insurance companies are sound but a few have, in the past, failed to honor GIC promises because of financial difficulties. Retirement plan managers usually blend their GIC offerings, minimizing the risk that you will lose out because any one insurer gets into financial hot water, but it's still important to recognize that the "guarantee" in a GIC is only as good as the issuing insurer. GICs resemble certificates of deposit issued by banks, but no federal insurance is backing the GICs' principal.

A guarantee that does come with a GIC applies only to a specified rate of interest for a specific period of time. A GIC is a contract between your employer-sponsored retirement plan and one or more insurance companies. The plan invests a specified amount of money for a set period, and the insurance company pays interest on the money at a fixed rate over the life of the contract. The insurance company, in turn, invests the money in a portfolio of securities that includes bonds and mortgages and is typically set up to mature when the GIC contract ends. When the insurer reinvests the portfolio, the interest rate may change.

If you are interested in GICs for a portion of your 401(k) investment mix, ask about the ratings of the insurance companies issuing the contracts. Stick with insurers that have been rated "AA" (or better) by at least two rating agencies.

GICs lost some luster in the wake of well-publicized insurance company difficulties a decade ago. Insurers are generally sound today, but a new version of conservative retirement investment—"stable value funds"—is currently found in three out of five defined contribution plans offered by large companies. Stable value funds are similar to GICs in many ways; in fact, they provide a steady stream of income by buying guaranteed investment contracts or wrap agreements from banks and insurance companies. As Sheldon Jacobs, editor of *The No-Load Fund Investor* explains, the banks and insurance companies selling these arrangements to employer plans demand that the funds own high-quality debt securities—not mortgages as such, but U.S. government and agency obligations, along with the highest rated corporate and mortgage-backed bonds. "Stable value funds," Jacobs notes, "should be considered as a core position for investors wanting to hold cash long-term."

Stable value funds generally offer better returns than money market mutual funds, and less risk than short- and intermediate-term bond funds. In terms of total return, when they are compared to regular bond funds, stable value funds perform best when interest rates are rising. In terms of generating income, they perform best when interest rates decline.

Stable value funds are a relatively new concept; they have not yet been tested in a period of high inflation. But John Hancock Financial Services and the Stable Value Association tested the performance results of various portfolios from 1962 to 1996, a period that included both rising interest rates (1962–1983) and declining interest rates (1983–1996). When they examined the average annual return, the risk level, and the relationship of returns, the researchers found that investors who choose a stable value fund for the fixed income portion of a retirement portfolio can boost their equity allocation, and hence their returns, without increased risk.

Those findings held true when the study was extended to 1999. According to the data, the risk level in a portfolio consisting of 60 percent stocks and 40 percent intermediate bonds was exactly the same as in a portfolio consisting of 75 percent stocks and 25 percent stable value funds. Yet the compound return from 1983 to 1999 was 14.81 percent on the first portfolio and 16.3 percent on the second. *If* this trend continues—as all the ads must say, "past performance is no guarantee of future results"—keeping a portion of your retirement portfolio in stable value funds could allow you to maintain a larger position in equities.

A bond/stock portfolio may match the return, but with higher risk and volatility. A money market/stock portfolio can match the risk and volatility, but with lower returns. Stable value products, according to this study, "anchor a portfolio so participants may sleep better even if the stock market tumbles."

But too much of a good thing isn't necessarily better. You may want stable value options to make up part of your 401(k) investment mix; just don't overdo it. The trade-off for greater potential reward is a willingness to assume some investment risk. If you are unwilling to gamble just a little, you face the certainty of a smaller retirement nest egg.

Employer Stock

There's gambling and then there's *gambling*. You definitely should hold growth investments among your retirement plan assets, but those investments should be diversified. Yet, despite the increased number of mutual funds being offered, there is a parallel move toward concentration. One of every five plans now offers employer stock as an investment option, and PSCA reported, in its 1999 survey that fully 43 percent of plan assets are invested in company stock. The larger the company, the more likely that participants own company stock as a portion of their retirement assets.

Is this a wise move? Many advisers think not. If employer stock makes up a large portion of your retirement portfolio, you are not adequately diversified. If your industry suffers a downturn, so will your retirement assets. If your company does not do well, neither will you. Think about this: In owning company stock, you are showing loyalty to your employer. But you are also relying on the fortunes of a single company for both your present well-being (in the form of salary) and your future well-being (in the form of retirement income). If you also hold stock options, you may be in for a triple whammy.

Think about what may happen if your company is acquired or merged, or goes out of business, or suffers financial reversals. Can't happen, you say? Yes, it can. Even the biggest of the big can suffer reversals in the financial markets. And it isn't just Internet and high-tech stocks that can suffer. When Procter & Gamble stock lost half its value early in 2000, retirement accounts held by its employees and retirees also plummeted. As *Smart Money* put it in its report, "No stock is totally 'safe' . . . even a slight earnings disappointment can translate into a massive selloff."

That said, you may not be an entirely free agent. Some employers insist that plan participants invest in company stock or make their own matching contributions solely in the form of company stock. Worse yet, some companies won't let you sell your shares until you're ready to retire. Procter & Gamble (P&G) required its employees to hold at least half of their retirement assets in P&G stock—and offered no other stock choices. If your employer has such a restrictive plan in place, take whatever steps you can to diversify your investment portfolio outside your retirement plan.

No matter how promising the company, in other words, don't buy more of the stock than you must. Mark Riepe, head of research at Charles Schwab, told *Forbes* magazine recently that his guideline for overconcentration is 30 percent of a portfolio in a single stock. At that point, the odds more than double that a portfolio will lose 10 percent or more of its value each year, over a period of three years.

If you do own company stock in your retirement plan, be sure to minimize the tax consequences when you start to withdraw money or roll it into an IRA. (Chapter 11 details the special rules that apply.)

Mutual Funds

The most extensive investment choice within retirement plans lies with mutual funds. Those most frequently offered (and the percentage of plan assets they hold) include an actively managed domestic equity fund (16.6 percent), an indexed domestic equity fund (10.9 percent), and a balanced stock and bond fund (10.4 percent). But, with some plans offering 10, 15, and as many as 20 mutual funds—to say nothing of open-ended brokerage windows through which virtually any fund is available—you may have to do considerable research before you select specific funds.

Which funds are right for you? Review your investment objectives as outlined in Chapter 4, evaluate your approach to investing (passive or self-powered), and then consider specific choices among stock, bond, and balanced funds. Be sure to mesh your tax-sheltered retirement investment strategy with your personal investment portfolio, as described in Chapter 6.

The *passive* approach to 401(k) investing is based on "ready-made" portfolios. Here are some examples.

Balanced Funds

These conservative funds are a mixture of stocks, bonds, and cash. They typically maintain a proportion of about 60 percent in stocks, 30 percent in bonds or other fixed-income investments, and 10 percent in cash equivalents. At a minimum, the fixed-income portion of the portfolio should be no less than 25 percent. The idea is to provide a reasonable return with reduced risk. Choosing a balanced fund also eliminates the need to select both equity and fixed-income investments—assuming that the mix in your particular fund is appropriate for your age and risk tolerance.

Lifestyle Funds

These funds, also called "life cycle" funds, simplify investment choice because they are targeted to meet the needs of various age groups and risk tolerance levels. In general, the investment choices are more aggressive for young investors and more conservative for people nearing retirement. A few of the funds in this category change the investment mix automatically as you age; most require you to switch funds as your needs

NOTE

Investment risk bears a relationship to investment return. Investments with the least risk generally have the lowest return. On a spectrum from low risk/return to high risk/return, you might see:

- **Stable value and money market mutual funds.**
- **Bond funds.**
- **Balanced funds.**
- **Large-cap value stocks and stock funds.**
- **Large-cap growth stocks and stock funds.**
- **Mid-cap value stocks and stock funds.**
- **Mid-cap growth stocks and stock funds.**
- **Small-cap value stocks and stock funds.**
- **Small-cap growth stocks and stock funds.**
- **Global/international stock funds.**
- **Emerging markets stock funds.**

change. Currently, one out of five 401(k) plans includes lifestyle funds in the investment options.

Although lifestyle funds are designed as a no-fuss/no-muss approach to investing, a recent study by Hewitt Associates, a benefits consulting firm, indicated that many "plan participants may be using these funds in ways that defeat their intended purpose." Instead of selecting a single lifestyle fund tailored to their time horizon and risk preference, these participants are mixing lifestyle funds with other mutual funds. Some employees even select more than one lifestyle fund. The end result is that many young plan participants, who should be investing in equities to build plan assets, have too much of their retirement investments locked into the fixed-income side.

Index Funds

Index funds mirror the market or a particular segment of the market. The most popular index funds—and the ones probably best suited for a 401(k) plan—hold all the stocks represented in the Standard & Poor's 500 Composite Index. The S&P itself reflects about 85 percent of market capitalization and therefore presents a pretty accurate picture of overall market trends. An S&P 500 index fund will do well when the market is generally trending upward but will do poorly when the market is trending downward. One potential problem is that index funds tend to be fully invested. Little cash is on hand, so when shareholders redeem shares, the fund must sell some of its holdings. If the market takes a sharp downward turn and many investors decide to pull out, there can be a cascading effect on the fund's share price.

Index funds are not actively managed; portfolio holdings change only when companies merge or the S&P itself adds or drops a company. If you hold shares in an S&P 500 index fund, the performance of those shares should mimic the overall market. Other index funds represent market segments—the Nasdaq for high-tech stocks, and the Russell 2000 for small-cap stocks—but these are less likely to be among a 401(k) plan's investment choices.

Index funds have lower expense ratios than actively managed funds and are therefore less expensive to own. They may also have some tax advantages, although these are irrelevant within the context of a tax-sheltered retirement plan because nothing is taxable until the money is withdrawn. See Chapter 6 for more on the pros and cons of index funds within your overall investment portfolio.

If you prefer a *self-powered* approach to investing, you'll make specific choices among actively managed mutual funds. Although almost 8,000 mutual funds (more than twice the number available in 1990) are currently available to individual investors, you're likely to find no more than 10 or 12 in your 401(k) plan. These may include:

- One or more large-cap domestic stock (equity) funds with the objective of capital appreciation. Your plan will probably offer a growth fund investing in high-quality common stock.
- An aggressive growth fund, investing in start-up, high-tech, and other more speculative issues.
- An international fund investing solely in foreign issues, or a global fund holding both domestic and foreign stocks. Investing a portion of your portfolio outside the United States is one way to reduce risk. Although less true in this era of a globalized economy, foreign markets do not usually move in lockstep with U.S. markets.
- Sector funds, still a relatively rare menu choice, focus on the stocks of companies in a specific area such as health care, technology, or telecommunications. Although sector funds are more aggressive than most equity funds, a small position in one may boost returns in your 401(k) while providing additional diversification.
- A fixed-income (bond) fund. This choice can diversify your portfolio and reduce the risk associated with investing in equities. In some plans, stable value options such as GICs take the place of fixed-income funds.

TIP

Does your 401(k) money belong in "old economy" or "new economy" investments? The "new economy," consisting largely of Internet stocks with high prices but little or no earnings, was all the rage in the 1990s and the early part of 2000. The "old economy," the tried-and-true companies that make up much of the industrialized United States, seemed somehow old-fashioned in its reliance on earnings. Yet the tide has turned, as the market moves down from its bull-market euphoria. The message: Diversify, diversify, diversify. Own some of several types of investment vehicles, and don't expect the superheated stock market returns of the 1990s.

If your plan offers a self-directed account (see below), you may have access to hundreds of mutual funds as well as individual securities. If not, you may want to consider diversifying your overall portfolio by making other types of investments outside of your tax-sheltered retirement plan. See Chapter 6 for a rundown of investment choices and advice on how to coordinate your tax-sheltered and taxable portfolios.

Making Your Picks

In deciding which funds belong in your 401(k) plan, the first step is to match your investment strategy to your investment goals. It's easy to say that young plan participants should concentrate on growth investments and those close to retirement should shift toward income, but this formulaic approach to investing ignores your personal time horizon, objectives, and risk tolerance.

Think about when you plan to leave the workforce, your life expectancy at that point, and what you expect to do in retirement. An extensive trip around the world or the purchase of a second home may require more immediate cash than puttering in a basement workshop and spending time with your grandchildren.

Whatever your plans, you want to be prepared for a long life in retirement. (I can't put too much emphasis on our longer life expectancies.) And you also want to be prepared for the unexpected. That means maintaining a diversified portfolio with a significant portion devoted to growth.

The word *diversification* keeps coming up. But what does it really mean? Does investing in four mutual funds mean that you are adequately diversified? Not if three of them are growth funds holding many of the same stocks. If you want to adequately diversify your investment portfolio, you should hold a mixture of securities providing growth *and* income. Then, within the equity (growth) side of the portfolio, you should hold the stock of large *and* small, domestic *and* international companies.

Within equity funds, you may also want to have representation from both the "value" and "growth" investment strategies. Value managers seek stocks with low prices relative to the company's current earnings and assets. The ultimate value manager may actually buy the shares of companies in bankruptcy. Growth managers look for fast-growing companies, at almost any price, whose stocks are likely to show rapid appreciation.

After you select two or three funds based on their investment objectives and investment strategy, monitor their performance. Information is easy to obtain if your plan offers publicly traded funds;

their performance data are reported in the daily newspapers and the financial press. Information may be less easy to locate if your plan offers proprietary funds (created solely for the plan) or institutional funds (designed for retirement plans and similar bulk purchasers). You may have to rely on plan documents and statements (see Chapter 8), or ask your benefits office for additional information.

You don't want to jump in and out of mutual funds—that's a losing proposition—but you do want to be sure that your fund choices measure up over a fair span of time. Here are some things to check:

- *Consistency.* A portfolio manager skilled in the strategy of value investing shouldn't jump into a growth strategy just because growth is "hot." The manager should continue doing what he or she does best, and you should stick with the program.
- *Management.* When a portfolio manager leaves, this can be a good time for investors to leave as well—not because the new manager won't do well but because a change at the top often means a change in portfolio as the new leader switches to his or her favorite securities. Changes in portfolio are costly; in addition to transaction costs, they generate capital gains distributions. The only exception to this rule is when a fund is truly managed by committee.
- *Total return.* Total return, not yield, is the best measure of fund performance. *Yield* is the fund's current income (dividends and interest minus expenses). But *total return* includes dividends and capital gains distributions, along with changes in share price. More important, total return, expressed as a percentage of an initial investment in a fund, shows change in the fund's value over a given period of time. Compare the returns of different funds for the same period—five years, ten years, or since the fund's inception. (Your return may differ from a fund's reported return because you may have owned your shares for a period other than the reported period.) Information on publicly traded funds is easy to obtain; read your newspaper's business pages or check Morningstar reports in your library. If your plan offers funds that are not publicly available—either institutional funds or proprietary funds—you may have to seek information from your plan sponsor or provider.
- *Risk-adjusted return.* This is a way of looking at how much risk it takes to achieve a particular investment's reward. As an

example, a technology fund specializing in volatile "dot-com" stocks might produce dramatic returns—but only at equally dramatic risk. Some fund-rating services provide risk-adjusted returns, as do some annual mutual fund reports in magazines such as *Forbes*.

- *Benchmarks.* Compare fund returns against an appropriate benchmark or index. As the Vanguard Group explains on its useful Web site, "So your stock fund was up 22 percent last year. Does that make it a big winner? Maybe, maybe not. It all depends on how funds with similar objectives, or an index with similar holdings, fared over the same period." Each piece of your portfolio, in other words, should be measured against the appropriate benchmark. That's the only way to tell whether you are meeting your investment objectives over a period of time. If you are invested in a large-cap growth fund, the S&P 500 Index may be an appropriate benchmark. For small-cap growth stocks, look at the Russell 2000 Growth Index. For small-cap value funds, look at the Russell 2000 Value Index. For international securities, the Morgan Stanley EAFE index reflects trends in the major industrialized nations outside the United States. In the bond arena, the Lehman Brothers Aggregate Bond Index tracks corporate bonds, and the Lehman Brothers Municipal Bond Index tracks municipal bonds. Check the prospectus for each of your funds to see which benchmark is used.

There are other, more technical ways to review fund performance. *Beta*, for example, measures the volatility of returns against a benchmark index. The benchmark is assigned a beta of 1.0. A stock fund with a beta of 1.5 has therefore moved up and down in price one and one-half times more than the market as a whole. But beta doesn't tell you how much risk you're assuming with a given fund; it just tells you, as a relative measure, how much the fund's value has changed relative to the market index. *Alpha* is another measure of risk; it indicates how much the fund's performance differed from expectations. A positive alpha shows better-than-expected performance, and a negative alpha shows the opposite. *Standard deviation*, a measure of volatility, shows performance relative to returns over a particular time period. You can see variations in performance by adding the standard deviation to (or subtracting it from) the fund's performance. Lower standard deviations are generally preferable.

On fixed-income funds, *duration* is a measure of volatility. The higher a fund's duration, the more its share price reacts to interest rate fluctuations. Duration is not the same thing as maturity. A bond fund, unlike individual bonds, never matures because the portfolio managers maintain a rolling portfolio of bonds within a specified maturity range. Duration is an accurate measure of risk based on portfolio characteristics such as maturity dates, the amount and frequency of interest payments, and the rate at which those interest payments can be reinvested.

In the absence of information about average duration, it's generally safe to assume that bond funds holding long-term bonds are more volatile and react more sharply to changing interest rates than funds holding short-term bonds. In recent years, the additional risk has not produced very much in the way of additional returns. As an example, in the fall of 2000, bonds with a two-year duration were yielding 6.4 percent, and bonds with a six-year duration were yielding 6.6 percent—a spread of two-tenths of 1 percent accompanied by considerably greater risk of a drop in value. If your 401(k) plan menu does not include a short-term bond fund, a good alternative may be a stable value fund.

Time to Go

Although buy-and-hold investors tend to do better in the long run than investors who make frequent trades, there can be times when it's better to switch than fight. But how do you decide when it's time to sell a fund?

If returns are down over several consecutive quarters, review the fund's performance against appropriate benchmarks. Then try to determine the cause of the poor performance, and whether it is likely to continue into the future. Scott Lummer, chief investment officer of mPower, suggests that you ask yourself whether the actions that caused the fund to do poorly were consistent with your overall objectives in investing in the fund. In other words, if an equity fund did poorly because it put too much of its portfolio in bonds or cash, it might be time to get out. Similarly, if a fund that claimed to be well diversified put a large chunk of its portfolio into high-tech or Internet stocks, it might be time to sell.

Lummer goes further; he suggests that good performance produced by inappropriate actions may also mean that it's time to sell.

"Why? Because outstanding returns generated for the wrong reasons," he says, "tell me the fund is taking risks that are not consistent with my desires. So when a fund betters its benchmark by shifting money into different asset classes, taking an undiversified position in a stock or an industry, or changing the investment objectives, that's my cue to sell. I consider myself fortunate that the additional risk helped me, but I don't take the chance that the fund, and I, will get lucky again."

As noted above, you may want to sell fund shares if the portfolio manager leaves. By the same token, be alert when a fund group is sold to another. Such acquisitions, increasingly frequent these days, may mean that expenses may rise, loads may crop up on previously no-load funds, and, in a worst-case situation, the fund you know and love may actually disappear. If your fund and a fund in the acquirer's family have similar objectives, one fund may be merged into the other. If this happens, check the track record of the surviving fund to determine whether you want to stay invested.

Self-Directed Accounts

The number-one option being added to 401(k) plans these days, according to the Profit Sharing/401(k) Council of America, is the self-directed account. The concept didn't even exist in 1993, yet today some 10 percent to 15 percent of plans offer self-directed accounts—and the number is growing rapidly. Among new plans, in fact, self-directed accounts are all the rage. At Charles Schwab, three of every four plans started in 2000 offered this option.

If this option is in your employer-sponsored retirement plan, you can customize your investment portfolio. Instead of choosing your retirement investments from a preselected menu, you may have almost unlimited flexibility—assuming that your plan is unrestricted and includes a brokerage "window" through which you can trade in individual securities.

Many companies place restrictions on the self-directed portion of retirement accounts. Typically, no more than 20 percent or 25 percent of an individual's plan assets can be invested in individual securities.

Some plans offer a slightly different version of self-directed accounts. Under this arrangement, instead of the wide world of individual securities being available to you, there is an increased selection of mutual funds. You might, for example, have access to a mutual fund "supermarket." Run by such giants as Charles Schwab and Fidelity Investments, these supermarkets offer access to a large number of load and no-load mutual funds.

But there's a downside to unlimited choice, in addition to pure confusion. You can expect to pay an annual administrative fee of as much as $100 plus commissions on individual transactions. For an employee earning $40,000 a year and contributing 6 percent of salary to a 401(k), a $100 fee means contributing $2,300 a year to the 401(k) instead of $2,400—a significant drag on long-term results.

Many financial planners are concerned that individual securities may pose too much risk. Despite years of a bull market, stocks are volatile. What goes up can also come down. If you elect a do-it-yourself approach for part of your retirement assets, be prepared to do some research on the securities or funds you select and to monitor their performance. And don't jump in and out of the market just because you can. In investing, as in many other activities, slow and steady generally wins the race.

One more point to keep in mind: Employer-selected investment options may offer employees some legal protection because the employer has a fiduciary responsibility to the plan, but you're completely on your own when you go outside the plan menu to choose your own investments. Karen Friedman, director of the Pension Rights Center, is uneasy about self-directed options. She is concerned that employees may be taking on too much responsibility and letting employers off the hook.

On the whole, plan participants are doing well. The most recent statistics released by the Employee Benefit Research Institute (EBRI) and the Investment Company Institute show that, although asset allocation varies with age and income, just over half of all plan balances were invested in equity funds at year-end 1999. At the same time, 19 percent was in company stock, 10 percent in GICs, 7 percent in balanced funds, 5 percent in bond funds, 4 percent in money market mutual funds, and 2 percent in other stable value funds.

Not surprisingly, younger participants tend to favor equity funds and older participants are more likely to stick to GICs and bond funds. Workers in their twenties invested 63.4 percent of their assets in equity funds in 1999; those in their sixties invested 44.2 percent of their assets in equity funds. Conversely, the younger set put 3.8 percent in

GICs and 3.8 percent in bond funds, while older participants reported 19.2 percent in GICs and 6.8 percent in bond funds. Those earning under $40,000 a year put 62 percent of their plan assets in equity funds, against 76 percent for those earning more than $100,000.

Avoiding Common Errors

Fewer than one-quarter of the plan participants surveyed by the Gallup Organization (for John Hancock Financial Services) in 1999 considered themselves savvy investors. Familiarity with specific investment options peaked in 1995 and has declined ever since. The very fact that you're reading this book puts you well ahead of the average plan participant. Now you know more about how various investment options can fit into your retirement plans. You also know that there are common investment errors that you can avoid. For example:

- *Failing to diversify.* Portfolios heavily focused on a single type of investment are a recipe for disaster because they are either too risky or too conservative. Yet only 44 percent of the plan participants in the 1999 John Hancock survey had an asset allocation in place. Of that group, only slightly more than half were at or near their target asset allocations. Not only should you have an asset allocation strategy for your plan assets, but you should review and rebalance your allocation periodically. You should also consider your retirement plan and your outside investments as a single investment pie. (Chapter 6 offers more detail on developing a strategy for all your investments.)
- *Choosing the right investments for the wrong reasons.* A money market mutual fund may have a place in your portfolio, but not as a substitute for an active investment. Money funds are good places for a cash cushion. They can also be temporary parking places pending investment opportunities. But it's important to understand what you're buying when you buy into a money fund. At least half of those surveyed by John Hancock either believed that money funds contain some combination of stocks, bonds, and short-term securities or frankly admitted that they had no idea what backs the funds. In fact, money funds invest in commercial paper, bankers' acceptances, government securities, repurchase agreements, and certificates of deposit—

all short-term, highly liquid investment vehicles that can replace cash but cannot produce growth.

- *Holding tax-free investments in your retirement plan.* This is a mistake because, by definition, qualified retirement plans are tax shelters. You can't shelter the same money twice. So, if you want to invest in municipal bonds or a tax-deferred annuity, it's best to do so outside of your retirement plans.

CHAPTER 6

The Big Picture

So far, we've been looking at investing within your employer-sponsored retirement plan. But your 401(k)—or 403(b) or other plan—doesn't exist in a vacuum. It's vitally important to mesh your 401(k) investments with your outside investments and develop an overall investment strategy that will help you reach your objectives.

We talk a great deal about reaching goals and objectives. I like to break them down, to make the idea real. When I speak of *goals*, I mean your long-range look-ahead vision of what is most important to you. When I speak of *objectives*, I mean the step-by-step path you'll take toward your goals. The third part of the equation is *action*—the hard core of a financial program, the behavior that will make both goals and objectives possible.

For example: You are in your early fifties. Your children are grown; the nest is empty. You've decided that your primary goal, right now, is to ensure a worry-free retirement. A worthy goal, indeed, but a bit vague. It needs to be reduced to manageable objectives. Your specific objectives might include funding your 401(k) and other tax-sheltered retirement plans to the maximum and then investing additional money in taxable accounts while maintaining an adequate cash cushion against emergencies. The action you take to meet those objectives and thereby achieve your long-term goal might include developing a budget, cutting back on spending to free funds for investment, and seeking the advice of a financial adviser.

As you develop the investment strategy that will implement your action plan, a major factor is your attitude toward risk.

How Much Risk Can You Tolerate?

The proportion of your investment pie devoted to growth, and the proportion dedicated to income, will depend on your age, your circumstances, and how close you are to retirement. But it also depends, perhaps to an even greater extent, on your tolerance for risk. Two married empty-nest 50-year-olds, each with 15 years to retirement, may have vastly different comfort levels when it comes to risking their money.

Potential investment rewards are linked very closely to the amount of risk you are willing to assume. A money market mutual fund or Treasury obligation promises a safe return, but neither investment will appreciate. Before you decide how to invest both inside and outside your tax-sheltered retirement plan, consider the different types of risk and then think about your own attitude toward risk.

When most people think of investment risk, they think of losing principal—putting $100 into an investment, for example, and having it lose value until it is worth $50 or even less. But there is more than one type of investment risk. Seemingly secure fixed-income investments can harbor several types of risk:

- *Credit risk* refers to quality and is the risk that a bond issuer will not meet regularly scheduled interest payments or will be unable to repay the principal amount at maturity. A decline in an issuer's credit rating can cause a decrease in the bond's value. Inability to pay principal or interest on time puts the bond in default.
- *Interest rate risk* also applies to bonds because there is an inverse relationship between bond prices and interest rates. The relationship looks like a child's seesaw: When interest rates fall, bond values typically rise. Conversely, when interest rates rise, bond values typically fall. Assuming that the issuer is creditworthy, you will receive the full principal amount at maturity. If you have to sell earlier, however, you could lose money.

- *Prepayment risk* refers to the possibility that a bond will be redeemed ("called") before its scheduled maturity date. Because bonds are typically called when interest rates fall and the issuer can borrow money at a lower interest rate, holders of called bonds are forced to reinvest at a lower interest rate.
- *Reinvestment risk* is the risk that you won't be able to reinvest the proceeds from a maturing investment at a comparable rate of return.
- *Inflation risk* is the risk that purchasing power will lose ground to inflation. This is virtually a certainty if you stick to fixed-income investments with little or no chance of capital growth.
- *Market risk* is the risk that your investments will lose value because of changes in interest rates or economic circumstances.

It's impossible to entirely avoid risk in investing. But some people are more comfortable than others in incurring risk for the sake of potential reward. Although there are no guarantees in the world of investing, the classic illustration of risk-versus-reward lies in the extensive research conducted by Ibbotson Associates of Chicago. In data tracking from 1926 to year-end 1999, the compounded annual return on ultrasafe U.S. 30-day Treasury bills was 3.79 percent. Over the same period, the compounded annual return on the S&P 500 was 11.35 percent. Both figures include reinvested interest and dividends.

I am not suggesting that your investment portfolio be entirely in the stock market. In fact, a balanced portfolio, as described in Chapter 7, can produce almost as much return as an all-stock portfolio, with considerably less risk.

Before you decide exactly where to invest your money, take the short Investor's Quiz on page 110 to evaluate your tolerance for risk.

One way to minimize risk is to practice *asset allocation*. This strategy builds on the idea of using a diversified portfolio to spread risk among different asset classes. With asset allocation, you determine the proportion of your investments that you want to allocate to various investment categories. Then, to keep the proportion steady, you review and rebalance your portfolio periodically. Lest you think that asset allocation is just a buzzword that doesn't mean much, several academic studies have found that the choice of investment categories has far more to do with investment success than either the choice of specific investment vehicles or the timing of transactions.

INVESTOR'S QUIZ

Place a checkmark (✓) alongside each statement that indicates your status or choice.

1. My retirement is still 15 years away. I keep my money in:
   (a) A money market mutual fund, certificate of deposit, or guaranteed investment contract. ____
   (b) A mix of stock and bond funds. ____
   (c) Stock and stock funds. ____

2. If, within two months of putting money into an investment, the value of the investment falls by 20 percent, I will:
   (a) Sell all my shares. ____
   (b) Hold on, in the hope that the investment will come back. ____
   (c) Buy more at the lower price. ____

3. Instead of going down, if my stocks double in value, I will:
   (a) Sell all my shares. ____
   (b) Sell half my shares to lock in some profits. ____
   (c) Buy more shares. ____

4. Today's stock market is so volatile that I will take my year-end bonus and:
   (a) Stay on the sidelines until the market calms down. ____
   (b) Invest gradually over an extended period. ____
   (c) Plunge right in and hope to catch the upswing. ____

5. In choosing stocks or stock funds, I am most likely to choose:
   (a) Large blue-chip companies with proven track records. ____
   (b) Small-capitalization companies with good earnings. ____
   (c) New dot-com or high-tech ventures with no earnings but lots of promise. ____

If all your answers are (a), you tend to be a conservative investor—and you can expect to lose ground to inflation. If you consistently chose (c), you're an aggressive investor with a high tolerance for risk. With (b) choices, you're likely to have a well-balanced portfolio, with stocks for growth and bonds to reduce risk.

Let's say you decide to put 55 percent of your investments into growth mutual funds, 35 percent into fixed-income funds, and 10 percent into money market mutual funds (for a cash reserve). The market does exceedingly well. At the end of a year, you find that you now have 65 percent of your portfolio invested for growth. To get back to your ideal allocation, you might sell some of your stock and take the profits. This is tough for many investors to do because it means selling some winners but think of it as following the investment mantra: "Buy low and sell high." When you sell some winners, you can put the money into investments that are currently out of favor. Or, if this approach won't work for you and you have additional cash to invest, you can achieve the desired balance by putting the new cash into the fixed-income side. You can also arrange to have dividends from growth mutual funds invested in fixed-income funds.

Rebalancing a portfolio probably isn't worth the effort, the paperwork, the transaction costs, and the taxes (in a taxable account) unless there is a differential of at least 10 percent. In other words, don't bother reshuffling your securities if growth stocks move from 55 percent to 58 percent of your total portfolio, but *do* rebalance when the shift is from 55 percent to 65 percent. In fact, if you follow the advice of mutual fund guru John Bogle, former head of The Vanguard Group, you might not rebalance at all. In his book, *Bogle on Mutual Funds*, he reports on the minimal difference in returns between a portfolio left "as is" and one that is rebalanced every year. But another mutual fund guru, Sheldon Jacobs, editor of the *No-Load Fund Investor* newsletter, notes that rebalancing may not improve performance but it does reduce the risk level in the portfolio. Take an annual look at your portfolio to see whether it is still roughly in line with your targeted allocation.

Don't limit your asset allocation thinking to the three broad categories of stocks, bonds, and cash. There are additional subcategories. On the cash front, you may want some money in money market mutual funds as both an emergency fund and "opportunity money" a stash that you can tap for new investment opportunities. You may also want some cash in short-term Treasury bills. Within the fixed-income category, you may want both short-term and intermediate-term bonds. (Most investors should steer clear of long-term bonds. They are as volatile as stocks.) Corporate bonds may be a good choice within your tax-sheltered retirement account, and tax-free municipal bonds and bond funds can be tucked into your taxable portfolio. Within the growth portion of your portfolio, consider large-cap and small-cap growth and value funds, an international fund, and an index fund.

As you think about allocating your assets, be sure to consider *all* of your assets: those in your tax-sheltered retirement plan and in your spouse's tax-sheltered retirement plan as well as those you hold in taxable accounts. Failing to consider the whole picture can result in a woefully unbalanced portfolio. Start by examining the investment options within any employer-sponsored retirement plans held by you and your spouse. Because these options are generally limited, you may want to make these choices first and then select other investments in your taxable accounts to fill out your allocation. The types of investment vehicles most often offered in employer-sponsored plans are described in Chapter 5; others are covered later in this chapter.

The most appropriate asset allocation is the one you create to meet your own investment objectives, time horizon, and tolerance for risk. As an example, however, Sheldon Jacobs suggests three "model" portfolios for three life stages. His "wealth builder portfolio," with 85 percent in domestic equities and 15 percent in international equities, is designed for working investors whose goal is capital accumulation. The equity allocation takes above-average risks to meet that goal.

The "pre-retirement portfolio" described in Jacobs' book, *Guide to Successful No-Load Fund Investing*, is designed for investors who are within 10 years of retirement and is somewhat more conservative. The portfolio avoids aggressive growth funds and sticks primarily to equity income, growth-and-income and lower-volatility growth funds along with fixed-income or money market funds. The breakdown is 65 percent in domestic equities, 15 percent in international equities, and 20 percent in bonds.

Jacobs' "retirement portfolio" emphasizes income and capital preservation along with growth. Designed for investors in their sixties and early seventies, who can anticipate many years in retirement, this portfolio has 55 percent in domestic equities, 10 percent in international equities, and 35 percent in bonds or money market funds for current income and reduced volatility.

Just to demonstrate that there are other approaches—"different strokes for different folks"—Kevin J. Cress, an analyst with mPower on the 401kafe Web site, describes three different portfolio allocations for roughly the same age and stage of life. For plan participants in their forties, an allocation might be 40 percent large-cap stocks, 15

Investment risk can be expressed with a pyramid in which the safest investment vehicles are the foundation and the most speculative buys are at the peak:

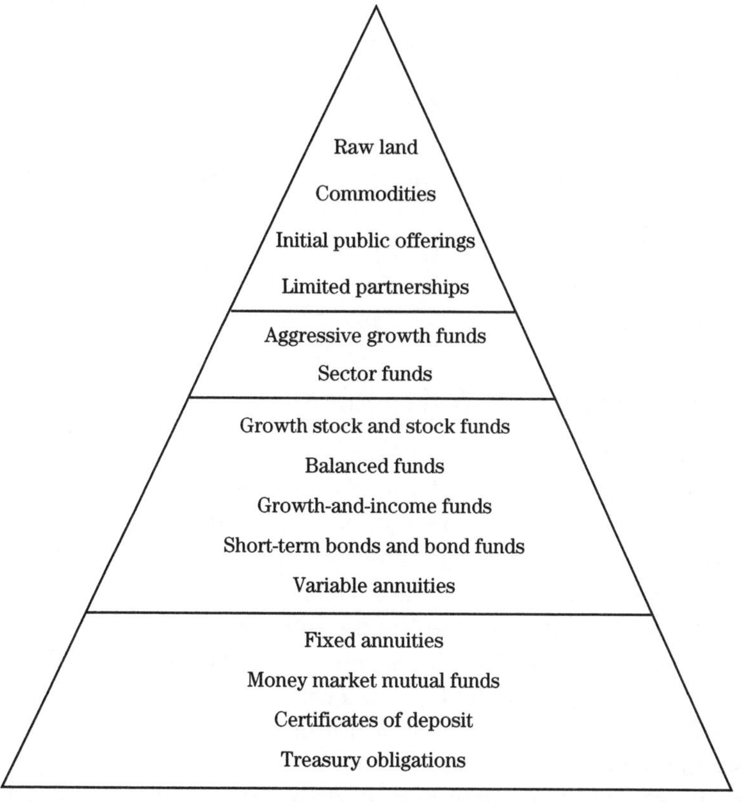

Every investor needs some of the safe investments that form the foundation of the pyramid. Then, depending on your age and your risk tolerance, a large portion of your portfolio should be invested for growth, and a small portion should be reserved for more aggressive growth funds. Only the most aggressive investors will look at the possibilities at the top: raw land, commodities, initial public offerings, and limited partnerships.

percent small-cap stocks, 25 percent international stocks, and 20 percent bonds. For those in their fifties, moving closer to retirement, he suggests 30 percent large-cap stocks, 10 percent small-cap stocks, 20 percent international stocks, and 40 percent bonds. And for those in their sixties, a recommended allocation might be 15 percent large-cap stocks, 5 percent small-cap stocks, 10 percent international stocks, 65 percent bonds, and 5 percent money market.

I disagree with this last recommendation. Years ago, retirement age was the time for shifting to fixed-income investments. Now, lengthening life expectancies must be considered. Will a portfolio with only 30 percent invested in equities generate enough growth to provide the lifestyle you want for the next 20 or 30 years? Read Chapter 7 for more insight into investing during the pre- and post-retirement years.

Which Investments for Which Account

Investment experts agree on the importance of viewing your entire portfolio as a single unit, but there's an ongoing discussion as to whether fixed-income investments belong in your tax-sheltered plan, with growth investments in a taxable account, or vice versa. A logical position is that income-producing investments—e.g., bonds—belong in the retirement plan because the income they generate every year can accumulate untaxed until the money is withdrawn. Following this theory, stocks should be held in a taxable account where capital gains will be taxed at the lower preferential rate and where capital losses can be used to offset gains.

But two studies have demonstrated that many people will come out ahead by placing income-producing investments in taxable accounts and stocks in tax-deferred accounts. A 1997 study by T. Rowe Price and a 2000 study by James Poterba of MIT and John B. Shoven and Clemens Sialm of Stanford both reported that capital gains taxes on the sale of equities are only part of the equation.

When stock mutual funds are held in a taxable account, investors are taxed each year on both dividends and capital gains distributions. Dividends and short-term gains are taxed at ordinary income rates. Long-term gains are taxed at the capital gains rate.

Frequent turnover within a stock fund generates income tax that you must pay even while you hold on to your shares. Owning stock funds within a tax-deferred retirement plan eliminates this annual tax. The saving may offset the difference between the lower capital gains tax when stocks are sold in a taxable account and the ordinary income tax that must be paid when retirement money is withdrawn.

In tracking investments from 1962 through 1998, Poterba and his colleagues found greater wealth accumulated by investors holding equity mutual funds in tax-deferred accounts and tax-free municipal bonds in taxable accounts. The T. Rowe Price study found similar results over the period from 1977 through 1996.

However, in a period where returns are lower and stocks do not outperform bonds by as great a margin, it may be better to hold bonds in a tax-deferred account.

How to decide? Samuel F. Beardesley, vice president of T. Rowe Price, suggests holding equities in a tax-deferred account if you actively manage your stock investments. That way, gains won't be taxed until money is withdrawn. Place equities in a taxable account if you tend to buy and hold index or tax-efficient funds.

And, if possible, determine your post-retirement income tax bracket. The worst situation for putting stocks in a tax-deferred account, according to Beardsley, is when the investor is in a high tax bracket both before and after retirement. The accumulated capital gains in a tax-sheltered account will be taxed as ordinary income, instead of at the lower capital gains rate, when the money is withdrawn. For taxpayers in the highest income tax bracket, the spread can exceed 20 percent: the maximum long-term capital gains tax rate is currently 20 percent (18 percent on securities held more than five years), and the maximum federal tax rate on ordinary income (pending anticipated cuts) is 39.6 percent.

As you decide what to put where in your own accounts, consider three other factors:

1. Are your taxable equity investments tax-efficient? If your answer is "Yes," your stocks may belong outside your retirement plan. If it is "No," think about holding stocks inside the plan. Unfortunately, many investors—and many portfolio managers—pay too little attention to the tax consequences of investment transactions. "Money managers who are truly tax-efficient," Barbara J. Raasch of Ernst & Young writes in the *CCH Estate Planning Review*, "are willing to continue to hold a security with a low cost basis even when they expect the return to be less than that of an alternative investment." They are aware that the after-tax investment proceeds are what counts.

2. How close are you to retirement? The more years you have, the better off you will be with growth investments in your retirement plan. With 10 years or less until retirement, you may want to keep equities in a taxable account and bonds in your tax-sheltered plan.
3. What is the income tax situation in your state? According to Beardsley, in 37 states, capital gains are taxed at the state's ordinary income rate. If you currently live in a high-tax state or think you will after retirement, it may be more advantageous to hold stock funds in the tax-deferred retirement account.

Keep one other fact in mind. There is a difference between Roth IRAs and other tax-deferred retirement plans. With a Roth, under current rules, withdrawals are not taxed at all if you are at least age 59½ and have had the plan for at least five years. That makes stocks and stock funds the best bet for a Roth because dividends *and* appreciation will never be subject to tax.

Others Pieces of the Investment Pie

Mutual funds are the investment of choice for most retirement plan participants because they offer built-in diversification along with professional management. But many other investment vehicles are available to fill out a portfolio. Some are tax-free, some are taxable, and some (like the annuities discussed in detail in Chapter 3) are tax-deferred. Some are mutual funds, of a type that may be best suited for investment *outside* your retirement plan, and some are individual securities. The next several pages describe some investment vehicles you may want to consider.

Municipal Bonds and Bond Funds

Municipal bonds and bond funds are the investments of choice for investors seeking completely tax-free income. Individual bonds can be purchased with maturity dates that will coincide with a specific need; mutual funds never mature. On the other hand, it's easier and less expensive to buy and sell shares of a mutual fund. A mutual fund also gives you the choice of receiving monthly income or automatically reinvesting the interest to buy additional shares. Mutual fund expenses are clearly expressed in the prospectus; it can be difficult to understand the cost associated with buying an individual bond.

Chapter 4 contains a more complete description of the pros and cons of individual securities and mutual funds.

If you're considering buying municipal bonds, either individually or through a fund, there are several things to remember before you commit to a purchase:

- They are generally tax-free only if issued in your state. If you buy a bond fund that contains issues from many states, you will receive a year-end statement showing the proportion of fund income subject to tax by your state. If you are holding individual bonds issued by one state consider selling the bonds if you move to another state.
- They don't make sense unless you are in at least the 31 percent federal income tax bracket. Consider your combined federal-state-local income tax bracket before you decide.
- The interest on municipal bonds is counted in determining whether your Social Security retirement benefits are subject to income tax.
- The interest on certain private-activity municipal bonds, such as those issued to finance airport construction, may push some investors into paying the alternative minimum tax.

Treasury Obligations

The U.S. Treasury raises money to finance government operations by issuing bills, notes, and bonds. All are fixed-income debt obligations. All are issued at a minimum price of $1,000. Because they pay income subject to federal income tax but not to state and local income tax, all are advantageous for investors in high-tax states. All are as risk-free as any investment can be, because they are backed by the full faith and credit of the U.S. government. You will get your money back if you hold an individual Treasury obligation to its maturity date. However, you can lose money if you sell an individual obligation before maturity. Treasury obligations are sensitive to interest rates, as are other bonds, and may be worth less when interest rates rise. Conversely, they may be worth more when interest rates decline.

Treasury bills (T-bills), with their 3-month, 6-month, and 12-month maturities, are generally considered cash equivalents; they can take a place in your portfolio alongside certificates of deposit and money market mutual funds. Unlike most investments, T-bills are sold at a discount; the interest is deducted from the purchase price. Because you effectively get the interest up front, the actual yield is higher than the stated yield. If a $1,000 T-bill sells for $950, the $50 is your interest. Because you get the $50 up front, the bill's yield is 5.3 percent, not 5 percent.

Treasury notes and bonds, like other bonds, pay interest twice a year. Notes have maturity dates of from 2 to 10 years, and bonds have terms of 10 to 30 years. Uncle Sam has recently cut back on issuing new Treasury obligations, however, so you may not be able to get exactly the maturity you want unless you buy on the secondary market where a note or bond is being resold by its original purchaser.

Inflation-indexed obligations, a recent addition to the Treasury menu, add a new meaning to the term "no-risk investment." With Treasury Inflation-Protected Securities (TIPS), the principal amount is adjusted every six months by the amount of increase in the Consumer Price Index (CPI), with the additional amounts stemming from each adjustment paid to investors at maturity. A 4 percent increase in the CPI would boost the value of a $1,000 bond to $1,040. And you can't lose money. If the principal should decrease, the U.S. Government will make up the difference. Interest is paid to investors twice a year, with a pre-set fixed rate applied to a principal amount that has increased or decreased depending on changes in the CPI. As the principal goes up, so do semiannual interest payments.

Inflation-indexed Treasury obligations can provide peace of mind if, as an investor, you are worried about the impact of inflation on your purchasing power. The bonds will really pay off if inflation returns in force. If inflation remains low, they may pay a bit less. In the unlikely event of an actual deflation, TIPS would turn out to be a very bad bet. The real downside, though, is that you owe federal income tax on the semiannual inflation adjustment, even though you don't receive it in cash. To avoid paying the tax on this phantom income, you may want to hold inflation-indexed obligations in an IRA. Or consider buying U.S. Government Series I bonds instead. (More on this option later.) Their yields may be slightly lower, but you can defer paying tax on the increasing value until the bonds are redeemed.

New Treasury securities may be purchased (at no charge) directly from the Federal Reserve Bank, or (at a nominal fee) through a bank or stockbroker. Older securities are available only through a bank or stockbroker, and the transaction will be more costly. Either way, there will be nothing to safeguard in a bank vault. The securities are issued in "book-entry" form, with electronic record keeping. You will receive a confirmation of your purchase, and periodic statements showing interest credited directly to your bank account.

You can also purchase Treasury obligations through mutual funds, although it rarely makes sense to do so. Mutual funds have many advantages, but you don't need professional management, diversification, or management fees when you're investing in Treasury obligations. They are easy to buy and they are completely safe.

NOTE

Call 1-800-722-2678 or go online to www.treasurydirect.gov to:

- **Request a copy of the Treasury Direct Investor Kit.**
- **Buy or reinvest securities.**
- **Check your account balance.**
- **Change your address and phone number.**

Agency Obligations

U.S. Treasury obligations are the safest of the safe among fixed-income investments. Other government agencies, such as the Federal National Mortgage Association (Fannie Mae) and the Federal Home Loan Bank, also issue notes and bonds to finance their projects, but these securities are not backed by the full faith and credit of the U.S. government. As a result, although they are considered very safe, their yields are often a bit higher than those on comparable Treasury issues.

As with Treasury obligations, the interest earned on agency obligations is subject to federal income tax. But there are differences. The interest on *some* agency obligations, but not others, is subject to state and local income tax, so ask before you buy. Unlike Treasury issues, however, these notes and bonds cannot be purchased directly from the issuing agency. You must buy them through a stockbroker or a commercial bank and pay a transaction fee. Compare these fees before you buy; they can be substantial. Also find out whether the bonds can be called; if so, you may lose your high-paying investment earlier than expected and be forced to reinvest the proceeds at a lower rate of interest.

Securities issued by the Government National Mortgage Association, familiarly called "Ginnie Maes," fall into another category. These *are* backed by the full faith and credit of the U.S. Government, but they do not pay semiannual interest or return the principal at maturity. Instead, as a Ginnie Mae investor, you receive monthly payments representing both interest and a partial return of principal. The interest is taxable on both the federal and state levels; the return of principal is not. But, because each check includes a partial return of principal, you won't have a lump sum to reinvest at the end.

Ginnie Mae certificates—or shares in a Ginnie Mae mutual fund—represent shares in a pool of government-backed mortgages. Although mortgages typically run 25 to 30 years, the average life of a new Ginnie Mae pool is generally projected at 12 years. But mortgages may be prepaid, if interest rates drop and homeowners can refinance at lower cost. So the precise term of your investment is unpredictable and so is the precise yield.

Tax-Efficient, Tax-Managed, and Index Funds

Within tax-sheltered plans, tax efficiency doesn't matter. There are no tax consequences in connection with capital gains distributions or when you sell shares. Outside your retirement plans, taxes can matter a great deal. A study published in the *Journal of Investing* showed an enormous difference: Over a 25-year period, based on the S&P 500 stock index, investors kept just 41 percent of the returns. They forfeited fully 47 percent to taxes and 12 percent to management fees. Reducing taxes, according to James Garland, author of the study, could raise the return to 73 percent.

Most mutual fund managers don't pay much attention to taxes because they are rewarded for performance. But investors can find tax efficiency, and hence the potential for greater returns, in many index funds as well as in funds that are labeled tax-efficient or tax-managed.

Index funds have been the darling of investors for the past several years. These mutual funds, mirroring the performance of a market index such as the S&P 500, have been a painless way to ride an upward market. Index funds are low-cost because they don't require active management. Their portfolio mix changes only when stocks in the underlying index are changed. As a result, index funds are generally tax-efficient; the lower turnover rate translates into fewer capital gains distributions and a smaller annual tax bite for investors.

But index funds are not always tax-efficient. Some analysts caution that a market downturn may leave investors surprised and unhappy. Because index funds are fully invested at all times, with little or no cash reserves, the funds would probably have to sell holdings—thereby generating taxable capital gains—to meet investors' demand for redemptions in a market downturn. On the other hand, Gus

Sauter, who heads Vanguard's index funds, points out that high-basis shares would be sold first, generating losses rather than gains. In his view, a major bear market, with a sustained drop of 20 percent or more of market value, would have to develop before redemptions could force the realization of gains.

If tax efficiency is your goal, look to large-cap index funds with low portfolio turnover. Small-cap index funds, such as those based on the Russell 2000, have more turnover because the most successful stocks move up into the mid-cap range and are removed from the index.

Or, look for a fund that is labeled tax-efficient or tax-managed. When this is a stated objective, portfolio managers consider turnover, yield, and unrecognized capital gains. Turnover generates realized capital gains. Yield matters because dividends throw off taxable income. A large-cap growth fund holding dividend-paying stocks will usually generate more taxable income than funds holding small-cap stocks geared toward appreciation rather than current income. And unrealized capital gains can have a particularly significant impact on new investors in a fund. Because these gains build in a fund over time, says Gordon Forrester of the Putnam Funds, newer investors "can be saddled with a huge tax liability without having enjoyed the benefits of the investment gains." For this reason, it can be preferable to invest in a relatively new fund. Just remember that taxes should never be the tail that wags the investment dog. Performance matters more than tax efficiency.

Exchange-Traded Funds

The new kids on the investment block, exchange-traded funds (ETFs), are hybrids. They are similar to index funds because they are designed to mirror the performance of a market index or stock market sector. They are similar to stocks because their shares trade on stock exchanges (primarily on the American Stock Exchange) and can be bought and sold at any time. The first ETF was introduced in 1993. It is called the Standard & Poor's Depositary Receipt (SPDR, or "Spider"), and it tracks the S&P 500. Today, there are at least 79 ETFs, including Diamonds to track the Dow Jones, and iShares from Barclays Global Investors (iShares alone offered 57 ETFs in December 2000) with new versions being introduced all the time.

ETFs have some advantages. They are tax-efficient, they generally have low expenses (although brokerage commissions can boost the cost), and they can be readily bought and sold. On the down side, information may be hard to find. Share prices are available in daily newspaper stock tables. But the major data providers in the mutual fund world—Morningstar and Lipper—are, at this writing, just beginning to grapple with how to present basic information about portfolio holdings and year-to-date total return in their databases. Complicating the issue, says Karen Damato, writing in *Investor's Business Daily*, there are "some key structural differences." Some ETFs are legally structured as ordinary mutual funds, but, because prices can vary from net asset value during the trading day, the Securities and Exchange Commission (SEC) won't let ETFs be called mutual funds. Other ETFs are more like closed-end funds (see below); they hold a fixed portfolio of stocks. And some are technically unit investment trusts (discussed later). You may want to investigate ETFs, but try to get as much information as possible before you invest. That advice applies to any investment, but particularly to something new.

Closed-End Funds

Although they are losing ground to the newly popular ETFs, closed-end funds are still available. Closed-end funds may contain stocks or bonds, both domestic and foreign, although the most popular varieties are single-country funds and municipal bond funds. Unlike the garden variety of mutual fund (technically called "open-ended"), closed-end funds have a fixed investment portfolio and a fixed number of shares. Unlike other mutual funds, too, the shares trade on stock exchanges. Shares are purchased through a stockbroker, and brokerage commissions are charged on each trade.

But shares usually trade at a discount to the net asset value—often a steep discount—after the initial public offering of a new closed-end fund. If you are interested in a closed-end fund, therefore, your best bet is an older one that is now available at a discount. Be aware, though, that the discount may never be made up.

Unit Investment Trusts

Unit investment trusts (UITs) are similar to closed-end funds in having fixed portfolios, but they are very different because they are unmanaged. The holdings in the portfolio are fixed at the time of purchase; change only takes place when bonds are called or mature. Although UITs appeal to investors seeking a steady stream of income, that income is not guaranteed. When bonds within the portfolio are called, or mature, investors receive a distribution of capital. Monthly interest checks also become smaller in amount as bonds are retired.

There is no management fee because the portfolios are unmanaged. But UITs are sold by stockbrokers, and brokerage commissions typically run 4 percent to 5 percent of the purchase price. There are also annual administrative costs. A single unit is priced at $1,000 but UITs may typically be purchased only in minimum amounts of $5,000.

Unless you are reasonably certain that you can hold the units to maturity, you are probably better off in a no-load open-end bond fund. Sponsors must redeem shares if investors want to sell before maturity, but doing so almost always means taking a loss.

Real Estate Investment Trusts

Real estate is expensive to buy and a chore to manage. Buying shares in a publicly traded real estate investment trust (REIT) is the best way for most investors to tap the income potential associated with real estate. You can purchase shares in one or more REITs directly or invest in a group of REITs through a mutual fund.

Buying shares of a REIT is like buying shares of any common stock, except that REITs offer some special tax advantages. Unlike corporations, REITs are not subject to double taxation. No income is taxed at the corporate level so long as at least 75 percent of the company's income is derived from real estate, 75 percent of the company's assets are in real estate, and 90 percent of taxable income is paid out to shareholders. Because most of the income goes directly to shareholders, REITs typically generate high yields when compared with other fixed-income investments. In addition, some dividends may be considered either capital gains or return of capital, thereby reducing the tax bite. And there is always the potential for growth if the properties appreciate in value.

REITs may invest in mortgages but today's most popular REITs, called equity REITs, invest directly in the development, acquisition, and renovation of real estate. Equity REITs may own shopping malls, apartment houses, office buildings, nursing homes, industrial parks—or virtually any form of real estate. REIT mutual funds may also be diversified among building types.

Individual Securities

These are the stocks and bonds you purchase individually rather than through a mutual fund, an exchange-traded fund, or a unit investment trust. The biggest argument for selecting and buying individual securities is that you retain control of the buying and selling decisions and, hence, of the tax consequences. You will pay brokerage commissions on each trade instead of the annual management expenses (and, possibly, an up-front or back-end load) associated with a mutual fund. But you will not owe capital gains taxes until you sell. As noted earlier, you may face a large tax bill on realized and unrealized capital gains within a mutual fund, even if you never see the money and even if you bought into the fund after most of the profits were reaped by earlier investors.

EE Bonds, HH Bonds, and I Bonds

U.S. government savings bonds are fixed-income investments that may be bought for as little as $25 at most financial institutions and through payroll deduction plans at many employers. But "fixed income" doesn't mean that there is a guaranteed rate, or that you can easily figure out how much particular bonds are paying. Uncle Sam has devised an enormously complicated system for paying interest on EE bonds. The interest rate is pegged, at this writing, at 90 percent of the average yield on five-year Treasury notes, and a new rate is set every six months. Bonds issued in May 1997 and thereafter earn the full rate of interest from the outset, as long as they are held for at least five years. There is a three-month interest penalty if bonds are redeemed before five years. Different rules apply to bonds issued earlier.

Series EE bonds issued after May 1, 1997, earned 5.54 percent from November 2000 through April 2001. Some bonds issued earlier earned 5.41 percent for the same semiannual earnings period; others issued at a different time earned 5.15 percent. For more information, go online to www.savingsbonds.gov, the official Web site of the U.S. Treasury, Bureau of the Public Debt. Other useful Web sites are: www.ny.frb.org, for bond values, and www.bondhelp.com to request a customized statement (for a fee starting at $15) for up to ten bonds. The Savings Bond Informer is not an official government source, but it provides information not available elsewhere. In addition to the bond help Web site, it may also be reached at 1-800-927-1901.

Series I bonds may be a better bet. These bonds are sold at face value but pay interest in a combination of a fixed rate and a variable inflation rate. The fixed rate in effect when the bond is purchased remains in effect for the life of the bond. For Series I bonds purchased from November 2000 through April 2001, the fixed rate, guaranteed for 30 years, was 3.4 percent. The variable rate is adjusted every six months to align with changes in the Consumer Price Index. Series I bonds purchased from November 2000 through April 2001 paid a variable rate of 3.04 percent. These bonds are similar to TIPS, the inflation-adjusted Treasury obligations discussed above, but are available for as little as $50.

In one more variation on the theme, you may choose to convert maturing Series E and EE bonds to Series HH bonds. Series E and EE bonds pay interest for no more than 30 or 40 years, depending on when they were originally issued. If you're still holding World War II vintage Series E bonds, in other words, it's past time to cash them in. If cashing in will leave you with a bigger tax bill than you care to pay—if you've been deferring the annual income tax on the interest until the bonds are redeemed, as most people do—you can exchange the bonds for Series HH bonds.

Converting to Series HH bonds lets you continue to defer tax on the accumulated interest in the EE bonds for as long as 20 more years, but you will have to pay tax, each year, on the twice-yearly interest payments received from the Series HH bonds. These bonds can be acquired only through conversion, not by direct purchase. To convert, you must have at least $500 in Series EE bonds that are at least six months old. If you have more than $500 but less than a multiple of $500, you can either make up the difference in cash or take the difference in cash.

If you own older savings bonds, pay attention to their final maturity date:

ISSUE DATE	FINAL MATURITY DATE
Series E bonds issued before December 1965	40 years
Series E and EE bonds issued after November 1965	30
Series H bonds issued between 1959 and 1979	30
Series HH bonds issued since 1980	20
Series I bonds	30

Taxes and Investing

The income from some investments, especially some municipal bonds and bond funds, may be entirely tax-free (although you will owe tax on any profit when you sell). Some investments, including annuities and anything within your 401(k) and other tax-sheltered retirement plans, are tax-deferred—no tax is due during the holding period, but everything is taxed at ordinary income tax rates when the money is withdrawn. And some investments are entirely taxable; income in the form of dividends or interest is taxed as it is received, and appreciation is taxed when the investment is sold.

Many Americans have a knee-jerk reaction when it comes to taxes, avoiding them at all costs. But it doesn't always pay to seek out tax-free investments. Unless you are in a fairly high combined federal/state income tax bracket, the chances are that you will come out ahead in a higher-yielding taxable investment, even after you pay the tax. (Refer to Table 4.4 for equivalent taxable and tax-free yields.)

In any case, profits in both tax-free and taxable investments—all investments except those within a tax-sheltered retirement plan—are taxed when the investment is sold and the profit is taken. One of the only drawbacks to tax-sheltered retirement plans, in some investors' minds, is that all the money is taxed at ordinary income tax rates when it is taken out, rather than at the lower capital gains tax rate. As a rule, however, long periods of tax-sheltered growth more than make up for the tax difference.

For taxable investments, the rules are:

- Profits on assets held less than one year are taxed at ordinary income tax rates.
- Profits on assets held one year or more are taxed at a maximum capital gains rate of 10 percent for taxpayers in the 15 percent tax bracket, and 20 percent for all others.
- Profits on assets held for at least five years are taxed at a preferential capital gains rate of 8 percent for taxpayers in the 15 percent tax bracket and 18 percent for all others.

The lower capital gains rate for assets held at least five years was enacted in the Taxpayer Relief Act of 1997 but became effective on January 1, 2001.

Note the subtle difference in the five-year requirement: For people owing capital gains tax at the lower 8 percent rate, the assets must be held for five years but could be sold as early as January 2, 2001. For everyone else to get the lower rate, the assets must have been acquired after December 31, 2000, and then held for five years before they are sold.

There is one exception to this rule, but it must be acted upon by October 15, 2002. If you hold securities acquired before January 1, 2001, and you want to qualify for the five-year holding period and the lower capital gains tax rate, you can make a special election to treat the securities as being acquired on January 1, 2001. To do so, you must attach Form 4797 to your federal income tax return for 2001. With extensions, the final date for filing that return is October 15, 2002. File earlier? No problem. You can file an amended return for 2001 up until October 15, 2002, and make the election as of January 1, 2001.

You must then pay any capital gains tax that is due. The payment will be out-of-pocket because you won't actually have sold the securities. But this up-front payment could be worth making if you currently have a modest gain in the securities (the tax will be low), but you expect a more substantial gain that will be taxed, when you do sell, at the lower 18 percent rate.

The above tactic may work with securities you want to keep. If you own securities that you're ready to sell, Laurence Foster, a Certified Public Accountant and personal financial specialist with Richard A. Eisner & Co. in New York, suggests that the difference in the five-year holding period presents a planning opportunity. Instead of selling appreciated securities, he recommends giving them to a child or grandchild who is age 14 or over and is in the 15 percent federal income tax bracket. The child can then turn around and sell the stock, producing a capital gains tax of 8 percent instead of 20 percent. The 12 percent spread means that your family saves $2,400 in tax on a joint gift, from you and your spouse, of $20,000 in appreciated securities.

But don't get greedy. Giving to a younger child won't work (unless the child holds onto the stock until age 14) because children under age 14 are taxed at their parents' highest bracket. Giving more won't work either. Gifts of up to $10,000 per person, or $20,000 for a married couple filing jointly, are free from gift tax. Make a larger gift and you will have to file a federal gift tax return. Then, when all your lifetime gifts exceed the amount excluded from gift and estate tax ($675,000 in 2001, $700,000 in 2002, and rising to $1 million in 2006 and thereafter), gift tax must be paid.

Giving too much can also backfire when a youngster applies for college. Earlier gifts may reduce his or her chances for financial aid and/or the dollar amount that may be offered. Perhaps more important, a child's or grandchild's sale of a larger gift could generate enough income to bounce him or her right out of the 15 percent tax bracket. At higher brackets, you're right back where you started because the five-year holding period starts at the beginning of 2001.

Investments don't always produce a profit. As some stockbrokers like to put it, "Trees don't always reach the sky." Inevitably, you will sell some securities at a loss. Within tax-sheltered plans, neither capital gains nor capital losses register on the tax screen. Outside tax-sheltered plans, capital losses can be put to some use.

Because losses can be applied against gains for the year, they reduce the total tax that is due. If losses exceed gains in any one year, a maximum of $3,000 may be used to offset ordinary income. Any capital losses in excess of $3,000 may be carried forward to later years.

Mutual Funds and Taxes

Owning mutual funds in your personal investment portfolio (outside your tax-sheltered plans) has other tax consequences.

First, be aware of tax filing requirements while you own mutual fund shares. Dividends and interest, whether taken in cash or reinvested to purchase additional shares, are taxable as ordinary income.

Capital gains distributions, as the fund itself profits from buying and selling securities, are generally received and reported annually. Whether those distributions are reported as long-term or short-term gains depends on how long the fund held the securities before the sale, not on how long you have owned shares in the fund. Funds with high turnover rates, because they buy and sell frequently, generate a heavier tax burden for shareholders. (A bill introduced in Congress in 2000 would allow investors to postpone paying tax on up to $3,000 in capital gains—$6,000 for a married couple—if they reinvest the gains in the same mutual fund. Watch for future action along these lines.)

"Return of capital" is another distribution category that occasionally occurs. When you see a return of capital on your year-end tax information forms, it represents a return of your investment in the fund. Because it is a return of investment, the distribution is not taxable; instead, it has the effect of reducing your cost basis in the shares. Keep track of these distributions against the eventual day when you sell. Meanwhile, if the distribution is larger than your cost basis, you will have a taxable gain on the excess amount.

When you sell mutual fund shares, taxes are another story. It's an easy tale to tell if you bought your fund shares all at once and sell them all at once. It's a very different and far more complicated tale if you reinvested dividends or bought more shares at various times. You then have a different "cost basis" for each purchase. If you keep careful records as you go along, you'll be able to sell specific shares, selecting short-term and long-term capital gains or losses to your tax advantage. If not, you can use an average cost basis. The IRS recognizes both methods for calculating taxes on fund sales.

Selling specific shares gives you maximum control of the tax consequences because you can reduce the tax bite by selling shares that cost more. This strategy can be pursued in one of two ways:

1. If you have kept very good records and can identify the shares you're selling by their purchase date and price, you can sell shares bought at a certain price. You can then sell the highest-cost shares and achieve the smallest spread (and therefore the smallest tax) between the purchase price and the sales price. To do this, you must give written instructions to your broker or mutual fund and receive a written confirmation of your instructions.
2. Use a first in-first out (FIFO) approach (the shares you are selling were the first shares you purchased). This method generally works to your best advantage (it produces the lowest tax bill) only when the fund has lost money and the current share value is below your purchase price. Otherwise, when a fund has done well over the years, the first shares purchased probably cost the least, and selling them will produce a higher tax bill. Perhaps this is why this is the IRS default position. If you don't indicate which accounting method you're using, the IRS assumes that you are using FIFO.

Using an average cost basis, you simply divide the total cost of all your shares (including those purchased with reinvested dividends) by the number of shares you own. This is the easiest method to use—some fund companies will do the arithmetic for you—but it doesn't always produce the best results. Also, once you start using this method, you need written permission from the IRS to switch to another method when you sell shares in the same fund.

A variation on the average cost basis method is called *double category averaging* and involves averaging your cost on both short-term and long-term holdings. When you are in a high tax bracket and most of your holdings are long-term, this method typically yields a more favorable result. To use it, you must tell your fund or broker which category of shares you are selling and, again, the fund or broker must provide written confirmation. Also, once you use this method you must continue using it.

TIP

For more information on mutual fund taxation, request:

- **IRS Publication 564, Mutual Fund Distributions.**
- **IRS Publication 550, Investment Income and Expenses.**

Both publications are available by calling the IRS, toll-free, at 1-800-829-1040.

Here are some cautionary notes for fund shareholders:

- When you sell your shares, remember that you've already paid taxes on reinvested dividends. Don't pay taxes again on the same money by basing your profit calculations on the simple difference between your initial purchase price and your sales price. Good records can avoid this trap.
- Funds are required to make year-end distributions of capital gains. If you buy shares in a fund just before that distribution is made, you will wind up paying income taxes on profits you didn't receive. To avoid this trap, find out the fund's distribution date and invest after the distribution is made.
- The market may be down and your particular fund may have lost value, but you may still be faced with a tax bite for capital gains distributions. If your fund made a profit on some sales, you'll owe tax on your share of that profit even if you bought shares later and didn't benefit from the upturn. This has been a big shock to some shareholders in recent volatile markets.
- Switching funds within a fund family—a task that can be accomplished with a simple phone call—is a taxable event. You will have to report any profit or loss on the sale.
- States with income taxes usually treat mutual fund distributions the same way the federal government does. But there are exceptions:

—If funds invest in U.S. government obligations, states generally do not tax dividends stemming from those federal obligations.

—Income from municipal bonds held either directly or through a mutual fund is generally not taxed by the state issuing those obligations. If you own shares of a national municipal bond fund, you will receive year-end information about which proportion of the dividends is taxable in which state.

CHAPTER 7

As Time Goes By

As a general rule, young people can invest aggressively because they have a long time horizon. As working people move closer to retirement, their investment objectives and strategies tend to change, and they become more directed toward hanging on to principal. Older investors, those well into the retirement years, often become even more conservative and risk-averse. They focus on investing for income.

Chapter 6 provided information on asset allocation and sample portfolios at various ages. But each investor is an individual, and age is not the only consideration. Financial responsibilities are at least as significant. Young or old, the key question is: Do you have dependents? Single folks can often invest more aggressively than married couples with children. But a single woman with dependent parents has concerns that are different from those of a single woman of the same age with no dependents. You may be middle-aged with grown children, or middle-aged with young children from a second marriage. You may even be middle-aged with young children *and* aging parents.

So think in terms of your life circumstances along with your anticipated life expectancy as you plan your investment strategy for your pre-retirement and post-retirement years.

The Pre-Retirement Years

Traditional "wisdom" holds that investment objectives should shift from growth to income as you near retirement. You can no longer afford to take chances, the theory goes, so you should "guarantee" your retirement income by putting most, or all, of your money into safe income-producing investment vehicles. That theory no longer holds. In your grandfather's time, when few people lived much beyond retirement (and few people were invested in the stock market to begin with), it may have made sense. Today, with an average life expectancy of about 20 years for a 65-year-old retiree, investing entirely for income may guarantee only that you run out of money before you run out of years.

Nonetheless, when you reach age 60 or so, you may want to change your investment mix both inside and outside your 401(k) plan. You may want to shift to a less aggressive position in stocks, perhaps making balanced growth-and-income funds a larger portion of your portfolio. As described in Chapter 6, a sample pre-retirement portfolio, as recommended by Sheldon Jacobs in his book, *Guide to Successful No-Load Fund Investing,* might be 65 percent in domestic equities, 15 percent in international equities, and 20 percent in bonds.

Another piece of traditional wisdom may bear examination as you near retirement: the assumption that you should continue contributing to your 401(k) or other tax-sheltered retirement plan just as long as you can. For most people, the answer is clearly *Yes.* For those who are in a high income tax bracket and expect to continue their high-tax status in retirement, the answer is less clear.

The downside to continued tax-sheltered investment is exactly what I've pointed out earlier: All the money that comes out will be taxed at ordinary income rates—currently, a maximum of 39.6 percent for taxpayers in the highest federal income tax bracket. Capital gains realized in a regular taxable account are currently taxed at no more than 20 percent. For assets held for at least five years, starting January 1, 2001, the maximum capital gains rate is 18 percent. In addition, if you die while you have assets in a taxable account, your heirs get a "step-up" in cost basis so that no tax at all may be due when those assets are sold. There is no step-up in the cost basis for assets in a tax-sheltered account. In fact, if you die while you have assets in a tax-sheltered account, as much as 75 percent of the account may be lost to a combination of income and estate taxes.

A taxable account also has some drawbacks. Taxes must be paid each year on dividend and interest income, realized capital gains, and capital gains distributions made by mutual funds. These taxes can be held down, as described in Chapter 6, by using tax-managed or tax-efficient funds that are focused on avoiding large taxable distributions.

The mutual fund family at T. Rowe Price recently conducted a study that compared tax-deferred and taxable investing for plan participants nearing retirement. Which approach is best? The study found that the answer depends on your tax bracket both before and after retirement, how much time you have until retirement, the rate of return on your investments, and whether your plan matches contributions. But an overriding consideration is whether you can and will invest the same amount in a tax-sheltered and a taxable account. The $10,500 that you might put into a 401(k) is pre-tax. Invest the same $10,500 after tax, and you may actually be investing just $7,560 if you are in the 28 percent federal income tax bracket.

Your choice of a strategy depends on your individual circumstances, but, in general, a 401(k) with an employer match is usually a better choice than a taxable account. The study suggested two rules of thumb that may be helpful:

1. Compare a pre-tax investment in a 401(k) with a lower after-tax investment in a taxable account, and the 401(k), even without an employer match, comes out ahead—unless you will move into a higher tax rate after retirement.
2. Compare investments of the same dollar amount and the taxable account, particularly if it is invested in a tax-efficient growth fund, may be a better choice than a 401(k) plan that has no employer match. "This approach," according to T. Rowe Price, "becomes even more attractive for those who expect to be in relatively high tax brackets after retirement."

Post-Retirement Investing

"Retirement," these days, doesn't mean a closing door. It doesn't mean the end of life. And so it doesn't mean the end of investing.

There has been significant change within the past few decades. As recently as 1950, according to trend-watcher David Pearce Snyder, lifestyles editor of *The Futurist* magazine, the average working person retired at age 67 and died at age 68. By 1990, the average American worker was retiring before age 60, and the average lifespan had increased to 77. With 20 years in retirement—considerably more for people who outlive the averages—retirement investing and spending deserve serious consideration.

Retirement is not a seamless continuum. Sociologists have identified at least three stages of mature adulthood: (1) healthy-and-active retirees up to about age 75, (2) those between ages 75 and 85 who are beginning to slow down, and (3) frail elderly persons over age 85 who are probably less active and who may be spending more on health care.

Younger retirees may still be working—part-time or full-time, in the same field or in new ones, as employees or consultants. Older retirees are spending rather than earning. But every retiree, at every age, should continue to invest at least partially for growth. The old rule of thumb—that growth investments should be traded in for income investments at age 65—no longer applies. With 20 to 30 years in retirement, your money must grow if it is to outpace inflation.

One of the first considerations, as you collect your gold watch and pass "Go" into retirement, is which investments to tap first to provide retirement income. Once the calendar moves past the April 1 after you reach age 70½, you must start taking the required minimum distributions from your tax-sheltered accounts (see Chapter 11). Before that date, you should almost always tap taxable accounts first, in order to continue tax-sheltered growth in your retirement accounts. Moreover, favorable capital gains rates on taxable accounts mean a smaller tax bite on the sale of assets in those accounts. All withdrawals from tax-sheltered accounts are taxed as ordinary income.

In an example from the Vanguard Group's useful new booklet, "Investing During Retirement" (available free by calling 1-800-992-0855), selling a $10,000 asset that you've owned for more than a year in a taxable account could leave you with more than $8,000. Selling the same $10,000 asset from a tax-sheltered plan could leave you with little more than $6,000. Why the difference? Because only the increase in the asset's price is taxable in the first instance, and the tax can be no more than the maximum long-term capital gains rate of 20 percent. But retirement plan distributions are taxed as ordinary

How can you simplify your finances when you retire—and have more time to enjoy life? The Vanguard Group suggests:

- **Consolidate your retirement assets by rolling all of your employer-sponsored plans into an IRA at one company. You'll receive a single statement, and calculating your required minimum distributions will be easier.**
- **Consider using a single mutual fund company for your taxable investments. At many companies, including Vanguard, you can also hold the shares of other companies' mutual funds. You'll receive a single statement and reduce the number of documents needed for income tax filing.**
- **Have your mutual fund company automatically calculate your required minimum distributions and transfer the distributions to the account of your choice. Remember that while you can't take less than the required minimum, you can take more.**
- **Have money automatically transferred each month from your mutual fund account to your bank checking account.**
- **Have your bank automatically debit your account and pay bills for fixed expenses such as mortgage payments and insurance premiums.**
- **Hire professional help, to free yourself from the chore of preparing tax returns and—unless you enjoy investment research—managing your investments.**

income, at rates as high as 39.6 percent, plus any state or local income taxes that apply.

As you plan an investment strategy for your retirement years, consider these three factors, suggested by the Strong Funds:

1. How much money you have to work with (your level of assets).
2. How much you need to maintain your desired lifestyle (your spending rate).
3. Whether your expectations are realistic (the risk/return trade-off).

All of these factors are essentially the same elements you consider at any stage of your investment life. The difference, once you have retired, is that your income stream comes from a different source. Instead of a paycheck, you'll have Social Security (which is indexed

WORKSHEET

A list of everything you own that can throw off income is an invaluable aid to planning as you enter your retirement years. Use this worksheet to list all of your financial assets.

401(k) plans and IRAs:	____________
Annuities:	____________
Pension plan:	____________
Bank accounts:	____________
Certificates of deposit:	____________
Individual securities:	____________
Mutual funds:	____________
U.S. Savings Bonds:	____________
Business interests:	____________
Life insurance (cash value):	____________
Rental real estate (market value):	____________
Royalties:	____________
TOTAL:	____________

to inflation), savings, your defined contribution plan, and, maybe, a traditional defined benefit pension.

Don't fall into the common but out-of-date traps of thinking that you must live off income and never tap your principal, or invest solely for income. The principal—your nest egg—is what you've been saving toward retirement. There's no reason not to tap it, now that you're in retirement, as long as you have reasonable expectations about your own longevity and market performance.

Investing solely for income means that you may eventually have to tap more of your principal than you mean to, just to keep pace with inflation. Move entirely to income, money manager Kenneth L. Fisher wrote in *Forbes*, and you must hate your wife. An all-income portfolio won't last long and such "a short-term approach regularly leaves a wife—and women tend to outlive men—poor after her husband's death."

Before you decide how long you need your retirement portfolio to last, Fisher urges, consider genetics. "Average your parents' ages at death and then add four years. Average all your grandparents and add eight years. Each generation lives longer on average. . . . Find the average of these two sets of numbers, and you'll know how long you likely have." If you don't die in a plane crash or come down with a life-shortening illness, you should plan on living at least as long as your ancestors did. And, Fisher concludes, "if you're married, remember that the money must last for two."

Use Table 7.1 to determine how long your assets will last at various rates of withdrawal, rates of inflation, and rates of return.

If you design a portfolio to provide the needed income, without considering growth for the long term, you are likely to have a cash shortfall when interest rates are down. Worse, you may be tempted into high-yielding but inherently risky investments. Instead, Florida wealth manager Harold Evensky strongly suggests focusing on total return—balancing your need for current cash flow with the need for long-term growth.

Following this strategy means taking cash flow from interest, dividends, and capital gains—periodically liquidating a portion of the portfolio to provide the needed cash. To avoid having to sell shares when the market is temporarily down, create a "cash flow reserve" and deposit enough money to supply your cash flow needs for two years. With the reserve invested in a money market mutual fund, you'll be cushioned against selling into a market downturn. If the market stays down and you've used all of your cash reserve, selling part of your fixed-income portfolio can build in another three years of protection. To this end, Evensky puts his clients in a mix of Treasury bills and short-term bond funds.

Bear in mind, though, that some circumstances are beyond your control. Identical retirement portfolios can produce very different results at different times and in different economic circumstances. The Vanguard Group, in a useful booklet called "Preparing to Retire," describes two investors who had two things in common. Both invested conservatively, with half the portfolio in stocks and half in bonds. And both withdrew, aggressively, 6 percent a year.

The first investor, "Dennis," retired at the end of 1972 with a $300,000 portfolio. Dennis assumed that he could safely withdraw 6 percent or $18,000 of his portfolio in the first post-retirement year and an equivalent inflation-adjusted amount in subsequent years. But

TABLE 7.1 Your Assets: How Long Will They Last?

WITHDRAWAL RATE	INFLATION RATE	YEARS OF INCOME IF ASSETS GROW AT:				
		5%	8%	10%	12%	16%
5%	2%	31	*	*	*	*
	4	23	39	*	*	*
	6	19	26	38	*	*
6	2	24	*	*	*	*
	4	19	28	*	*	*
	6	16	21	27	*	*
7	2	19	33	*	*	*
	4	16	22	31	*	*
	6	14	17	21	31	*
8	2	16	24	*	*	*
	4	14	28	23	*	*
	6	12	15	18	23	*
9	2	14	19	28	*	*
	4	12	15	19	27	*
	6	11	13	15	19	*
10	2	13	16	21	*	*
	4	11	13	16	20	*
	6	10	12	13	16	32
12	2	10	12	15	19	*
	4	9	11	12	14	30
	6	8	10	11	12	18
15	2	8	9	10	12	20
	4	7	8	9	10	14
	6	7	8	8	9	11
20	2	6	7	7	8	10
	4	6	7	7	7	8
	6	5	6	6	7	8

* Withdrawals could be sustained more than 40 years.

Source: Taming Taxes in Retirement, American Century Investments. For a free copy of a "Post-Retirement Calculator" to help you determine how long your tax-deferred retirement accounts can provide the annual income you need, call American Century, toll-free, at 1-800-345-2021.

Dennis retired at the wrong time. Inflation was running very high, and the stock market lost almost 40 percent of its value in the bear market of 1973–1974. The result: Dennis had used up his portfolio by 1986.

The second investor, "Sandy," retired at the end of 1982, early in the recent record-setting bull market. Thanks to a combination of low inflation and a rising market, Sandy still had more than $2.5 million in her portfolio in 1999, after the market dropped from its 1998 high. In effect, thanks to good luck and good timing, her planned 6 percent withdrawals actually amounted to little more than 2 percent.

These scenarios demonstrate extreme circumstances. Chances are that you'll retire in more moderate times. Nonetheless, there is a lesson here. As the folks at Vanguard put it, "It's prudent to make conservative initial assumptions abut investment returns (assume they'll be lower than historical averages) and inflation (assume it will be higher than historical averages)." Then you can make adjustments as time goes on. Moreover, "as a rule of thumb, you might consider limiting your initial withdrawal to no more than 3 percent to 5 percent of a portfolio that you want to last 30 to 35 years after you retire."

Todd Cleary, head of financial planning for T. Rowe Price, agrees, noting that a relatively safe withdrawal rate is about 4 percent to 5 percent of assets during the first year. "No analysis can predict the future," he says, "but history suggests that this withdrawal rate gives you a high probability that you won't run out of money using a reasonably diversified investment strategy."

Cleary also points out that there are risks in basing retirement income decisions—how much you can safely withdraw from your investments—on average rates of return. The future is not predictable, and, in the real world, "Investment returns vary not only year to year, but month to month, day to day."

His point becomes very real if you consider the 30-year period from 1968 through 1998. During this period, a portfolio composed of 60 percent stocks, 30 percent bonds, and 10 percent cash produced an average annual total return of a very healthy 11.7 percent. Could a retiree have withdrawn that much each year? No way. In fact, an 8.5 percent annual withdrawal rate would have made the portfolio last exactly 30 years, given *average* annual returns, but only 13 years, given *actual* annual returns. "This reflects," Cleary says, "the impact of disappointing performance relatively early in retirement, particularly the vicious bear market of 1973–1974." In other words, even though the average annual return skyrocketed to 15.3 percent from

T. Rowe Price has introduced a free Retirement Income Calculator that simulates the impact of 500 potential market scenarios on different asset allocations and allows you to estimate the probability of maintaining an income strategy throughout retirement. The Calculator, available online at www.troweprice.com, offers a reality check so that you can find the probability of success for your retirement income projections.

Want more detail? For $500, T. Rowe Price also offers a personalized plan called the Retirement Income Manager. Using analytical techniques, including a variety of portfolio combinations, and taking into account the individual's financial priorities and life expectancy, along with the variability of market returns, the program projects the likelihood of success for various investment strategies. Call toll-free, 1-800-566-5611, for more information.

1982 to 1998, annual withdrawals during the prior years of mediocre market performance didn't leave enough money in the portfolio for this retiree to reap the full benefit of the bull market when it finally rolled around.

If you had a crystal ball and could accurately predict the average real-world returns during your own retirement years, you still wouldn't have total control. In short, the sequence and variability of returns, as well as their average, affect how much income you will have. A rise in inflation, a drop in stock values, shifts in interest rates—all have an immediate and a long-term impact.

Because this is so, financial analysts have begun to use something called "Monte Carlo simulations" to predict the likelihood that a retirement nest egg will last through retirement. When variables such as those above are fed into a computer, the result is a wide range of predictable outcomes and a statistical probability of achieving an investor's goal. Some financial planners have begun to use the simulations, as has at least one mutual fund company: T. Rowe Price.

A Balanced Portfolio

For most people, a "retirement portfolio" emphasizes income and capital preservation along with growth. One such portfolio is designed by Sheldon Jacobs for investors in their sixties and early seventies who can anticipate many years in retirement. The portfolio has 55 percent in domestic equities, 10 percent in international equities, and 35 percent in bonds or money market funds for current income and reduced volatility. Your portfolio may be slightly different but should maintain a targeted asset allocation consistent with your investment horizon and your tolerance for risk.

Your investment horizon is important at any age. Even if you're having trouble deciding where to invest, because you're worried that the long bull market is turning into a longer bear market, don't stay on the sidelines. Don't buy stocks or stock funds with money you'll need in a year or two, but do buy stocks or stock funds with an eye to growth over at least five to eight years. Stock prices will go up and down, and it would have been wildly unrealistic to expect the bull market of the 1990s to continue indefinitely, but a five-to-eight-year investment horizon gives you time to ride out most market turbulence.

And don't ignore bonds. Even if you don't need the current stream of income that bonds can produce, bonds and bond funds can reduce the volatility of a portfolio by evening out the bumps produced by stock market highs and lows. Bonds generate income and can help to offset declines in the value of a portfolio. Bonds typically respond differently than stocks to economic circumstances; they may perform well when stocks are performing poorly. Owning a portfolio composed of both stocks and bonds keeps risk down yet typically produces returns that can be almost as high as those from an all-stock portfolio.

Consider this example from T. Rowe Price:

- For the 20 years ending December 31, 1999—a period that included an extraordinary bull market—stocks produced an annualized return of 17 percent.
- For the same 20 years, an aggressive portfolio composed of 80 percent stocks and 20 percent bonds, would have produced an average annual return of 15.9 percent. This represents 93 percent of the return and 83 percent of the risk of an all-stock portfolio.
- A moderate portfolio made up of 60 percent stocks, 30 percent bonds, and 10 percent cash would have garnered 83 percent of the all-stock return with about two-thirds of the volatility.
- A conservative portfolio of 40 percent stocks, 40 percent bonds, and 20 percent cash would have earned nearly 75 percent of the all-stock return with less than half the volatility.

What kind of bonds should you buy? Short-term bond funds and money market funds can be good choices when interest rates are heading upward. In addition to providing an essential cash cushion, they can quickly take advantage of those rising rates. Intermediate-term bonds and funds become more attractive as the economy slows and interest rates stabilize. And long-term bonds and bond funds should do well when interest rates begin to decline.

You may also want to consider adding convertible bonds to your investment mix. Convertibles are just that—bonds that may be converted to shares of stock at a predetermined price. Meanwhile, they pay a fixed rate of interest. As a mixed breed, convertibles typically offer the potential for greater appreciation than ordinary bonds, and higher income than most stocks.

The combination works well in most markets. As Nick Calamos of Calamos Asset Management told *Investor's Business Daily*, when the stock market is rising, you may gain by converting to stock. When the stock market is flat, you can continue enjoying high interest. And, should the stock market fall, convertibles are less likely to decline as much as common stock because of the inherent value in the interest. One possible sour note, if you buy individual convertibles: The timing of the conversion may not be in your hands. The issuing company typically retains the right to exchange the bonds for shares of stock at any time within the first five years. You may want to consider investing in a convertible bond fund instead.

As you invest, remember: It's impossible to successfully "time" the market—to buy only when shares are at their lowest price and sell only when they are at their peak. Professional money managers can't accomplish this feat, and neither can you. But consistent investing is more important. A report by the investment management firm of Neuberger Berman demonstrates that the difference between investing on the "best" day of the year and the "worst" day of the year, over a 10-year period, was just about 2 percent. Each year, from 1989 to 1998, an investment of $10,000 on the day the market hit its high would have produced an average annual return of 22.44 percent and a total value of $338,777. The same $10,000 a year, invested on the day the market was at its lowest point, would have returned 20.39 percent for a total of $269,691. The difference is significant, but staying out of the market isn't the answer either. Stick with certificates of deposit or a money market fund and you might, just might, earn 5 percent. After inflation and taxes, 5 percent won't cut it.

Sources of Retirement Income

In addition to modifying your investment strategy for your retirement years, you may want to purchase an immediate annuity to guarantee a stream of income. You should consider cutting down on debt. And you may want to tap the equity in your home or in a life insurance policy if you need additional cash. Let's look at each source in turn.

To ensure a steady stream of income to supplement your investment earnings, consider purchasing an *immediate annuity* with part or all of a retirement distribution. An immediate annuity can provide peace of mind by guaranteeing enough income to cover recurring bills. As David Littell of The American College wrote, in the *CCH Journal of Retirement Planning*, his father sleeps much better knowing that fees for his retirement residence will always be paid without the need to sell stocks or rely on fluctuating income from bonds.

Annuities are discussed in some detail in Chapter 3, but that discussion focuses on deferred annuities. At retirement, you can purchase an annuity, either fixed or variable, that will start regular payments right away. The payments are based on life expectancy. The older you are at the time of purchase, the larger the payments.

Fixed annuities live up to their name. They do not increase to keep pace with inflation. If a 70-year-old person puts $100,000 into an immediate annuity in exchange for $650 a month in income (this is just an example; actual payments differ, depending on the issuing company and prevailing interest rates), two things would happen: (1) the person would have to live almost 13 more years to get back the $100,000, and (2) the income of $650 a month would almost certainly lose its purchasing power as prices rise.

Variable annuities have fluctuating payments, depending on the performance of the underlying investments. You may receive more than you expect, if the investments do well. Or, you may receive less.

Although many advisers recommend immediate annuities as a component of a retirement portfolio, the conservative investors subscribing to T. Rowe Price's Retirement Income Manager service overwhelmingly preferred to maintain control of their investment strategy rather than have the certainty of annuity income. They may also be aware that annuities often come with fees that eat into the value of the investment. If you are considering purchasing an annuity, reread Chapter 3. Then shop around. Compare expenses *and* guarantees.

Cutting down on debt as you move into retirement may have a larger financial impact than is immediately apparent. Paying off high-cost debt is always the best "investment." It doesn't make much sense to carry credit card debt at 18 percent while you're earning investment income of 5 percent or 6 percent. It may not even make sense to continue carrying a 7 percent mortgage, once it is past the midpoint of the term and most of the tax deductions are used up, if you are earning 5 percent or 6 percent on your savings.

Scott Burns suggests, in *Worth* magazine, that you need to figure out how much principal you will need, to produce enough income to pay your bills. Let's say you're actually earning 3 percent on your overall investment portfolio. At that rate of return, if you are in the 28 percent federal income tax bracket (forgetting about state taxes for the moment), you would need $552,000 in principal just to cover a $1,000 monthly mortgage payment. "Add in everyday expenses," Burns writes, "and suddenly a portfolio of $700,000 seems barely sufficient." In these circumstances, a move to a lower-cost area may be something to think about. Reducing mortgage debt can go a long way toward freeing investment income for other spending.

Tapping home equity through a reverse mortgage can help older people who may be house-rich and cash-poor. Reverse mortgages let you convert an otherwise stagnant asset to cash—either a lump sum or regular monthly payments. No repayment is due as long as the home is your permanent residence. Moreover, if you live a long time and the payments exceed the value of the house, you will still never owe more than the proceeds when the house is sold. On the downside, these loans can be expensive.

You can take a reverse mortgage if you own your own home, have little or no mortgage left on that home, and are at least age 62—although these arrangements make the most economic sense for borrowers who are at least age 70 or 75. More money is available to older borrowers because, given their shorter life expectancy, lenders can expect quicker repayment. If you (or your parents) are interested in a reverse mortgage, free advice is available from the U.S. Department of Housing and Urban Development. Go online at www.hudhcc.org or call 1-800-569-4287. A state-by-state listing of government-approved counseling agencies is available through the nonprofit National Center for Home Equity Conversion, online at www.reverse.org (click on Sources).

Life insurance cash values can be another financial resource. If you own permanent life insurance that you no longer need, perhaps because you no longer have anyone financially dependent on you and the money won't be needed to cover federal estate taxes, you can tap the cash value by:

- Surrendering the policy and receiving the cash value as a lump sum. Bear in mind, however, that tax will be due on the amount by which the cash value exceeds the premiums you have paid over the years.
- Exchanging the cash value for an immediate annuity. This is a tax-free transaction under Section 1035 of the Internal Revenue Code, if the insured is the same person and the exchange is made directly from company to company.
- Borrowing against the policy and using the cash value as collateral for the loan. This is probably the least desirable option, assuming that you no longer need the insurance, because interest will be due on the loan. You don't have to repay the principal but, if you don't pay the interest, you will owe interest on the interest.

Retirement Taxes

Uncle Sam doesn't let you off the tax hook just because you retire. Quite the contrary. Taxes can eat up more of your post-retirement income than you may expect.

Retirement plan distributions—all the money you've accumulated in your IRA and 401(k) over the years—are taxed as ordinary income. This is payback time for all the years of tax-sheltered growth, when no taxes were paid on dividends, interest, and capital appreciation. In addition, any money remaining in your retirement accounts when you die may be subject to federal estate tax if your total taxable estate is larger than the excluded amount of $675,000 in 2001. Under current law, the ceiling will rise gradually to $1 million in 2006 and thereafter—although legislation introduced in 2001 may raise the limits or eliminate the tax. (Ways to reduce the impact of income and estate taxes on retirement distributions are given in Chapters 11 and 12.)

Social Security benefits are also likely to be subject to income tax. Up to half of your benefits are taxable if your "provisional income" exceeds $32,000 for married couples filing jointly or $25,000 for single taxpayers. As much as 85 percent of your Social Security benefits are taxable if your "provisional income" exceeds $44,000 for married taxpayers filing jointly and $34,000 for single taxpayers. "Provisional income" is defined as modified adjusted gross income plus one-half of the Social Security benefit. Here's where it gets tricky; modified adjusted gross income is adjusted gross income (the figure normally used in tax calculations) *plus* tax-exempt interest.

Catching tax-exempt income in the Social Security tax net makes many people cry "Foul!" Unfortunately, it's true. The municipal bonds and bond funds you counted on to provide a tax-free stream of income during your retirement years will still provide the income. But that income will count toward the taxability of your Social Security benefits. Keep this in mind as you evaluate the after-tax rate of return on taxable and tax-exempt investments and decide where to invest during the retirement years.

Worse yet, the provisional income amounts are not indexed. They have remained the same since Social Security benefits were first subject to tax, and they catch more people each year as incomes rise.

There is no benefit to filing separately if you are married, unless you really are separated from your spouse. The provisional amount is zero for married taxpayers who lived with their spouses at any time during the year. Translation: In this situation, your Social Security benefits will be partially taxable, regardless of your income level. What if you receive Social Security benefits and your spouse does not? You must still add your spouse's income to yours to determine whether any of your benefits are taxable.

Courtesy of the accounting firm of Ernst & Young, here are some strategies that may minimize the tax bite on your Social Security benefits:

- Defer the receipt of income by investing in U.S. Government Series EE bonds. The interest on these bonds is not taxed (unless you elect current taxation) until the bonds are redeemed.
- Stagger the receipt of income so that your benefits are taxed in alternate years. Depending on your income level and the sources of your income, you might be able to surrender savings bonds or sell appreciated assets in alternate years. You could also buy Treasury obligations maturing in alternate years, if doing so would keep your total income under the provisional income levels.
- If you continue to earn income, consider contributing to your employer's 401(k) plan or your own deductible IRA. Doing so

would have the double-barreled effect of decreasing your adjusted gross income and thereby reducing the taxable portion of your Social Security benefits.

Give Uncle Sam His Due

While you're working, income tax is withheld from your paychecks. You must file quarterly estimated tax payments only if you have additional income, such as dividends and interest, not covered by withholding. During retirement, you will almost definitely have to file quarterly estimated tax payments.

Pension, profit-sharing, and annuity payments are subject to withholding tax, although you may elect not to have tax withheld by filing Form W-4P. Tax is generally not withheld on Social Security benefits, although you may elect withholding by filing Form W-4V.

For all other income—interest, dividends, capital gains, rents, royalties, self-employment income—you must make estimated tax payments if you owed any income tax for the past year and will owe at least $1,000 in federal income tax for the current year. Estimated tax payments are due on April 15, June 15, September 15, and January 15 of the following year, or on the first business day thereafter if the due date falls on a weekend. You won't get any reminders from the friendly folks in Washington, DC, so put a note on your calendar. Missing a payment date could lead to penalties and interest.

You may also be penalized if you fail to pay enough estimated tax to meet your obligations. The rules are a little complicated (of course), but you will escape penalty if you pay at least 90 percent of the tax you ultimately owe for the year when you file your return the following spring. This solution is easy—if your income is predictable. If you may owe tax on capital gains, to name just one less predictable item, the above method won't work. You can also avoid penalty if you pay (1) 100 percent of the prior year's tax if your adjusted gross income is $150,000 or less, or (2) 110 percent of the prior year's tax if your adjusted gross income exceeds $150,000. For these higher-income taxpayers, the "safe harbor" for avoiding penalties on estimated taxes increases to 112 percent for the 2001 tax year and then (unless the law is changed) falls back to 110 percent for 2002 and beyond.

PART 3

Details, Details

CHAPTER 8

Checking Up on Your 401(k)

It's boring, I know, but if you want to understand what happens to your money once you contribute to a defined contribution plan, you need to know how the plan operates. That means understanding who operates the plan (an amazingly long cast of characters) as well as the documents you're given.

In words designed for financial advisers but equally applicable to plan participants, tax publishers CCH Incorporated observed: "The 401(k) rules may appear straightforward. However, they contain many twists and turns." Navigating those twists and turns will help you to make the most of your 401(k).

The Cast of Characters

The players involved in operating a specific 401(k) plan always include the plan sponsor (your employer) and a trustee (sometimes called a custodian) designated by the employer to keep the plan's assets safe and to make disbursements. Depending on the wording of the plan document, the trustee may be a company officer or an outside entity such as a bank. Either way, your money is protected because, under the rules of the Employee Retirement Income Security Act (ERISA), any entity with discretionary control over plan assets is considered a "fiduciary" and is required to act "solely in the interest of the participants and beneficiaries" in providing benefits. Additional players may include an administrator, a record keeper, an investment manager, and, sometimes, an investment adviser. The plan sponsor and the trustee are always fiduciaries. A separate investment manager, if one is designated in the plan document, may also be a fiduciary.

Despite the maze of laws and regulations, however, there is no standardized one-size-fits-all defined contribution plan. Sticking within the rules, plan sponsors may adopt specific provisions governing their plans. As an example, contributions may be deducted from paychecks in each pay period or once a month. You may be vested in employer matching contributions all at once at any time within three years, or gradually over no more than seven years. Federal law permits a plan to include a provision for hardship withdrawals, but a sponsor is not obligated to allow withdrawals at all.

Your point of contact for the plan could be your employer's human resources unit or employee benefits department. These folks manage the contributions and make sure that paycheck deductions are directed to the trust for investment. As noted in Chapter 2, contributions must be invested no later than 15 business days after the month in which the money is deducted from your paycheck. That's the maximum period allowable by law; most large companies deposit the money into the trust much more rapidly.

Most sponsors now use a "daily valuation" method; your individual plan balance is updated every day to reflect new contributions and any changes in the value of your invested funds. With this method, payroll contributions are typically invested rapidly. With daily valuation, you have immediate access to information either online or via a telephone voice response system. And you are in control of your own account.

Some sponsors, usually smaller companies, may still use a "balance forward" method. Under this arrangement, your money may be pooled with that of other plan participants in a short-term investment such as a money market mutual fund. At a set time, perhaps monthly, all the money is invested. Depending on the plan, it may be invested according to participants' instructions or at the trustee's discretion. Either way, there is a huge difference in your access to information.

Unlike the immediate access of daily valuation, under the balance forward method—labeled a "dinosaur" by some in the business—you may not find out for six months or a year what is going on in your account.

A large company may hire an outside administrator to handle many of the chores otherwise done in-house. According to a 1999 survey by Hewitt Associates, 62 percent of plans use outside providers to interact with plan participants on 401(k) issues. Only 13 percent rely on internal staff. But Hewitt (and other consultants) typically conducts surveys among large companies. Only 9 percent in the 1999 survey had fewer than 1,000 employees, and almost 60 percent had between 1,000 and 10,000 employees. If you work for a very small company, the owner may be the plan administrator. Not surprisingly, perhaps, many of the problems surrounding 401(k) plans arise in smaller firms where the owner/administrator is wearing several hats at once. Problems in 401(k) plans—from delays in crediting contributions to the pitfalls in company mergers—are discussed in Chapter 10.

In a "bundled" approach to managing the defined contribution plan, a company can go to a single provider and contract for all the needed services. This single provider may be a financial institution, such as a mutual fund family or an insurance company, or it may be an independent third-party administrator, a company dedicated to this purpose. The bundled approach is increasingly popular because it clearly is easier for the employer.

In an "unbundled" approach, the plan sponsor chooses "one from Column A, one from Column B," in an effort to find the best or lowest-cost trustee, record keeper, and investment manager. The plan sponsor may also hire a benefits consultant to help with the selection of providers and the investment menu, and then to monitor the providers' and investments' performance. According to the 1999 Hewitt survey, 83 percent of plans use outside record keepers. Mutual funds/investment firms serve as record keepers for 36 percent of plans; benefits consulting firms provide the service for 22 percent of plans.

Does it make much difference to you whether your employer goes with a bundled or unbundled approach to the 401(k) plan? Not really, although, in some instances, the bundled approach limits the available investment options to the offerings of a single mutual fund family. Counteracting this drawback, however, is a move toward what Patricia Pou of benefits consultants William M. Mercer, Inc., calls "alliance arrangements." Driven by demand for more investment choice, an alliance arrangement uses a single vendor to provide the trustee, the record keeper, and some of the investments, but allows some outside investment choices as well. In this scenario, a mutual fund family acting as the provider might also offer funds from other mutual fund families. For participants, this may be the best of both worlds.

But some observers believe that there is an inherent conflict of interest when a mutual fund family or other financial services firm administers employer-sponsored retirement plans. Ted Benna, often credited with inventing the 401(k) plan, notes that mutual fund companies, banks, and insurance companies may be tempted to push their own products. He also notes that plan participants currently have little control over their own investments. As described more fully in Chapter 10, employers can change providers and thereby force a switch from one mutual fund group to another.

Benna would like to see a 401(k) arrangement in which participants have more choice, lower costs, and more control over their investments. To this end, he has teamed up with a new Web-based provider, Persumma Financial. In this 401(k) model, "core" mutual fund portfolios will be offered to participants who may be more comfortable with packaged offerings, while every mutual fund and individual stock will be available to plan participants who want more choice. Morningstar, the mutual fund research firm, builds the core portfolios and provides a recommended list of mutual funds. At the service's launch, in late 2000, the cost to participants was $12.99 a month.

The idea is that employees will benefit from more choice *and* lower costs. However, most employees don't take full advantage of the choices they already have. The average plan now offers eleven investment alternatives; yet most employees pick three or four funds and rarely make a change. Furthermore, most fund administrators offer choices well beyond their own in-house products. At Fidelity Investments, as just one example, some 40 percent of the 401(k) plan assets the company administers are invested in non-Fidelity funds.

Meanwhile, under the current system, when separate outside vendors are hired, there may be a record keeper to keep track of contributions, disbursements, and loans. The record keepers compile periodic account statements, although you may actually receive your statement from your employer. Record keepers also conduct the antidiscrimination testing discussed in Chapter 2, to make sure that highly compensated employees aren't getting a better deal than the rest of the work force.

The last actor in the play, but one of the most important, is the investment manager. This is the vendor—often, but not always, a mutual fund family—that offers the investment menu for your plan. An independent investment adviser may also be used to monitor performance and recommend changes where appropriate.

Paperwork

To protect your interests as a plan participant, the plan sponsor or administrator must file regular reports with the federal government and make information available to you.

What documents do you receive? The first one you see, an explanatory brochure, may be followed by an employee enrollment form on which you elect the amount you want to contribute and how you want that contribution invested among the available options. Of course, in these days of automated everything, you may not see an enrollment form at all. More and more plans are going paperless, allowing you to enroll through a voice response system (VRS) or electronically through the Internet. Pou points out that, even with automated enrollment, you still generally receive an enrollment kit containing the Summary Plan Description (see page 158).

You should also receive information, either in or accompanying the enrollment kit, about the investment options available through the plan. In addition to prospectuses for mutual funds (the most common investment alternative), these options may include employer stock, guaranteed investment contracts (GICs), and a direct brokerage window through which you can purchase individual securities. Reread Chapter 5 for a refresher course on investment options.

One cautionary note: Although you will always receive a prospectus when you invest in a mutual fund that is not in a tax-sheltered account, there is some disagreement as to the necessity of providing mutual fund prospectuses to each participant in a 401(k) plan. Some vendors claim that the plan itself, rather than the individual participant, is the true owner of the fund. Where vendors believe that providing a prospectus to the plan sponsor fulfills the requirement, participants may be provided with summary descriptions instead of a full prospectus.

In 401(k) plans conforming to so-called "404(c)" rules, where the plan sponsor must provide at least three investment choices with accompanying information (see Chapter 5), most sponsors provide the prospectus as a form of employee education. In other cases, it's "hazy under the law," says John Doyle, vice president of marketing and communications for T. Rowe Price Retirement Plan Services, but "our position is that we need to treat the participant as the retail investor and provide the prospectus." In short, if you don't receive the prospectus, ask for it. And read it.

Next—and very important—is the Summary Plan Description (SPD). If the SPD is not in your enrollment kit—it generally is included—you must receive it, together with a statement of your rights under the plan, within 90 days of your enrollment in the plan. You should then be given a copy every five years if the plan has been amended, and every 10 years if it has not. But such a time lag would be very unusual, Pou notes, in this era of rapid plan changes. "Material modifications" to the plan must be disclosed to participants no later than 210 days after the close of the plan year in which the change was adopted.

The Summary Plan Description is worth reading. It spells out the details of your employer's plan, including:

- How much you may contribute and when.
- Matching contributions, if any, and when they become vested.
- Provisions for loans and hardship withdrawals.
- Investment options.
- Rules governing distributions.
- How to get a copy of the plan document.
- How to contact the administrator.
- What to do if you have a complaint.

The plan document itself won't be given to you unless you request a copy. It may be more than you want to read under ordinary circumstances, but, if you run into a problem, it may be worthwhile to check it out. Remember, within the framework of laws and regulations, the plan document governs. Uncle Sam may say that the plan sponsor can make unlimited matching contributions, for example, but the plan document may limit contributions to 50 cents on the dollar. It need not make provision for any matching contributions.

A Summary Annual Report (SAR) must be provided to each plan participant within nine months after the close of the plan year. It will usually be distributed at work and mailed to retirees, but it may be published as a special insert in a company magazine or newspaper. The SAR will tell you how the plan as a whole is doing—total contributions for the year, how much money is in the plan at year-end, and so on. An SAR typically shows:

- The plan's total administrative expenses for the year.
- How the plan's investments performed during the year.
- Loans made by the plan, and whether any outstanding loans have not been repaid on time.
- Financial arrangements with individuals or organizations closely connected to the plan (these may be suspect).

The SAR, as its name implies, is a summary of plan activity for the year. In addition, if you ask for it in writing, you must be given a copy of the full annual report that the plan files with the federal government. Plans covering 100 or more participants file a Form 5500 as an annual report every year. Plans covering fewer than 100 participants may file the simpler 5500-C/R form every three years. Both forms provide regulators with information on the plan's financial condition and operations. For plans with more than 100 participants, an independent auditor must also review the financial statements.

Information must also be filed with the federal government when a plan is amended or terminated, and when there is a merger or consolidation that affects the plan. And, of course, the IRS gets copies of the 1099R forms with which the plan sponsor reports distributions to employees. You must file a 1099R form with your individual income tax return for any year in which you withdraw money from the plan. The IRS can then match the information you report with the information provided by your employer. When taxes are withheld from any distributions you receive, the plan sponsor reports the withholding on Form 945. (You may elect not to have taxes withheld from distributions but you may then have to file quarterly tax estimates, accompanied by payment.)

You can request a copy of Form 5500, and your employer must supply it, but there will usually be a copying fee for each page. Although Form 5500 won't give you any information about your individual account, it can provide a useful overview of the plan's financial circumstances if you suspect a problem. For example, according to the Pension and Welfare Benefits Administration of the U.S. Department of Labor, Form 5500 will show how much is paid in salaries to people running the plan, as well as total fees and commissions paid to accountants, actuaries, investment managers, lawyers, plan trustees, and other consultants. The form will even show the costs of rent, office supplies, telephone, and postage billed to the plan. Note that these administrative costs are separate from the asset-based investment management fees that make up a large part of the costs you pay as a plan participant.

Your Own Account

The most important document you'll receive, under most circumstances, is the Individual Benefit Statement summarizing your individual account balance and activity. The statement should spell out your investment allocation and investment performance, and show the account balance at the end of the period. Federal law requires statements to be distributed to participants once a year (request it in writing if you don't receive it), but, depending on your plan, you may receive a benefit statement monthly, quarterly, or annually. The 1999 Hewitt survey found that 95 percent of all plans provide account statements to participants on a quarterly basis—again, as a reminder, these surveys focus on larger plans. Where plan sponsors maintain a Web site or an interactive voice system, you can probably receive daily updates.

The statements themselves are not standardized. Some plan sponsors provide much more information than others. As Clifton Linton noted, on the 401kafe Web site, one statement might be a half-page in length but crammed with data. Another could run five pages, with a "snappy summary showing beginning and ending balances and a personal rate of return" followed by mind-numbing detail.

At the very least, you want a statement that accurately reports your name, address, Social Security or account number, and account balances at the beginning and end of the reporting period. It might also be useful to see—and some statements do include—a breakdown of your own pre-tax and after-tax contributions, along with your employer's matching contributions, if any, and how much of the match is vested. Any outstanding loan should be reported, along with the repayments made and the balance due. Investment allocations may also be shown, sometimes via a pie chart that represents the percentages for your current investment mix.

The personal account statement offered to sponsors by the Vanguard Group may be viewed as a model. The six-page statement starts with an overview of the plan balance, the current asset mix, and earnings for the current reporting period and the year to date. The second page continues with a plan summary listing the opening balance, current quarter, and year-to-date information for pre-tax contributions, employer matching contributions, earnings (dividends, capital gains, and unrealized gains and losses), withdrawals, and other transactions such as loans.

The Vanguard statement continues on page three with pie charts showing asset allocations and with lists of pre-tax, matching, and after-tax allocations to each investment choice. Changes in the value of each investment for the reporting period are on this page and the following page. The history and current activity of any outstanding loans are shown here as well.

This particular statement concludes on pages five and six with performance information on each of the participant's investment choices, market news for the period, a recap of beneficiary designations, and educational messages from the plan sponsor.

There is great variation among statements from different plan sponsors. Some statements contrast, via pie charts, the participant's asset allocation and how a typical investor of the same age might invest. (Comparative pie charts might be informative, but don't take the "typical investor" chart as gospel. It probably doesn't include important variables such as risk tolerance. Chapters 4 through 7 offer more information on tailoring your own investment allocation.)

There is a noticeable trend toward benefit statements showing each participant's individual rate of return. Your statement might indicate how much you personally have made, based on how you invested, and how you shifted money among investment choices. This is a beneficial departure from most mutual fund reports of rates of return, which are based on what $1 would have earned from the beginning of the reporting period to the end of the reporting period. As a 401(k) investor, you don't make one-time investments at the beginning of a mutual fund's reporting period. Instead, you put money in every payday, or you stop and start, or you move money around among funds. As Pou notes, each participant in the plan, even after choosing the same investment options, could have very different rates of return.

There is also a miniscule trend toward hand-tailoring benefit statements. Typically, plan providers allow plan sponsors to choose from among various statement formats. The chosen format is then used for the statements that are sent to all participants. But there is, reportedly, at least one provider who lets participants choose the type and sequence of information on the statement—balance first or performance first, or some information not at all. Even before statement customization becomes a real trend, however, a number of providers are allowing participants to set up "quick paths" on voice response systems or Web sites so that the information most desired—by that participant—is always presented first.

Your statement may even contain reminder notices that resemble the nagging voice from your childhood that told you to wear your raincoat. As Doyle describes "personalized messaging," plan sponsors can direct messages to plan participants based on age, position in the firm, recent transactions, and so on. If you've taken a loan from your 401(k) plan (see Chapter 9), your statement might comment on the cost of borrowing money from the plan. If you're not contributing enough to get the full employer match, your statement might tell you that you're leaving money on the table. If your asset allocation is heavily tipped toward equities, the statement might gently suggest that you should reallocate your portfolio.

More Paperwork

The periodic statement of your benefits may be the most important piece of the paper storm generated by your 401(k) plan, but there are other documents that you may receive. Among these are confirmations of:

- *Initial enrollment in the plan.* You should read everything you're sent, but this document is particularly important. Read it carefully and confirm the accuracy of your name and address, Social Security number, effective date, beneficiary designation, and initial allocation among investment choices. If you realize, years later, that your money has been going into Fund A when you meant it to go into Fund B, you will have no recourse. Confirm that your allocation jibes with your initial intent.
- *Individual transactions.* Every time you trade in or out of a specific investment, you should receive a confirmation of the trade. When you do, read it carefully and verify all of the information.

- *Changes in investment allocations.* If you decide to shift your allocation in a given mutual fund—say from 25 percent to 50 percent—you should receive a confirmation of your request. Read the statement and make sure it correctly reflects your intent.
- *Account changes.* If you move, change your name, or designate a new beneficiary, you should receive a confirmation of the action.
- *Loans.* If you take a loan from your defined contribution plan, the loan balance and repayment schedule should appear on your benefit statement. In addition, when you receive a check for the loan amount, you should receive a detailed statement showing the loan amount, annual interest rate, scheduled number of payments, and amount of each payment. The Vanguard statement also shows the scheduled final payment amount, total repayment amount, total interest paid, total principal paid, loan fee deduction, and net distribution amount.
- *Distributions.* When you withdraw money from your defined contribution plan, either in a lump sum or in periodic payments, you should receive an accompanying statement. Some providers include tax details, showing taxable and nontaxable distributions, as well as any federal and state tax withheld.

Your "To Do" List

It may be tedious to do so, but you should read the relevant documents and request additional information if something isn't clear. Plan sponsors and record keepers believe that most participants do not read the plan literature and periodic statements. In fact, legislation introduced in late 2000 that would greatly improve retirement plans in terms of how much you can contribute, would also loosen the requirements for providing information to plan participants. Increased contribution levels would be beneficial; less information could be harmful. Former Senator William V. Roth, Jr., the Delaware Republican who sponsored many improvements in retirement plans (the Roth IRA is named for him), has been quoted as saying that because most workers throw out retirement fund reports, they are "a wasted administrative effort that can be very costly to companies." The Senator may be right, although he reportedly later changed his mind. Many participants don't bother reading the reports. At the very least, however, you should compare your pay stubs with your benefit statement to be sure that deducted amounts were actually invested. Check the cumulative total of your contributions for the year; once you reach the legal limit for the year ($10,500 at this writing), contributions should no longer be deducted from your paycheck.

Be sure that your contributions have been invested in the funds you chose. Finding out years later that an administrative mistake caused your money to sit in a money market mutual fund instead of the growth fund you selected can do you out of a large part of your retirement income. Other things to verify periodically are: your employer's matching contributions and how they are invested, and the accuracy of reports on your vesting status. (See Chapter 10 for a further discussion of what to do when things go wrong.)

Recent reports of a scam that has cost at least 100,000 workers a major chunk of their retirement income (see below) led Senator Roth to rethink his position. Before he left office, he hoped to change his bill to address workers' concerns about adequate information.

I can't stress strongly enough that you should pay attention to your plan's provisions and the periodic benefit statements you receive. They may provide an early warning signal that something is amiss. You can't assume that your 401(k) money is safe just because it has been invested as you instructed. In a recent case, the U.S. Department of Labor, the Securities and Exchange Commission, and Portland members of the Oregon Laborers Union jointly filed civil suits against the trustees of the union's retirement plans. The plaintiffs claim that $225 million was lost through the trustees' malfeasance.

Approximately half of the money was in traditional defined benefit pension plans, so workers will be made at least partially whole by insurance from the Pension Benefit Guaranty Corporation. The rest was in 401(k) plans, where there is no government protection. The first clue to the looming problem was in the plan's summary annual reports two years earlier, when a discrepancy of $1.8 million was noted. Plan participants who read their statements and saw the discrepancy asked the Labor Department to begin an investigation.

The case is still in litigation. What is known at this writing, however, is that the money management firm hired by the plan's trustees made ill-considered investments into a risky loan portfolio. Then, when losses became evident, they attempted to conceal the problem by pouring money into what the Securities and Exchange Commission referred to as a scheme to create the appearance that interest payments were being made on the original investment. At the same time, in what may have been a telltale clue, the money managers were charging annual fees of 3 percent, well above the typical asset-based fees of about 1 percent.

As you review your statement, go beyond reconciling it with your pay stubs. Do the following:

- Verify the amount of your contributions and any employer matching contributions.
- Confirm that your contributions were deposited to the investments you chose.
- Confirm that you are vested in the correct amount, based on your years of participation in the plan and its vesting policy.
- Look for appropriate benchmarks to evaluate fund performance. Generic benchmarks such as the S&P 500 are good, but benchmarks related to the specific type of fund are better.
- Find out how much you're paying in fees and transaction charges. It may be hard to pin down all the costs, but you should be able to find out what the annual management fees are on each mutual fund.
- Review your asset allocation and decide whether to make changes. Reread Chapters 4 through 7 and consider *all* your investments, both inside and outside your tax-sheltered retirement plans, in making your allocation decisions.

CHAPTER 9

When You Need Your Money

If you're frequently strapped for cash, you may be reluctant to contribute to your employer-sponsored retirement plan. Like the 11-year-old who once told me that she didn't like to put money in the bank because "it gets stuck," you may fear that your 401(k) contributions are lost and gone forever—or, at least, until you retire.

Fear not. Most plans offer some way to get your money out if you truly need it, through either a loan or a hardship withdrawal. Neither is a particularly good idea if you have any other way to raise cash (I'll discuss some alternative strategies later in this chapter), but you do have an out. And because you have an out, you should always contribute as much as you can to your retirement plan. At the very least, you should contribute the amount your employer will match. Those matching contributions are found money. As I noted earlier, if your employer matches 50 cents on each dollar you contribute, that's a guaranteed risk-free 50 percent return on your money. You can't get that anywhere else.

Then, if you do need money down the road, consider *all* of your options.

Borrowing from Your 401(k)

Most plans, but not all, permit participants to take loans. The larger the company, the more likely it will permit loans. Nine out of 10 plans with more than 5,000 participants have provision for loans, compared to fewer than half of the plans with 10 or fewer participants. Across the board, 58 percent of plans, accounting for 80 percent of all participants, offer loans.

In plans with a loan feature, according to the PSCA survey, one out of every four participants has an outstanding loan. The average loan amount is just under $7,000. Many companies permit multiple loans, although proposed federal regulations would set a limit of two loans in any twelve-month period.

Where loans are permitted, plan sponsors must follow federal guidelines. These rules apply if you are a plan participant:

NOTE

Size of 401(k) loans:

Less than $2,500	**19%**
$1,500 to $4,999	**19**
$5,000 to $9,999	**23**
$10,000 to $19,999	**15**
$20,000 or more	**12**
Don't know	**12**

Reprinted by permission of the Investment Company Institute (www.ici.org)

- You may borrow up to half your account balance, to a maximum of $50,000, or your entire balance if it is $10,000 or less. There is no regulatory minimum, but many plan documents set the smallest loan at $1,000 (the cost of processing small loans is as high as processing large ones).
- The account balance is defined as your own contributions plus any vested employer contributions.
- You may borrow for any purpose at all, as far as Uncle Sam is concerned. But your plan may restrict loans to specific situations akin to the rules for hardship withdrawals (discussed on pages 173–176). That may mean that you can borrow to buy a house but not to take a much-needed vacation. Such rules may seem arbitrary but are actually in your best interest because the tax-sheltered money in your retirement plan is really meant for retirement. Read your plan documents or check with your plan administrator to determine the rules in your plan.
- If you're married, your spouse's consent may be required before you can take a loan. Because this requirement technically applies only to plans offering annuity payments, it is found in 403(b) plans more often than in 401(k) plans. Most 401(k)s

provide only lump-sum or installment payment options and are therefore not required to secure spousal consent to a loan. But some do, so check your plan's provisions.

- Loans must be repaid within five years, in equal installments, at least quarterly. In practice, loans are typically repaid through payroll deductions.
- Employers must charge a "market rate" for plan loans—usually, 1 or 2 percent above prime rate.
- Failure to make any installment payment within the grace period granted by your plan (often, three months or until the end of the calendar quarter) will convert the entire outstanding balance of the loan, including interest, into a taxable distribution. If you are under age 59½, there will also be a 10 percent tax penalty. But making the loan taxable doesn't get you off the hook; you must still repay the loan. (Note: For some reason, the IRS recently proposed changing the term "grace period" to "cure period." The meaning is the same.)
- There is an exception to the five-year repayment rule when a loan is used to buy your principal residence. The law does not specify the maximum repayment period in this situation, but many plans limit repayment to a 10-year period. The extension does not apply to loans used to renovate an existing residence or to purchase a vacation home; loans for these purposes must be repaid within five years.
- The only other extension applies if you are on a leave of absence from your job. In this case, you must still repay the loan within the five-year period (or later, if the loan is for a home), but, while you are on leave, you may suspend payments for up to one year.
- Payments may be suspended longer than one year if your leave is for military duty. You must resume payments after completing your military service, and you must pay at least as much and as frequently as was required under the original loan agreement. And, the loan must be repaid in full, including any additional interest built up during the deferral period, by the end of the original term of the loan plus the period of military service.
- If you leave your job, you will have to repay the loan immediately, and you are not allowed to do so from your remaining 401(k) account balance.

EXAMPLE

The following example, from tax publishers CCH Incorporated, demonstrates how loan repayment might work after a leave of absence.

Your account balance is $90,000; you borrow $40,000. A payment of $825 is to be made each month for five years, to repay the loan. After nine months, you take a 12-month unpaid leave. The remaining loan amount will not be considered a taxable distribution if, upon returning to work, you either (1) resume making monthly installment payments in the increased amount of $1,130 until the loan is paid off at the end of the original five-year term, or (2) resume making payments on the loan at the original monthly installment rate of $825, and pay the remaining balance, in full, at the end of the original five-year term.

Applying for a 401(k) loan is easy—in some instances, as easy as picking up the telephone or, at most, walking into your company's benefits office and making the request. Because the money you're borrowing is your own, there is very little formality. You may have to sign an application, and you will probably have to sign an agreement to repay the loan—but, under federal legislation that became effective in October 2000, you may be able to do all this electronically if your state doesn't require written signatures on loan applications.

If your plan uses an electronic system, you should be given a reasonable opportunity to review, correct, or rescind the loan terms before the loan is finalized. That opportunity can also be given electronically, with two requirements:

1. You and your beneficiary must have reasonable access to the electronic means of confirmation.
2. No one but you and your beneficiary can get into the system to request a loan on your account.

Confirmation may also be given through a paper document. If it is not, you must have the right to request a free written copy of the loan agreement.

In more than three-quarters of the plans surveyed by Hewitt Associates in 1999, the money was available within two weeks. You may even carry two plan loans at once, so long as you don't exceed the allowable dollar limit, but 11 percent of companies specified one home loan and one general-purpose loan.

TIP

If you are self-employed and have the tax-sheltered retirement plan known as a Keogh Plan, you are not allowed to take a loan. Doing so, if you own more than 10 percent of the business, has two serious consequences:

1. **There will be a 10 percent penalty on the principal of the loan each year that there is a balance.**
2. **The entire plan may be disqualified and lose its tax-sheltered status.**

The Real Cost of a 401(k) Loan

It may be easy to borrow from your 401(k), but that doesn't mean it's a good idea. In fact, unless you really need the money and have no other means of getting it, a plan loan is generally a bad idea.

The upside is that money in your 401(k) plan is readily accessible and may be available at a relatively low rate of interest—typically, just 1 or 2 percent over the prime rate. There may also be fees—an initial processing fee, and, at some companies, an annual servicing fee. Three-quarters of companies have a loan origination fee; 30 percent charge annual fees. Smaller companies, where loans present more of an administrative burden, are more likely to charge fees than larger ones. Where they exist, fees can add up to as much as $650 over the period of a five-year loan. (The median origination and service fees in the Hewitt study totaled $110.)

The availability of the money—it's just sitting there in your 401(k)—makes it tempting to take a loan when you have a temporary cash shortfall. But you may want to think twice, because there are a number of disadvantages inherent in plan loans.

For one thing, even though you will pay back the loan, you lose all the growth in the interim. If you're invested in equities and the stock market is going like gangbusters, you'll really see the difference. In an example from Scott Lummer, chief investment officer of mPower, "Claudius" and "Polonius" each had $100,000 invested in stock funds within their retirement plans in January 1995. Claudius borrowed $50,000. Polonius did not take a loan. "Assuming they never invested another penny," Lummer notes, "by December 1999, Claudius would have had $247,000 in his plan, while Polonius would have had $357,000—a 45 percent difference!" The difference was exaggerated in this example because the stock market did so well in this period, but there will generally be a noticeable difference.

Here's another point: You've probably heard that you're paying interest to yourself. Not exactly. It's true that the loan repayments go back into your account. But those fixed-rate repayments probably can't come near the return of growth investments in your retirement account. Put another way, the money you took out is no longer invested, so you're losing out on the investment return you would otherwise be getting. At the same time, the additional money to pay the interest on the loan is no longer earning the money it was accumulating in a bank account or money market fund. All you've done is move money from one pocket to another. The end result is: You end up with less.

Worse yet, you'll wind up paying taxes twice on the same money. Hard to believe? You have to repay the loan with after-tax money. And you'll pay taxes again when the same money is withdrawn from the plan at retirement. You can defer the second tax bite by rolling the 401(k) balance into an IRA, but the tax must eventually be paid.

In addition, if you forgo making additional contributions while the loan is outstanding—after all, you wouldn't have taken the loan unless you were short of cash—you may put a permanent dent in your retirement nest egg. If you borrow $15,000 and don't keep making contributions during the five-year repayment period, you may have a $50,000 deficit when you're ready to retire. The deficit will be even worse if skipping your own contributions means that you're missing out on your employer's matching contributions as well.

Last, if you leave your job, you will typically have to repay the entire outstanding balance within 90 days. If you are unable to do so, the balance will be considered a fully taxable distribution. You will be subject to mandatory 20 percent withholding if you fail to roll over your distribution into an IRA or another employer's plan, and the 20 percent will be applied to the total of your plan balance and the outstanding loan. You will also be subject to a 10 percent tax penalty if you are under age 59½. The combination, especially if your state levies taxes as well, could mean losing more than half the distribution in taxes and penalties. That doesn't leave much for your future retirement.

If you leave your job, though, you may have a couple of options. Some plans will let you continue paying off the loan, so long as you leave the money in your former employer's plan. If you're fortunate enough to have this arrangement, be sure to keep track of when payments are due and write checks in a timely fashion. Once you leave the company, you will no longer have the benefit of automatic payroll deduction to repay the loan.

If you do take a loan, think about this: With a fixed-rate loan, you're effectively substituting a fixed-income investment for another investment in your 401(k) portfolio. If you have a choice, try to take the loan from a fixed-rate investment currently in your 401(k) portfolio. But you may not have a choice. Find out how your plan goes about getting the cash for your loan. Which securities or mutual funds will it sell out of your account? Then consider tinkering with your remaining investments to keep your asset allocation intact.

TIP

Why do 401(k) participants take loans?

Pay everyday expenses or bills	28%
Buy a car or other expensive item	23
Make a down payment on a home	16
Pay education expenses	6
Pay for an emergency expense	4
Something else	34

401(k) Plan Participants: Characteristics, Contributions, and Account Activity (2000). Reprinted by permission of the Investment Company Institute (www.ici.org)

Hardship Withdrawals

Federal law permits withdrawals from qualified retirement plans if the participant would otherwise suffer financial hardship. Nine out of ten 401(k) plans actually permit such withdrawals.

Hardship distributions must meet stringent IRS requirements. You may withdraw money from your 401(k) only if you have an "immediate and heavy financial need," *and* you have no other financial resources with which to meet the need. Be prepared to provide documentation to back up your request.

Let's look at each requirement. An "immediate and heavy financial need" is determined on the basis of "all relevant facts and circumstances." The determination of relevant facts can be subjective, but the IRS makes it easier by specifying four circumstances in which a hardship withdrawal is always permitted (assuming that a plan has provision for hardship withdrawals at all; plans are not required to do so):

1. Paying unreimbursed medical expenses for yourself or a dependent.
2. Buying a principal residence.
3. Paying college tuition due within the next 12 months.
4. Preventing eviction or foreclosure.

The expenses of buying a home and paying college bills don't come out of the blue. Both can be anticipated and, presumably, planned for. Nonetheless, the need to do either can be sufficient reason, under your plan's rules, to allow a hardship withdrawal. Note, though, that when it comes to buying a home, a hardship withdrawal may cover the down payment and associated costs; it may not be used for mortgage payments.

Some plans are a bit more lenient; they permit hardship withdrawals for such things as funeral expenses or significant uninsured damage to your home. Although employers are permitted to make case-by-case determinations, they are less likely to do so these days because standardized plan documents are often provided by third-party plan administrators, says Lynn Phillips, an attorney with benefits consultant Watson Wyatt. Again, check the plan documents or ask your benefits officer what types of withdrawals are permitted by your plan.

TIP

Why do plan participants take hardship withdrawals?

Home purchase	**45%**
Medical emergency	**28**
Bills or daily expenses	**21**
College costs	**7**

Reprinted by permission of the Investment Company Institute (www.ici.org)

The requirement that you have "no other resources" means just that. If you, your spouse, or your dependent children own anything of value, that asset must be tapped first. You would probably have to sell securities held in a taxable account, invade your IRA, and apply for a bank loan. You would have to use your kids' college savings, unless those college savings were securely protected in an irrevocable trust or a custodial account. You would even have to take a loan from your 401(k) before you could take a hardship withdrawal. The only exception would be if you could show that the loan repayments would, in and of themselves, constitute a financial hardship.

Assuming that you qualify for a hardship withdrawal, there are many reasons for avoiding it if at all possible. The money you take will be taxable and 20 percent will be immediately withheld by your employer. If you're under age 59½, the withdrawal will also be subject to a 10 percent tax penalty unless you are totally disabled or are using the money for deductible medical expenses exceeding 7.5 percent of your adjusted gross income. You are allowed to take out enough money to cover your pressing need and the taxes, but that means a larger withdrawal and a bigger hole in your retirement savings.

Don't underestimate the long-term damage. A $10,000 withdrawal at age 40 could mean missing out on about $175,000 by the time

THE IMPACT OF TAXES AND PENALTIES

If a 50-year-old plan participant who is in the 28 percent federal income tax bracket and a 4 percent state income tax bracket takes a hardship withdrawal of $20,000, here's what's left:

Withdrawal		**$20,000**
Less:		
Federal income tax	**5,600**	
State income tax	**800**	
Early withdrawal penalty	**2,000**	**8,400**
Net withdrawal		**$11,600**

Note that the early withdrawal penalty applies to the entire pre-tax amount.

you reach retirement. That additional amount in your nest egg could provide an annual income boost of $10,000 or more for the next 20 years.

A loophole that had enabled some plan participants to sidestep the 20 percent mandatory withholding was closed at the beginning of 2000, when hardship withdrawals were made ineligible for rollovers. Prior to the change, Lynn Phillips explains, participants could do an IRA rollover and then take the needed cash from the IRA, thereby avoiding the 20 percent mandatory withholding. The rollover also eliminated the 10 percent tax penalty if the money was being used to purchase a first home (up to $10,000 of IRA money can be used without penalty for this purpose).

After taking the hardship withdrawal, you will not be allowed to make any contributions to your 401(k) for a full year. Your allowable contributions for the following year will also be reduced by any amount you put into the plan during the calendar year in which you received the hardship distribution. This restriction can put a sizable dent in your hopes for a comfortable retirement. It's not that Uncle Sam is trying to penalize your attempts at thrift. According to tax publishers CCH Incorporated, the assumption underlying the suspension of contributions is that if you have the money to make contributions, you also have the money to solve your financial problems.

If a financial emergency forces you to invade your 401(k), try to minimize the damage. For example, if you get your finances back on track before you are allowed to resume contributions to your 401(k), put as much as you can into an IRA. Consider reallocating your assets toward growth; a little more risk may produce greater returns.

Other Sources of Money in an Emergency

Before you tap your 401(k) at all, through either a loan or a hardship withdrawal, investigate every other possible source of funds. Possibilities may include home equity loans and lines of credit, life insurance loans, a margin loan on a brokerage account, and borrowing from your family.

Home equity loans and lines of credit have one major advantage over money from your 401(k): The interest on loans of up to $100,000 is deductible. Interest on a 401(k) loan, even if the money is used to purchase a home, is not deductible. If you must take a hardship withdrawal to purchase a home, 401(k) guru Ted Benna suggests taking the money as early in the year as possible. Then the tax benefits of home ownership for most or all of the year will offset some of the disadvantages associated with the withdrawal.

A home equity loan is a plain old-fashioned second mortgage, usually paid to the borrower in a lump sum and repaid over a term of up to 15 years. The interest rate may be fixed or variable, depending on the terms of the loan. A home equity line of credit is just that—a revolving line of credit, to a pre-set maximum, that you can access as needed. You pay interest only on the amount you actually borrow. The interest rate is usually variable, so you'll pay the prevailing rate at the time you take the money. Adjustments thereafter are most often monthly but may be quarterly or pegged to market changes.

Lines of credit, because of their flexibility, are more popular. But a line of credit won't suit your purposes if you need a lump sum for a specific need.

Loans and lines of credit are widely available through financial institutions. Most permit you to borrow up to 80 percent of the appraised value of your home, minus any amount still outstanding on your first mortgage. But the amount you can actually borrow is limited by the factors that go into any application for credit: your income and how much other debt you have outstanding. According to the most recent study by the Consumer Bankers Association (CBA), the highest concentration of loans and lines of credit in the 12-month period ending June 30, 2000 represented what lenders call "loan-to-value" of less than 70 percent. During the same period, the average outstanding open-end home equity line was $30,852, and the average home equity loan was $34,318. The average new home equity line during the period was $56,067, and the average new home equity loan was $43,425.

Loans and lines of credit are like home mortgages, complete with closing costs and assorted other fees. The CBA reports that the average origination fee is about $85 and the average annual servicing fee is $26. Many lenders don't charge origination fees, and the field is highly competitive, so you may be able to find a loan or line of credit with cut-rate costs if you shop around. Just be wary of lenders offering higher loan amounts—sometimes as high as 125 percent of your actual equity. These loans come at a higher cost—and a higher risk of default, especially if you should have to move before the loan is repaid.

Before you commit to a home equity loan or line of credit, find out exactly what the money will cost in application fees and closing costs, as well as interest. If the interest rate is variable, find out how often the rate is adjusted and how much the payment may rise.

A *life insurance loan*, if you have a cash value policy, may be another source of cash. Unlike a loan against the equity in your home, interest on a life insurance loan is not deductible, but you don't have to pay the interest or repay the principal. This may be tempting—especially if you no longer need the insurance. If you do need it, ignoring repayment can be a big mistake.

As soon as you're out from under the immediate financial emergency, you should repay the loan. If you don't, the amount of the loan will be deducted from the death benefit; if your family will need the money after you are gone, you could be leaving them seriously strapped for cash. At the very least, pay the interest. If you don't, you will be charged interest on the interest until you've eaten away the value of the policy. At that point, if you took a large loan and the policy is forced to lapse, you will owe income tax on the amount by which the loan exceeds the total amount you paid in premiums.

There's one other thing you should know: Although policy loans may seem to carry a relatively low rate of interest, there is a hidden cost. The amount of interest earned within the policy is usually reduced while the loan is outstanding, effectively raising the actual loan rate by as much as 2 to 3 percent. Before you borrow against life insurance, ask your insurance agent or company for an illustration of exactly what will happen to the cash value and the death benefit.

A *margin loan* lets you borrow against the value of your investment portfolio. This may work in lieu of a loan against your 401(k), but it's not a substitute for a hardship withdrawal. If you are faced with the kind of pressing financial need that would warrant a hardship withdrawal, you would probably have to sell securities you hold outside your 401(k) plan.

Margin loans are most often used by investors seeking to leverage their available cash to buy more securities. But they are also available for other purposes, and you may want to consider covering a tuition bill by taking a margin loan instead of tapping your 401(k). The interest is not deductible, so this is second-best to a home equity loan, but it's an alternative to consider.

Federal guidelines limit margin loans to half the value of publicly traded securities. Brokerage firms may set more restrictive rules. The interest rate is typically 1 to 2 percent above the cost of money to the brokerage firm. Your investments stay invested while the loan is outstanding, so the amount you make in stock appreciation could exceed the cost of the loan. On the other hand, stocks don't always appreciate in value, so there is a risk of losing more money than you can handle. Even with winners, don't let a margin loan run too long. Interest charges can consume any gains in the value of the securities. And, if the value of the securities drops significantly, your stock may be sold to cover the debt.

Borrowing from family is an option born out of desperation for many people, but it may be an option to consider if you're in difficult but temporary straits. The only way to make such a loan work without harming relationships, however, is to keep it businesslike. Be aware of possible emotional fallout, and, at the same time, keep an eye on possible tax consequences.

The loan arrangement should state, in writing, the amount, the interest rate, and the terms of repayment. "Interest rate?" you say. "My family shouldn't charge me interest!" In fact, if the loan is $10,000 or more and your generous family member doesn't want to run afoul of Uncle Sam, he or she must charge what's called the *applicable federal rate* (AFR) of interest for the month in which the loan is made. If Uncle Joe makes an interest-free loan, he must report as income the interest he would have received if he had actually charged the AFR. If the loan is substantial, he could even face gift tax on the interest he should have charged.

There is one other exception to the interest requirement. If the loan is for under $100,000 and the borrower does not use the money to invest, no interest need be charged. However, in this instance, the lender must report as income, on his or her own federal income tax return, the amount of the borrower's taxable unearned income for the year. Your Uncle Joe will wind up paying tax on your interest and dividends—unless you have less than $1,000 in unearned income for the year, in which case the lender doesn't have to report anything at all.

You may be tempted to ignore the rigmarole and just shake hands on the deal, but it's not a good idea if substantial sums are involved. The IRS, long suspicious of loans between family members, considers them a gimmick to evade gift and estate tax.

CHAPTER 10

Know Your Rights

Being able to contribute to an employer-sponsored defined contribution (DC) plan gives you a big boost in saving for the retirement years. For the most part, the whole system works smoothly. You decide how much to contribute and where to invest, your employer may add to your stash with matching contributions, and the money grows nicely during your working years.

But, every once in a while, there is trouble—sometimes big trouble. Perhaps your company is acquired in a merger or, worse yet, files for bankruptcy. Perhaps there's a bureaucratic snafu with the plan administrator. Or personal problems, such as divorce or bankruptcy, may adversely affect your retirement savings. In each situation, there are actions you can take to avert disaster.

Mergers and Bankruptcy

In these days of megamergers, many 401(k) plans are under attack. High-level corporate negotiations may ignore details such as retirement plans, but employees ignore them at their peril. When the dust settles, employees of an acquired company may find their defined contribution plan somewhat the worse for wear.

Sometimes, a plan is simply terminated. If this happens, you'll get your money back—including your employer's contributions—and you can roll it into an IRA or, possibly, into the new company's plan. Note that when a plan is terminated, you are immediately fully vested in employer contributions made on your behalf. You could take a cash distribution, but you would be subject to an immediate tax bite. You'll owe income tax on the distribution, plus, if you're under age 59½, a 10 percent tax penalty. You're much better off keeping the tax shelter through an IRA or the new company's plan.

Occasionally, if the plans are so different that a combined plan might lose its tax-qualified status, a merged company may keep the old plan intact, side by side with the plan of the parent company. If this happens, new employees may have to go with the dominant plan. Employees of the acquired company who stick with the original plan may find matching contributions cut back.

Most often, the two plans are merged into the plan of the acquiring company. When this happens, your prior contributions will be automatically rolled into the new plan. But "automatically" doesn't mean "immediately." The plan will be frozen temporarily—from a couple of weeks to several months or more—while the details are worked out. During this lockout period, the money in the plan will remain invested but you won't be able to make contributions or withdrawals. You may even be forced into early repayment if you took out a loan from the prior plan.

The money will remain invested, but you may find that it has been moved without your consent. One of the biggest problems facing employees of acquired companies is that their investment choices in the new plan may not be nearly as good as their options under the prior plan.

Sometimes, the choices are so bad that disgruntled employees take to the courts. For example, a class-action lawsuit brought by former employees of Virginia's Signet Bank contested the arbitrary transfer of investments by the acquiring bank, First Union. Signet employees had had a wide-ranging choice of investment options. As First Union plan participants, they were limited to the bank's own house-brand ("proprietary") mutual funds. Worse yet, some participants were switched, without their knowledge or approval, from growth to fixed-income investments. One former Signet employee claimed to have lost at least $50,000 because First Union transferred his money from an appreciating stock to a stable value fund.

The former Signet employees claimed that they had a vested right to their investment choices. The court disagreed, on the grounds that the original plan provided that changes could be made in the investment alternatives. As long as the plan offered the minimum basic investment choices, the tax analysts at CCH report, "a participant's investment options could be modified or eliminated by a valid plan amendment."

But there are still unsettled issues revolving around the case. The court did not address the issue of "whether the successor company breached its fiduciary duties in liquidating the participants' investments in the plan and discontinuing non-proprietary investment options." Some analysts believe the liquidation, even though it was in line with plan documents, contravened employees' right to control their investments within the 401(k).

The court did note that First Union had a "fiduciary duty" to give participants timely notice of the merger and the change in investment alternatives, along with adequate opportunity to make decisions about their investment options. That might have meant giving employees the opportunity to cash out their plan accounts before the merger and roll them into IRAs, where they could stick with the mutual funds they wanted.

Many benefits consultants believe that the First Union case is just the beginning of what may be a series of lawsuits brought by unhappy plan participants, based on changes in investment choices or even on lagging investment performance. Other suits have been brought. One charges SBC Communications with shifting 401(k) assets into its own stock from the stock of a competitor, without participant approval. When SBC's stock stayed flat while the competitor's tripled in value, plan participants allegedly lost over $1 billion in the value of their 401(k) accounts. And another suit charges New York Life Insurance Company with using employee retirement money as start-up money for house-brand mutual funds.

The problems don't always stem from a merger. But merger negotiations may be well publicized, giving you some prior notice. To protect yourself in advance of a merger:

1. Make sure, to the extent that you can, that your asset allocation within the plan is in line with your current objectives. (You may

not be able to transfer into new investments for several months, once the merger takes place.)

2. If you leave the company, take a 401(k) distribution and roll the money into an IRA or a new employer's plan. Either way, arranging a direct trustee-to-trustee transfer will eliminate mandatory tax withholding on the distribution.

It may be tempting to leave the money in the prior plan if you like the investment options, but doing so leaves you vulnerable to unanticipated and unapproved (by you) changes in your investment mix.

Out-and-out mergers between two companies are nothing compared to the complexity that has faced employees who have become subject to what the IRS calls "same desk" rules. In this situation, you work for a division of Company X. The division is sold to Company Y. You keep right on doing the same job in the same location, working with the same people, but your paycheck comes from a different entity. Until a recent change of heart at the IRS, your 401(k) plan was frozen as if you had not separated from service. You might have been able to make contributions to the new employer's plan, depending on its eligibility requirements, but you were not allowed to make new contributions to the original plan or withdraw prior contributions in the form of a loan or cashout. About the only thing you could do was shift money among investments in the prior plan; to do that, however, you had to work through your former employer, who was charged with maintaining the plan.

The law has not been changed, but the IRS has agreed that employees in this situation will be treated as if they have indeed left the company. To be treated as if you separated from service, the division you worked for must have accounted for less than 85 percent of the company's assets. The rule must be applied if the sale of the division took place after September 1, 2000, and *may* be applied to earlier sales, although companies are not required to do so. Under the new ruling, you can have a lump-sum distribution rolled over into an IRA or (if the plan permits) into the new employer's plan. This is a boon for you and a benefit to companies that will no longer have the administrative chore of managing retirement accounts for workers they no longer employ.

If your employer goes into bankruptcy, it's a whole other story. Sometimes, companies file for bankruptcy under a "Chapter 11 reorganization" plan. When this happens, business generally goes on as usual while the company restructures its operations for greater profitability. (Continental Airlines, for example, is a healthy corporate entity today but has filed under Chapter 11 twice in recent years.) In this situation, you may be able to continue regular contributions to your 401(k) plan, although employer matching contributions may be suspended.

A plan may be discontinued during a bankruptcy reorganization. If this happens, the effect will be the same as if the company has been liquidated. The plan will be terminated, and you will receive your contributions, any employer contributions made on your behalf, and all the investment earnings on your account.

If your employer actually goes out of business, however, you may wind up out of pocket. Although the money in your retirement account is legally yours and can't be tapped by creditors, there may be a problem with contributions that have been deducted from your paycheck but not yet deposited in your account. Employers are required to deposit employee contributions to the 401(k) plan within 15 working days after the end of the month in which payroll deductions were made for those contributions. The most you could lose would then be 45 days' worth of contributions. However, when companies are on the verge of bankruptcy—especially small companies with few resources—they often face cash flow problems that may lead them to temporarily "borrow" employee contributions. This solution may work—if the employer can quickly replace the money. If the cash shortage turns into a real crunch, the borrowing can turn into outright fraud.

This was a bigger problem several years ago—prior to a Department of Labor (DOL) crackdown, and before steps were taken to mandate quicker deposit of employees' contributions. Until 1996, employers were supposed to deposit contributions "within 90 days or when it is reasonable to do so, whichever is shorter"—a rule that left employers with a lot of leeway. Some, according to the DOL, used the money as interest-free loans to top management. Others actually stole employee money. Only a handful of employers were bad apples, but those few did a lot of damage and left employees high and dry, with little recourse. Federal law prohibits using money earmarked for pensions for any other purpose, but that doesn't make the money easy to collect once it's gone. Meanwhile, as complaints are filed and lawsuits drag on, plan participants must work more years to save enough to retire.

Most of the problems occurred in companies with fewer than 100 workers, and a boss who wore double-duty hats, as plan sponsor and plan administrator. As the Pension and Welfare Benefits Administration (PWBA) noted in late 2000, "In recent years, considerable public attention has focused on the potential vulnerability of small plans to fraud and abuse." It doesn't happen often, but when it does it can devastate participants' hopes for the future. In response, the Department of Labor is taking action to beef up the security of pension assets and reinforce the accountability of persons handling those assets. These measures will strengthen the provisions regarding audit of small pension plans. Currently, pension plans with fewer than 100 participants are exempt from being required to have an independent qualified public accountant conduct an annual audit of the plan's financial statements. Under new regulations, there will still be an audit waiver, but plans will have to meet tougher criteria, including enhanced disclosure to participants and improved bonding requirements. The new conditions apply to the first plan year starting after April 17, 2001.

Sometimes, outside administrators or trustees have been culpable. In one well-publicized case involving a Connecticut company, the plan trustee was accused of covering up plan losses by using subsequent contributions to honor requests for distributions. It looked very much like an old-fashioned pyramid scheme. Employees sued their employer, claiming negligence in not monitoring the trustee's actions, but it may take years to resolve the lawsuit. In fact, the theft probably would not have taken place if someone in management had paid attention, or if an outside record keeper had been tracking the transactions.

What To Do When Things Go Wrong

If you suspect problems with your 401(k) plan—if your contributions aren't being deposited, statements aren't coming on time, or managers keep changing—don't sit idly by. Suspend any further contributions until you satisfy yourself that everything is okay, and consider turning to the federal government for help. But don't expect an immediate response to your individual complaint; federal agencies sometimes stockpile consumer complaints until they see a pattern emerge. Then they take action. Because government agencies have limited resources, you may also want to contact an attorney.

Three agencies have authority to investigate possible violations of the rules and to bring lawsuits or assess penalties against individuals engaged in illegal actions: the Department of Labor, the Internal Revenue Service, and the Justice Department.

WARNING SIGNS

Are your retirement contributions being misused? Here are 10 warning signs from the Department of Labor:

1. **Your 401(k) or individual account statement is consistently late or comes at irregular intervals.**
2. **Your account balance does not appear to be accurate.**
3. **Your employer fails to transmit your contribution to the plan on a timely basis.**
4. **Your statement shows a significant drop in the account balance, and it cannot be explained by normal market ups and downs.**
5. **Your 401(k) or individual account statement shows that your contribution was not deducted from your paycheck.**
6. **The investments listed on your statement are not those that you authorized.**
7. **Former employees are having trouble getting their benefits paid on time or in the correct amounts.**
8. **Your statement reveals an unusual transaction, such as a loan to the employer, to a corporate officer, or to one of the plan trustees.**
9. **There are frequent and unexplained changes in investment managers or consultants.**
10. **Your employer has recently experienced severe financial difficulty.**

If you think the plan trustees, or others responsible for investing your pension money, have been violating the rules, you should call or write the nearest field office of the U.S. Department of Labor's Pension and Welfare Benefits Administration (PWBA). The Labor Department has authority to investigate complaints of fund mismanagement. If an investigation reveals wrongdoing, the Department can take action to correct the violation, including asking a court to compel plan trustees and others to put money back into the plan. Courts can also impose penalties of up to 20 percent of the recovered amount, and bar individuals from serving as trustees and plan money managers.

If you suspect that individuals providing services to your plan have gotten loans or have otherwise taken advantage of their relationship to the plan, the Employee Plans Division of the Internal Revenue Service may want to take a closer look. The IRS is authorized to impose tax penalties on people involved in unlawful "party in interest" transactions. (The Department of Labor suggests that, if you are planning to provide information to the IRS, you should also consider filing a simultaneous claim for an Informant's Reward with the IRS Intelligence Division. If the IRS collects a penalty tax as the result of your information, you could possibly receive an award of up to 10 percent of the amount collected.)

Cases of embezzlement or stealing of pension money, kickbacks, or extortion should be referred to the FBI (part of the Justice Department) as well as to the Labor Department field office in your area. If illegal activities are found, the case may be referred to the U.S. Department of Justice for prosecution. Criminal penalties can include fines and prison sentences, or both. Many employees are justifiably fearful of blowing the whistle on their employers, but, for what it's worth, federal pension statutes make it unlawful for employers to fire or otherwise retaliate against employees who provide the government with information about their pension funds' investment practices.

Whichever federal agency you approach, the most effective way to do so is to present your concerns in a short written summary together with copies (not originals) of supporting documents. Those documents may include the summary plan description, the plan document itself, and any separate trust agreement governing the plan. (As described in Chapter 8, these documents should be available from your plan upon written request.) If you have trouble getting the documents from your plan, contact either the nearest PWBA field office or the PWBA Division of Technical Assistance and Inquiries, in Washington, DC.

If you would prefer not to ask your plan for the information, you can obtain a copy of the plan's tax file (ask for Form 5500) from PWBA's Public Disclosure Facility after the form has been filed with and processed by the government. If you find that your plan has not filed the Form 5500 (or Form 5500-C/R, whichever is required), or that the forms are incomplete or contain false or misleading information, you should immediately notify the nearest PWBA field office. The Labor Department has authority to assess civil penalties against plan administrators who fail to comply with annual reporting requirements.

If all else fails and you want to file a lawsuit, consider banding together with other employees to strengthen your case. Look for an

GOVERNMENT AGENCIES

Government agencies can help. For example:

In February 2001, the former trustee of two 401(k) plans sponsored by a Kansas City physician was ordered by the Department of Labor to repay $120,719.97 to the plans and their participants. The trustee had made improper loans, liquidated assets, and withdrawn money from the plans for his own personal use.

In January 2001, the Department of Labor filed a lawsuit against the trustees of a 401(k) plan established by GNM Associates, Inc., an engineering firm in Silver Spring, Maryland. The charge: commingling employer contributions with the company's general assets in violation of federal law.

In April 2000, the Department of Labor reported obtaining a final settlement in which the executive director of Community Action Agency of Calhoun, Cleburne & Cherokee Counties, Inc., in Anniston, Alabama, agreed to pay an additional $5,034.50 to participants in the agency's 401(k) plan. The money represented employee contributions, totaling $3,517.55, that were used to finance agency operations in 1996 instead of being properly deposited in plan accounts. It also included interest on that money as of the end of November 1999. Following an investigation conducted by the Atlanta Regional Office of the Pension and Welfare Benefits Administration, the money was to come out of the executive director's own plan account and be redistributed to the other plan participants.

attorney who is experienced in pension law and is willing to represent workers and retirees. If the cost seems prohibitive, bear in mind that the courts have the power to award attorneys' fees if you win a pension case.

Bureaucratic Hassles

Sometimes a problem with a 401(k) plan may not stem from a merger, bankruptcy, or fraud. Sometimes it's just plain red tape or messy bookkeeping that infuriates participants.

Contributing more than the annual limit, for example, can lead to a major snafu complete with tax penalties. Think it can't happen? With a midyear job switch, coupled with immediate eligibility for the new plan and slightly different payroll deduction schedules, you may wind up doing just that. In the case of a Californian who wrote to *Worth* magazine about his plight, the new employer refused to return the excess contribution because the plan administrator wasn't notified until after the plan deadline. Withdrawing the excess from the former 401(k), already rolled over into an IRA, would produce both taxes and penalties.

According to the IRS, contributions in excess of the limit must be reported as gross income. If the new employer allows the money to be withdrawn the following year (it's up to the employer), there won't be the 10 percent tax penalty otherwise imposed for early withdrawal before age 59½. If you can't or don't withdraw the money, it will still be taxable income in the current year—*and* in the year when you take it out of the 401(k) as retirement income. Taking it out of the IRA does indeed lead to both taxes and penalties. Either way, if the withdrawal of the excess isn't made until the following year, the withdrawal must include interest earned on the original excess amount. That interest must also be reported as income.

Then there are the bureaucratic hassles that can attend rollover requests. If you arrange a rollover of your 401(k) account to an IRA when you leave your job, as an example, you might expect the rollover to be completed right away. As many participants have found, however, it can take months to complete a rollover. Employers are not obligated to release the funds until you reach retirement age, although most are willing to do so when an employee leaves. But that doesn't mean they have to be in a hurry about it. With daily valuation of plan assets in place in more and more plans, payments are sometimes made within a couple of weeks. But the plan document may say that checks are distributed at the beginning of the calendar quarter following your departure. Red tape might delay the actual transfer for another month or two, and your loss of earnings during the time the money is in limbo could be substantial.

Bureaucratic bungles, even when they are in no way your fault, can lead to extra taxes and tax penalties. As CPA Michael J. Jones wrote, in *Ed Slott's IRA Advisor*, "if your IRA trustee or custodian mistakenly places money intended for an IRA into a non-IRA account, that may be treated as a taxable distribution." If you're under age 59½ when this happens, watch for a 10 percent tax penalty as well.

If you catch this kind of error quickly, it can probably be corrected (although you may still run into trouble if your income tax return is audited). But you could be in serious trouble if your first inkling of the mistake comes in the form of a 1099 information form filed by the financial institution with the IRS. Once taxable income has been reported to the IRS, it's very hard, if not impossible, to convince the tax collectors that the income was not in fact taxable. According to Jones, the IRS may even "treat the correction of the error as an illegal excess IRA contribution and penalize you, in addition to the penalties you may already face from a transaction treated as a premature withdrawal."

When a Rhode Island retiree named William Wood ran afoul of the IRS because Merrill Lynch mistakenly put the money intended for a rollover IRA into a taxable account, Wood fought the case all the way to Tax Court and won. Unfortunately, the IRS does not appear inclined to apply the precedent to other cases. So, while you, too, can fight the IRS, the best course is vigilance when it comes to handling rollovers.

Start by arranging a direct transfer from your employer-sponsored retirement plan to the rollover IRA. Doing so will forestall problems that could develop if you take possession of the money and then arrange the rollover IRA. It will also eliminate mandatory withholding. If for some reason a direct transfer isn't feasible, Jones suggests using a certified check or an electronic funds transfer. Jones also suggests that you:

- Give formal written instructions to the financial institution that will be acting as custodian or trustee.
- Have your tax professional review these instructions before they are submitted.
- Send in at least two copies of the instructions, and ask to have one copy signed and returned to you.
- After you receive it, keep the signed copy in a safe place, and tell your relatives and tax adviser where it is.
- After any IRA transaction, review your account statement to be sure that the institution's records accurately reflect your instructions.
- If you spot an error, follow up as quickly as possible to rectify the mistake within the allowable 60-day rollover window.

Some retirement plan problems, of course, have nothing to do with your employer. They crop up when you find yourself in personal difficulty. Perhaps you've left your job, leaving money behind. Financial difficulties are forcing you to declare personal bankruptcy. Or you're going through a divorce. Bankruptcy and divorce are problems you'll have to work out on your own, by and large, but this chapter can help you to understand the role of your retirement plan in each situation.

Money Left on the Table

When you leave a company that has good investment choices in its 401(k) plan, it may seem wise to leave your plan balance in place. If you do, be sure to notify your former employer if you change your address. Better yet, leave the money in place only temporarily, then roll it either into a new employer's plan or into an IRA. In an IRA you can direct your own investments.

If you leave a 401(k) at a former employer indefinitely, you're risking several problems. Companies change their names or their owners; they move, or are acquired, or go out of business. If even one of these events takes place, the 401(k) balances of former employees may not get much attention. When you go to retrieve your money, years down the road, you could be in for a rude surprise. There's no central clearinghouse for 401(k) plans, so you may have to become a sleuth to track the benefits that are coming to you.

If you can find the employer, file a written claim with the benefits or human resources department. Include your date of birth, Social Security number, and dates of employment. If your former employer has moved, and is a publicly traded company, the folks at 401kafe suggest looking for the new address on the most recent annual report.

If the company is privately held, check with the local chamber of commerce to see if the company has a new address. If the company was acquired, the plan may or may not still be operating. If it is, you can file a claim for benefits with the plan administrator. If it is not, you'll have to locate the trustee currently responsible for the plan's assets. If the company went into bankruptcy, the bankruptcy trustee should be able to distribute plan assets. Don't have any clue where to start? Clifton Linton, writing on the 401kafe Web site, suggests trying to find former co-workers who may have some information. Retirees are a particularly good bet; they may be receiving checks from the company.

Your job will be tougher if the company was acquired, and you are not the original participant but your spouse's beneficiary under the plan. In this situation, you may first have to prove your spouse's participation in the plan and then prove that you have a right to the money. It will help if you have pay stubs and plan statements. If you don't, try to reconstruct as many documents as you can: Look for benefits statements, W-2 forms, or tax returns—anything that might document participation in the plan. A pay stub or W-2 form, for example, will show payroll deductions as contributions to the plan. If you can't locate old tax returns, contact the IRS and request copies. If you have no other way to prove that your spouse was actually employed at the company, ask the Social Security Administration to provide a statement of earnings history; it won't prove participation in the plan but it may be enough to start the process. Be persistent. If necessary, hire an attorney to press your claim.

Bankruptcy

Personal bankruptcy is both a financial and an emotional hardship, but you can take some solace in knowing that assets in your 401(k) are generally safe from the clutch of creditors because qualified retirement plans are protected by federal law. IRAs, on the other hand, are under state jurisdiction. Most states have laws that shield IRAs from creditors, but, because there is some variation from state to state, some professional advisers suggest forgoing an IRA rollover if you might be vulnerable to creditors' claims. Leaving the money in a former employer's 401(k) plan might be preferable in this situation. Be especially cautious about a rollover within three or four months before declaring personal bankruptcy because this money may be open to attack on the grounds that you were using the IRA specifically to hide the money from creditors.

Keep these two facts in mind if you are considering filing for bankruptcy:

1. If you have a loan outstanding from your 401(k) plan, you can usually stop repayment once you file for bankruptcy. But that doesn't mean you're completely off the hook. The tax experts at CCH point out that any outstanding balance at the end of the five-year repayment period will be treated as a taxable distribution.
2. Declaring personal bankruptcy doesn't eliminate certain debts, including tax liens. One small consolation: In a recent case, the IRS was told that it could not have the money in an employee's 401(k) plan until the employee actually retired. At that point, the plan administrator would have to pay the benefits directly to the IRS to satisfy the tax lien. But the IRS could not have the

money in advance of retirement and it could not force the employee to retire. In addition, if the plan requires joint-and-survivor payments, as CCH puts it, "the IRS' ability to get the taxpayer's 401(k) plan benefits paid to it in a lump sum may be stymied by the rights of the taxpayer's spouse." Joint-and-survivor payments are more typical from a defined benefit pension plan than from a defined contribution plan such as 401(k), but some DC plans do have this provision.

Divorce

The breakup of a marriage isn't fun, no matter how you look at it, but it sure can put a crimp in your retirement savings. One of the biggest mistakes divorcing couples make is failing to plan for the disposition of their retirement accounts.

Forget the house. The money in a qualified plan is the largest single asset on many couples' bottom line. That money, like it or not, is going to be part of a divorce settlement. In fact, if you are smart, you will figure the *future* value of both assets before agreeing on a split. Your house and your 401(k) plan may each be currently worth \$200,000, but their value in 10 years may be radically different. If the diversified investments within the 401(k) grow at 8 percent a year and real estate in your neighborhood appreciates at 4 percent per year, the 401(k) will then be worth \$430,000 and the house will be valued at \$296,000. The disparity in dollar value will grow larger over time.

You should also recognize the tax differences. All of the retirement money will be taxed at ordinary income rates when withdrawn. But any profit on the house will be taxed at the lower capital gains rate when it is sold, and then only to the extent that the gain exceeds the \$250,000 exclusion available to a single taxpayer or the \$500,000 exclusion available to married couples filing jointly. If one of you takes the house, remarries, and then sells, it's quite possible that no tax at all will be due. If the other takes the 401(k), there is no way to avoid taxation on every penny when the money is withdrawn.

Let's take it from the top. Although tax-qualified retirement assets are protected by law—they aren't normally subject to creditors' claims, as discussed above—they are subject to division in a divorce settlement. Your state of residence may make a difference. Marital property is generally split fifty-fifty in the nine community property states (see page 195) but it is split "equitably" in all other states.

"Equitable distribution" is not fifty-fifty; it's whatever a judge decides is fair under the specific circumstances. Those circumstances could include your age, how long you've been married, and what each of you has contributed to the marriage.

Either way, however, the mechanism for dividing retirement benefits is a Qualified Domestic Relations Order (QDRO), a court order that gives an "alternate payee" the right to some or all of your plan assets. Obtaining a QDRO is essential. Without it, a split of assets could disqualify your account and erase its tax-sheltered status.

The QDRO must be properly prepared. According to the Society of Financial Service Professionals, it must specify that it is being established under the applicable section of the Internal Revenue Code and the particular state's domestic relations laws. In addition, it should include:

- The name and address of the plan participant and the "alternate payee."
- The name and number of each retirement account involved.
- The percentage or dollar amount of each plan that is to be paid to the alternate payee.
- The period of time or the number of payments covered by the QDRO.

Without the latter provision, you may find yourself liable for taxes that should be paid by your ex-spouse. In a case cited by the Society of Financial Service Professionals, a New Mexico orthodontist agreed to give his wife $1 million from his retirement plan as part of their divorce agreement. He assumed that his ex-spouse would be responsible for paying taxes on the money she received. The IRS, and then the Tax Court, disagreed. Because the divorce agreement was not a properly drawn QDRO, the orthodontist was left with a federal income tax bill of almost $400,000, and his ex-wife received the $1 million tax-free. The ruling was reversed in 1996—nine years after the divorce—when another court ruled in favor of the orthodontist. Meanwhile, there were legal bills and an emotional toll. It's better to get it right the first time.

> **NOTE**
>
> **The nine states that follow community property rules are (in alphabetical order):**
>
> 1. **Arizona**
> 2. **California**
> 3. **Idaho**
> 4. **Louisiana**
> 5. **Nevada**
> 6. **New Mexico**
> 7. **Texas**
> 8. **Washington**
> 9. **Wisconsin**

Normally, the QDRO will divide the retirement account in whatever proportions are ordered by the judge or agreed to by the parties, and will establish a separate account in the second spouse's name. Under this arrangement, you can continue to contribute to your account and manage its investments. If the plan document permits, your ex-spouse can leave his or her portion of the plan in place and make investment choices, but cannot make any contributions. Alternatively, your ex can roll his or her portion into an IRA. This is usually the best choice because it affords more flexibility and more control, as well as preserving the tax shelter. Your ex may also choose to take his or her share in cash, but this course is advisable only when there is a pressing need for cash. A cash distribution is subject to income tax although the 10 percent tax penalty otherwise levied when the individual is under age 59½ is waived in divorce distributions.

If both accounts remain with your employer, the general rule is that no distributions will be made from either account until you retire. A New Jersey court recently set a precedent by permitting a divorced spouse to receive a distribution well before her fireman husband's retirement, but the decision is being contested on the grounds that state law prohibits the plan from making any disbursements until an employee retires.

If you are contemplating divorce:

- Read your plan documents before talking to your attorney. You may even want to provide both attorneys—yours and your spouse's—with copies of the documents. Don't expect attorneys to be familiar with the provisions of a specific retirement plan. Plans have great flexibility in establishing rules, and those rules dictate what you can do.
- Talk to your plan administrator about your options. Some large companies even have "QDRO kits" to help employees work through the details.
- Talk to an accountant about any possible tax consequences. In general, you don't need to worry about any adverse tax consequences from transferring assets from one ex-spouse to the other. The transfer is tax-neutral if it is part of divorce proceedings and takes place no more than one year after the divorce is final.
- Talk to a financial planner about your entire financial picture, pre- and post-divorce. You may want to consult one of the new specialists called Certified Divorce Planners; these are financial

planners, accountants and attorneys who specialize in tax, alimony, and pension issues. For a referral, call the Institute for Certified Divorce Planners at 1-800-875-1760.

- Be sure that the QDRO is signed by the court and approved by the plan administrator; mistakes in the paperwork can come back to haunt you in later years.
- Give consideration to any outstanding loan; it may have to be repaid.
- Check out www.splitup.com for free general information and moderately-priced downloadable software that can help you address some of the issues before you consult your attorney.

If you rolled your 401(k) into an IRA before your divorce, you face a different set of rules. On the plus side, mandatory withholding does not apply to IRAs. On the negative side, there is no waiver of the 10 percent early withdrawal penalty when distributions are made from an IRA.

All or part of an IRA may be transferred to an ex-spouse under a divorce decree. You can direct the custodian to change the title of the IRA to put it into your ex-spouse's name, or you can request a transfer of the IRA directly from your custodian to the custodian chosen by your former spouse. Once the IRA is in your former spouse's name, you are totally out of the picture. The IRA is treated as if your ex-spouse was the original and only owner of the account.

I've said it before: The laws and regulations governing retirement plan distributions are exceedingly complex. Be sure to get knowledgeable advice.

PART 4

At the End of the Road

CHAPTER 11

When You Retire or Leave Your Job

As the years go by, you steadily put money away in your defined contribution plan until you have a tidy nest egg. The only decision you have to make is where to invest that nest egg. Then you retire or leave your job, and you face some serious decisions. Will you start to withdraw the money and pay income tax on the distributions? Or can you—will you—keep it working for you, building tax-sheltered money toward a later date?

Too many people—especially younger folks, for whom retirement seems like a very distant idea—take the cash and spend it. Perhaps $5,000 or $6,000—or even $10,000—doesn't seem like very much of a head start on retirement. But it could be just the right amount to replace your clunker of a car, or help to put together the down payment on a house.

TIP

Distribution decisions may have to be made—from a 401(k), 403(b), profit-sharing, or employee stock ownership plan—if you:

- **Retire.**
- **Take a new job.**
- **Become disabled.**
- **Work for a company that has been merged or acquired.**
- **Need to take distributions to meet financial need.**
- **Are the beneficiary of a spouse's retirement plan and your spouse has died.**

NOTE

What do employees do with their retirement benefits when they leave a job?

Roll over some or all to a new employer's plan	**8%**
Save some or all of the money outside an IRA or a new employer's plan	**23**
Spend some or all of the money, or pay off debt	**30**
Leave some or all of the money in their old employer's plan	**34**
Roll over some or all of the money into an IRA	**42**

Source: 1997 Retirement Confidence Survey by the Employee Benefit Research Institute, American Savings Education Council, and Mathew Greenwald & Associates

Think twice before you take the money and run. If you take $10,000 out of a 401(k) plan and pay taxes on it at 31 percent, you'll lose $3,100 right off the top. If you're under age 59½, you owe a 10 percent tax penalty, and that's another $1,000 down the tubes. If you keep the $10,000 intact by keeping it tax-deferred, either by leaving it in the 401(k) plan or rolling it over into an IRA, you'll have $21,500 after 10 years, if the money is invested at a steady return of 8 percent. That's if you never add another penny. If you keep on working, however, you can add to the account and reap the advantages of additional tax-deferred compounding.

People are getting the message. Studies by the Employment Benefit Research Institute (EBRI) sounded a dismal note a few years ago, reporting that two out of five employees leaving a job in 1993 took their 401(k) distributions in cash—and spent the entire distribution. Current studies show a marked improvement. A recent survey by American Century Investments found that only one in every 25 workers said they would cash out their retirement nest egg if they changed jobs.

What people say, of course, may be different from what they do. Thirty percent of the employees recently surveyed by EBRI reported actually spending at least some of the money, or using it to pay off debt. This ratio is much higher than the 1-in-25 reported by American Century, but it is still a marked improvement over the 40 percent of several years ago. However, when it comes to holding onto future retirement benefits, older workers are more likely to roll the money into an IRA. Younger workers are more likely to leave the money behind in a former employer's plan.

A lot depends, of course, on whether you are actually retiring or are leaving your job for another. Much also depends on your age and on the rules laid down by Uncle Sam and by your company plan. This chapter sets forth your options when you leave one job for another, and when you reach retirement.

Green Pastures

Moving on to another job? Choices about what to do with your 401(k) money depend on how much is in your account. If you leave a job when you have less than $5,000 accumulated in your employer-sponsored retirement plan, you will probably have to take the distribution in cash. When you have accumulated $5,000 or more, you may have as many as five choices for what to do with the money:

1. Take the money in a lump sum.
2. Take the money in substantially equal periodic payments over your life expectancy.
3. Leave the money in place, if your plan permits; let it continue growing.
4. Transfer the money to the 401(k) plan sponsored by your new employer.
5. Transfer the money to a rollover IRA.

Each of these options deserves a closer look.

1. Take the Money in a Lump Sum

A lump-sum distribution, as indicated above, is generally the worst choice for a pre-retiree. It will be hard to overcome the temptation to spend the money instead of keeping it growing toward retirement. More important, you will owe income tax on all of the money. The tax bite may be bigger than you thought possible.

When you take a cash distribution from a tax-sheltered retirement plan, your employer must withhold 20 percent for taxes. If you are in a higher tax bracket, you will have to make up the difference when you pay your federal income tax for the year.

In addition, if you're under age 59½, you will owe a 10 percent tax penalty, unless you qualify under one of the following exceptions:

- You are retiring or leaving your job and are at least age 55.
- You have become totally disabled.
- You will use the money for medical expenses that exceed 7.5 percent of your adjusted gross income.
- You will take the money in substantially equal periodic payments over your lifetime.

Fail to meet one of these exceptions—or, in one other exception, tap your retirement funds to meet a qualified domestic relations order (QDRO) during a divorce—and you will owe ordinary income tax plus the 10 percent tax penalty. The total tax bite, if you are under age 55 and in the 33 percent federal tax bracket, could be 43 percent, which would leave you 57 percent of your accumulated retirement funds—unless, of course, you live in a state where state income taxes will take an additional bite.

A tax strategy called "forward averaging" used to be available to ease the tax bite. But five-year averaging has been eliminated, and 10-year averaging is available only to people born before January 1, 1936, who are separating from service after participating in the retirement plan for at least five years. If you are in this group and receive your entire plan balance within one calendar year, you must pay all the tax in a single year but it will be taxed as if it had been spread over ten years. Or, if you were born before 1936, you can elect to treat any portion of the lump-sum distribution attributable to plan participation before 1974 as capital gains, which are taxed at the maximum rate of 20 percent. This is a once-in-a-lifetime option; no matter how many retirement plans you may participate in, it can't be used more than once.

EXAMPLE

Want to share your 401(k) plan with Uncle Sam? Take a lump-sum distribution. Want to keep it for yourself? Do an IRA rollover. These figures tell the tale:

Lump-Sum Distribution	IRA Rollover
$100,000	$100,000
Less:	
$20,000 (20 percent tax withholding)	
11,000 (balance of federal taxes)	
10,000 (10 percent early withdrawal penalty)	
$59,000	$100,000

The example assumes an individual under age 59½, in the 31 percent federal income tax bracket. The tax bite could be bigger if this individual owes state and local income taxes as well.

The tax may be lower if you qualify for 10-year averaging because it is calculated as if it is the only income received for the year by 10 different individuals. In other words, you calculate the tax on 10 percent of the distribution and multiply it by 10 to determine how much you owe. This generally means that most of the money is taxed at the lowest rate. A possible downside, though, is that the tax is calculated on 1986 federal income tax rates for single taxpayers. Tax rates in 1986 were higher than they are today, so a distribution of several hundred thousand dollars may be needed before it makes sense to use averaging. Run the numbers, and ask your tax adviser if averaging makes sense for you. Transferring the distribution to a rollover IRA may still be a better bet.

2. Take the Money in Substantially Equal Periodic Payments

If you are parting ways with your employer, you can avoid the early withdrawal tax penalty of 10 percent by electing to take your distribution in the form of substantially equal periodic payments based on your life expectancy. You don't have to retire—you don't even have to reach any specific age—but you do have to leave your job to take advantage of this loophole in the early withdrawal penalty for an employer-sponsored plan such as a 401(k). (Note: Don't confuse substantially equal periodic payments, sometimes referred to as SEPP, with the SEP-IRA. The latter is a totally different animal, as described in Chapter 3.)

The Internal Revenue Service has approved three ways to calculate the distributions you will receive under a SEPP arrangement:

1. The life expectancy method.
2. The amortization method.
3. The annuity method.

The *life expectancy method* is based on annually dividing the fund balance by your life expectancy (or the combined life expectancy of you and your beneficiary). It typically produces smaller payments at the outset because it does not reflect growth in the underlying investment. If your retirement funds grow through capital appreciation or accumulated dividends and interest, you will have larger payments as the years go by.

The life expectancy method is not particularly popular. Attorney Natalie Choate, the author of *Life and Death Planning for Retirement Benefits*, links its lack of popularity to the fact that it produces smaller payments at the wrong time. People expect or assume that their cash reserve will cover a specific need such as purchasing a new home or traveling. And, of course, the life expectancy method does not produce a steady predictable flow of income.

The *amortization method* is also based on life expectancy, but it assumes a steady rate of growth and therefore provides fixed-sum payments and a predictable stream of income. This is by far the most popular method.

An *annuity method*, in Choate's words, "allows more actuarial creativity." It also tends to produce the largest payments of the three methods. But it requires the selection of a "reasonable mortality table" to determine life expectancy, along with a "reasonable interest rate." These decisions might best be left to an actuary.

If you elect to take your 401(k) in the form of substantially equal periodic payments, you must continue the payments for at least five years or until you reach age 59½, whichever is later. If you make any change in the payments sooner, the 10 percent tax penalty will be applied retroactively to all of the payments received. Interest on the penalty will also be charged. Furthermore, distributions taken in the form of periodic payments are never eligible for rollover.

Suppose you don't want to take all of your retirement money in this manner, but you need access to some of your money. What do you do? If you have two retirement plans, you may be able to tap one of them and leave the other intact for tax-deferred growth. If you have just one plan, you may be able to split it into two to achieve the same result. Consult a knowledgeable tax adviser before doing so, however. This is a gray area in tax law.

3. Leave the Money in Place

If you have more than $5,000 in your 401(k), your present employer may allow you to leave the money in place. This can be a good choice if you are satisfied with your plan's investment options—and if you will be allowed the full menu of investment options once you are no longer with the company. But consider all the pros and cons before making your decision.

Several factors argue *against* leaving the money in place:

- Most corporate plans require that you withdraw all the assets within five years.
- The IRS allows several distribution methods, says Fleet Bank retirement expert Marvin Rotenberg, but many corporate plans are less flexible.
- Beneficiary designations may be limited. Because more paperwork is involved, you may not be allowed to split the plan assets among different beneficiaries.
- Some employers don't want to administer plans for former workers. Instead of refusing to do so, they may simply make the terms unattractive. Investment choices may be limited, and loans may not be available. Your company may also limit the frequency with which ex-employees may change investments.

On the other hand, there are some solid reasons for leaving the money in a 401(k) instead of rolling it into an IRA:

- You have made after-tax contributions and want to leave them in a tax-deferred retirement plan. At present, these contributions cannot be rolled over to another plan or to an IRA, so you may want to stick with your prior employer's plan.
- You want to keep your options open so that you will be able to borrow against your 401(k) in an emergency. You are never allowed to borrow from an IRA, although you can take money out without an early withdrawal penalty if you meet certain conditions.
- You are a professional or own a business, or have creditors breathing down your neck, and may need to consider bankruptcy. Employer-sponsored retirement plans are subject to federal law and can't be touched by creditors. An IRA, depending on the state in which you live, may be vulnerable.
- You own employer stock within your 401(k) plan, and you do not want to sell the stock or roll it into an IRA. (More on company stock later in this chapter.)
- You plan to continue working into your seventies, and you don't want to tap your retirement nest egg before you are required by law to do so. As an employee, you can defer taking minimum

distributions until April 1 of the year after you actually retire (unless company policy requires distributions at an earlier date). You must begin required minimum distributions from an IRA no later than April 1 of the calendar year after you reach age 70½, even if you are still working. If you are self-employed or own more than 5 percent of the business, you can't use this strategy.

If you leave money with a past employer, you need to monitor your account, make sure investment options remain satisfactory, and keep the plan informed if you change your address. Pay attention, in case the company is acquired or merges with another. (When this happens, plans are sometimes merged or dropped, as described in Chapter 10.) If you don't keep tabs on your money after you move on, it might not be available when you need it.

4. Transfer the Money to a New 401(k)

If you are moving on, and if your new plan permits an immediate contribution of former 401(k) assets, this may be your best bet. Check out the details of the new plan, following the guidance in Chapter 2, to avoid any surprises. You may have to reallocate your 401(k) investments among the fund choices in your new plan. Use that opportunity to ensure that your investments are in line with your long-term goals.

If there is a waiting period before you are eligible to participate in the new plan, keep your options open by using a rollover IRA as a temporary parking place for the money. Be sure to keep the money separate. If you commingle it with an existing IRA, you will not be permitted to transfer it to another 401(k).

If you are moving from a public-sector job to the corporate world, or vice versa, you may not be able to move your retirement money from one plan to another. At this writing, money can move between profit-sharing plans and 401(k) plans, but it cannot be transferred among 401(k) plans (in the corporate world), 403(b) plans (in the nonprofit universe), and 457 plans (in the governmental sphere). Legislation proposed in mid-summer 2000—and overwhelmingly approved by the House of Representatives—would make retirement money "portable" (in pension jargon, transferable from plan to plan).

If your career move is from employment to self-employment, you may be able to put your accumulated retirement funds into a Keogh Plan or a SEP-IRA. (Retirement plans for small businesses are described in Chapter 3.)

5. Transfer the Money to a Rollover IRA

If in doubt, do a rollover. The single best choice for most people is the rollover IRA, because it preserves flexibility. In a rollover IRA, your money continues to grow, tax-deferred. Once the money is in a rollover IRA, you may withdraw only the amounts you need at any given time (you'll pay tax on the amount actually withdrawn). If you are under age 59½, you will also owe a 10 percent tax penalty unless you meet one of the exceptions listed earlier.

After you establish a rollover IRA, you can arrange automatic monthly withdrawals or take out what you want when you want it. You have complete flexibility until the April 1 after you reach age 70½. Then, under the law, you will have to start taking required minimum distributions pegged to *your life expectancy* or—if your spouse is your beneficiary and is more than 10 years younger than you are—*the life expectancy of you and your beneficiary.* (You'll find more on beneficiary designations in Chapter 12.)

You can always take more but, once you reach this crucial birthday, you are not allowed to take less. The exception permitted under other tax-sheltered retirement plans—defer taking distributions until the April 1 after the calendar year in which you actually retire—is not available for IRAs. In fact, if you fail to withdraw the required minimum distributions, you'll face an excise tax of 50 percent of the difference between the amount that should have been distributed and the amount that was actually distributed during the year. The responsibility is yours. As noted in the *Ernst & Young Tax Guide 2000*, "Many financial institutions do not inform their IRA holders when it is time to begin receiving distributions."

In some respects (unless you plan to keep working and want to defer distributions), a rollover IRA is even better than a 401(k). Within a typical 401(k) plan (unless the plan has a brokerage window, as described in Chapter 5), you might have six to 10 investment options. With a rollover IRA, you have as many choices as are available through your custodian. Those choices may include individual securities and certificates of deposit, as well as mutual funds. If you have carefully planned your asset allocation and have selected from a menu of investment options to meet your retirement objectives, you'll be able to keep your allocation in place within your rollover IRA and change the allocation to meet your changing objectives as you near retirement.

But you must follow the rules, and the most important rule is that the money must move directly from your 401(k) plan to the IRA. Don't be led astray by the 60 days a year in which you are allowed to use IRA money without a tax penalty. Under current law, if the 401(k) plan money passes through your hands even briefly, your current employer must withhold 20 percent in taxes. Translation: *Do not* let your current employer send the check to you with your name as payee. If the check must come to you, make sure that it is made out to the new trustee, the institution holding your rollover IRA. *Do not* let the check be made out to you, even if you will immediately make it payable to the custodian of your rollover IRA. If the check is made out to you, taxes will be due on the distribution.

If you do receive the money and place it in a rollover IRA before the end of 60 days, you can get the withheld taxes back—but not until after you file your federal income tax return for the year. Meanwhile, you still have to deposit 100 percent of the 401(k) distribution in the rollover IRA or you will be hit with both income tax and, if you're under age 59½, a 10 percent tax penalty. As an example, if you take $20,000 from your 401(k) with the intention of rolling it into an IRA, 20 percent ($4,000) will be withheld in taxes. If you can't come up with $4,000 to replace the withheld amount, so that you can deposit $20,000 in your rollover IRA, the $4,000 will be treated as a taxable distribution and you won't get a refund for the withheld taxes.

The second important rule is: Your rollover IRA should be kept separate. If you mingle the funds with an existing IRA, you will lose the ability to transfer the money into a new employer's 401(k) plan when you become eligible to do so. Later, when you are well and truly retired, you can consolidate your IRAs for ease of record keeping. Until then, keep them separate.

COMPANY STOCK

A rule of thumb—accurate, for the most part—says that total 401(k) accumulations should be rolled into an IRA to preserve tax-deferred growth. True—but only up to a point.

SPECIAL NOTES ON ROLLOVER IRAS

- Rollovers may not be made to a Roth IRA, a SIMPLE IRA, or an education IRA. If you want 401(k) money transferred to a Roth, as an example, you must first transfer it to a rollover IRA and then convert that IRA to a Roth IRA. CPA Ed Slott, editor of the newsletter "Ed Slott's IRA Advisor," calls this "the Roth two-step."
- After-tax contributions may not be placed in a rollover IRA, although earnings on those contributions may be rolled over. A bill passed by the House of Representatives in 2000 and again in 2001 would permit rollovers of after-tax contributions themselves, as part of a larger package of retirement plan enhancements. Until such a measure is signed into law, you must take a distribution of after-tax contributions; the money is not taxable, because you have already paid taxes on it, but you will lose the opportunity for future tax-deferred growth on earnings.
- If you own a lot of appreciated company stock in your 401(k) plan, don't automatically include it in your rollover. You'll see why in the following section.

Let's say that you have been using retirement plan contributions to buy company stock over the years, or that your employer has made matching contributions in the form of company stock. If you now hold substantial amounts of greatly appreciated company stock and your plan document permits an "in-kind distribution," you may save considerable tax dollars by taking some or all of the stock out of your tax-sheltered retirement plan when you leave your job and placing it in a regular taxable brokerage account. Doing so may seem counter-intuitive, but it lets you take maximum advantage of what the Internal Revenue Service calls "net unrealized appreciation" (NUA).

The savings come about because everything that eventually comes out of your IRA, even if generated by capital gains, will be taxed at ordinary income tax rates. At this writing, those rates run as high as 39.6 percent. If you remove the company stock from its tax shelter, however, you will owe ordinary income tax only on the cost basis—the value of the shares at the time they were acquired by the 401(k) plan. (You may have to ask your employer to provide you with this amount.)

When you sell the stock—whether the next day or 20 years down the road—you will owe tax, at the lower capital gains rate, on the net unrealized appreciation. NUA is defined as the amount of appreciation between the date of purchase (in the company plan) and the date of distribution (when it is removed from the plan).

Any additional appreciation from the date of distribution until the date of sale is taxed as either a short-term or a long-term capital gain, depending on how long you held the stock before selling it. For long-term assets—those held more than 12 months—the maximum capital gains tax rate is currently 20 percent. For assets purchased after January 1, 2001, and held at least five years, the maximum capital gains rates is 18 percent.

Leave the money in a tax-sheltered IRA and you forfeit the capital gains tax break. Withdrawals will be taxed at ordinary income tax rates. And there's no escape. You must start withdrawing the money, in minimum amounts pegged to your life expectancy, by the April 1 after you reach age 70½.

NOTE

For taxpayers in the 15 percent tax bracket, a maximum capital gains rate of 8 percent applies to any asset held for at least five years, regardless of the initial purchase date. For taxpayers in this bracket, there is a maximum long-term capital gains rate of 10 percent on assets held more than 12 months but not more than five years.

Removing the stock from its tax shelter produces an additional break because you won't ever have to cash it in if you choose not to do so. You can leave it to your heirs, who will receive (unless the law governing gifts and estates is changed, as has been proposed) a "step-up" in value from the date you took the stock out of the plan until the date of your death. (Note: The step-up does not apply to any appreciation in value from the original acquisition of the shares in your plan account until the date they are transferred out of the account. You will already have paid ordinary income tax on these gains, as described above.)

This means that your heirs' cost basis in the shares—and the resulting tax liability when they sell the shares—is determined by the value of the stock at the date of your death. If they sell the appreciated stock right after your death, there may be no tax at all. If they hold the shares and sell later, capital gains tax will be due only on the appreciation from the stepped-up basis to the date of sale.

Moving company stock to a taxable account is a strategy that works best when appreciated company stock makes up a hefty part of your 401(k). If the amounts are not large, or if the stock has not gained much in value, you might do just as well by rolling your entire 401(k)—including the company stock—into an IRA. And, of course, there is no benefit to this approach if the stock has lost value since its acquisition.

Retirement

In this next scenario, you are leaving the workforce and joining the ranks of the joyfully retired. Here, too, you have some choices:

1. Take a lump-sum distribution.
2. Take an annuity (for a steady stream of lifetime income).
3. Leave the money in place.
4. Rollover to an IRA.

If you are leaving your job for the joys of retirement but have not yet reached age 70½, when you must start withdrawing your accumulated retirement funds, you may want to leave the money in place. Then it can continue to grow tax-deferred—so long as you have other funds that can be tapped for current living expenses. The longer your tax-sheltered money stays tax-sheltered, the better off you will be.

There is, however, an exception to the general rule that tax-deferred is always better. If you die owning tax-sheltered funds, they will be subject to income tax. They may also be eroded by federal estate tax. If you have over $1 million in your retirement accounts, some advisers suggest starting withdrawals early, well before age 70½, so that you avoid this double tax whammy. (See Chapter 12 for more details on distribution methods, beneficiary designations, and estate planning.)

One way or the other, you must make a choice. Some of the rules are the same as those for pre-retirees who are making a job change (discussed earlier in this chapter). Others are different. Each option is worth a closer look in the context of leaving your job for good.

1. Take a Lump-Sum Distribution

If you take the cash all at once, you may face a hefty income tax bill. Federal income tax is due, at ordinary rates ranging as high as 39.6 percent, on all of your contributions, your employer's contributions, and the earnings on both. The only 401(k) money that escapes taxation at withdrawal is after-tax contributions (the money was already taxed).

TIP

A lump-sum distribution from a defined contribution plan qualifies for special tax treatment only if all three of the following conditions are met:

1. **It represents a distribution of your entire retirement account.**
2. **It is the first distribution after you leave your job, retire, reach age 59½, or die.**
3. **It occurs in a single tax year, as either a single distribution or a series of distributions.**

In fact, if you have made after-tax contributions to your employer-sponsored retirement plan, you may be able to sidestep tax on distributions for the first year or two after you reach your required beginning date. As the accounting firm of Ernst & Young explains in its *Tax Guide 2000*, the strategy involves taking a lump-sum distribution, keeping the portion that represents the after-tax contributions (you can't roll it over, in any case), and rolling over the rest to an IRA. The IRS has indicated, in a Private Letter Ruling, that nontaxable amounts may be used to satisfy the minimum distribution requirement. Depending on how much you must withdraw and how much you have in after-tax contributions, your first year or two of distributions may be satisfied by these nontaxable amounts. They are not subject to tax because you have already paid tax on the money before contributing it to the plan. (So far, at least, earnings aren't taxed twice.)

If you want to take the entire distribution in a lump sum and are at least age 55 when you leave your job, you can take the money and pay only the income taxes that are due on the entire distribution, with no tax penalty. The tax bite may be eased, however, if you qualify for income averaging, as described earlier in this chapter.

2. Take an Annuity

If you are at least age 59½, you can choose to "annuitize" or take the money in a steady stream of income for your lifetime. Your employer may offer this option, or you can do it on your own by using a lump-sum distribution to purchase an annuity from an insurance company. (See Chapter 3 for a full discussion of annuities.) In either case, the amount of the annuity is based on how much your lump-sum distribution would buy, based on your life expectancy or the joint life expectancy of you and your spouse.

Annuities come with various payout options. If you are married, however, you may not have a choice. You may be required to take a joint-and-survivor annuity to guarantee ongoing income to your surviving spouse. Election of another option will require the written consent of both you and your spouse.

Annuities have definite advantages. Perhaps the paramount advantage is that you can't outlive your retirement income. Another feature may be appealing to some people: You won't have to make investment decisions. Once you purchase an annuity, there are no more decisions to make.

But annuities have disadvantages: They provide a fixed stream of income, but any fixed income is subject to erosion by inflation. At this writing, inflationary price increases are relatively modest. But you may remember the double-digit price jumps of the late 1970s, when inflation rose as high as 17 percent. At a 10 percent rate of inflation, a fixed annual annuity of $25,000 will have the purchasing power of $3,500 in 20 years. Even at a 4 percent rate of inflation, today's $25,000 will effectively be cut in half, giving you the purchasing power of $11,500 in 20 years.

Furthermore, if you choose the annuity option, you will receive the monthly payment and nothing more. If you transfer the money to a rollover IRA instead of taking an annuity, you can arrange automatic monthly withdrawals (with no guarantee that they will last a lifetime) but you can also take larger sums if you need or want the money.

WHAT RETIREES DO WITH DEFINED CONTRIBUTION FUNDS

Leave all the money in employer plan	32%
Leave some or all in employer plan, withdrawing required amounts	20
Leave some or all in employer plan, withdrawing as needed	27
Put some or all in IRA, no withdrawals to date	7
Put some or all in IRA, receive regular periodic payments	21
Put some or all in IRA, make withdrawals as needed	18
Annuitize some or all, receive regular payments	20
Put some or all in another form of savings	40

Source: 1997 Retirement Confidence Survey by the Employee Benefit Research Institute, American Savings Education Council, and Mathew Greenwald & Associates.

3. Leave the Money in Place

If you have more than $5,000 in your account, you may be able to leave your account in place with your former employer. Just be careful to scrutinize the investment options and flexibility of choice available to retirees. Although a growing number of large corporations are allowing retirees to leave the money in place, under the same terms available to active workers, some employers, not wanting to be bothered with plan administration for former employers, limit their choices as a deterrent to continued participation.

Here too, depending on how close you are to needing the money, you may want to reevaluate your investment choices within the plan. Review Chapter 7 and then decide on the best asset allocation for this stage of your life.

4. Rollover to an IRA

When you retire, as when you leave a job, you can transfer your 401(k) accumulations to a rollover IRA. You need not keep the accumulation intact; you can roll over part of your 401(k) and elect another option with the balance. However, you will have to pay income tax on any portion that you take in cash.

Tip: If you can arrange to be self-employed in the year in which you retire, the accounting firm of Ernst & Young suggests rolling your 401(k) or other qualified retirement plan into a Keogh Plan. This will preserve tax deferral—and also preserve the option to use 10-year

HOW RETIREES USE IRAS AFTER RETIREMENT

Leave all the money in the IRA	45%
Leave some money in the IRA, withdraw the amount required by law	50
Leave some money in the IRA, withdraw as needed	33
Leave some or all money in the IRA, receive regular periodic payments	29
Annuitize some or all of the payments, receive regular payments	7
Put some or all into another savings vehicle	45

Source: 1997 Retirement Confidence Survey by the Employee Benefit Research Institute, American Savings Education Council, and Mathew Greenwald & Associates.

forward averaging (assuming that you were born before January 1, 1936)—when you withdraw the money at a later date. You cannot use income averaging when you withdraw money from an IRA.

Arrange to have the rollover made directly from your employer's plan to your IRA rollover account. If you take the money, even temporarily, 20 percent will be withheld for taxes. If you make up the withheld amount to complete the rollover, you will get a tax refund after you file your federal income tax return in the following year. If you are unable to make up the withheld amount, the amount withheld is treated as a taxable distribution.

When you open a rollover IRA, you'll be asked to name a beneficiary. Don't wait until you must start distributions. Only by naming a beneficiary can you ensure that payments can be stretched out—and tax deferral can be preserved—for the longest possible time. In fact, in a worst-case scenario under newly issued IRS regulations, if you die before your required beginning date (RBD) and have not named a beneficiary, the account will have to be emptied within five years. If you die after your RBD without naming a beneficiary, the account would probably go into your estate (assuming your estate is the default beneficiary under your custodian's prototype retirement plan) and then would pass in accordance with the terms of your will. Ultimately, the recipient would have to use your remaining life expectancy to take the distributions. Name a beneficiary and, whether you die before or after your RBD, distributions can be taken over the beneficiary's remaining life expectancy.

TIPS FOR TAKING DISTRIBUTIONS

- If you have multiple qualified plans—for example, you have a 401(k) at each of two jobs—you must take the minimum required amount from each plan.
- If you have more than one IRA, you must calculate the required minimum distribution from each IRA, but you can elect to take the payment from any one or more of the accounts. Be sure to notify the custodian of each plan, in writing, to forestall the automatic distributions that some institutions will initiate at your required beginning date.
- Consolidating your qualified plans into a single rollover IRA before your required beginning date will make the distribution calculations—and the paperwork—much easier.

Distributions during your lifetime are always based on life expectancy—either yours alone or (if your spouse is your beneficiary and is more than 10 years younger) the joint life expectancy of you and your spouse. With IRAs, unlike other qualified plans, you may name any beneficiary. You are not required, if married, to name your spouse.

Under proposed IRS regulations issued in January 2001, it is no longer necessary to decide whether you want to: (1) take distributions fixed on your life expectancy at the date you start; (2) recalculate distributions each year; or (3) use a so-called hybrid method. All this complexity is out the window because, under a uniform life expectancy table, your minimum required distributions are automatically recalculated annually, based on your age. The table also permits smaller required distributions over a longer period. The new, greatly simplified regulations are a boon for taxpayers. (You'll find more details in Chapter 12.)

When you are well and truly retired, and no longer making contributions to any form of tax-deferred retirement plan, you should consider

Under prior regulations, mistakes in designating beneficiaries could not be corrected after you reached your required beginning date (April 1 of the year following the year in which you reached age 70½). You were locked into distributions based on the joint life expectancy of yourself and your designated beneficiary. If your beneficiary died first, you had to accelerate payments—unless you were able to convert your traditional IRA to a Roth IRA where no distributions are required.

Under proposed regulations issued in January 2001, you can change your beneficiary at any time, before or after you start distributions, without affecting the minimum amount you must withdraw each year from your retirement plan. Under a new uniform life expectancy table, distributions are recalculated each year, based on your life expectancy.

Although smaller distributions are required under the new life expectancy table, conversion to a Roth IRA may still make sense if you want to preserve your IRA for your heirs. To convert, your adjusted gross income cannot exceed $100,000, and you must be willing to pay the taxes up front, at the time of conversion.

consolidating your retirement accounts to reduce paperwork. You should also be sure—well before you reach age 70½, when required minimum distributions must begin—to designate a beneficiary or beneficiaries, as described more fully in Chapter 12. Don't leave beneficiary choice to chance, or assume that your retirement money will be distributed according to the provisions of your will. It doesn't work that way.

CHAPTER 12

Name That Beneficiary!

The money in your tax-sheltered retirement plans may make up a very sizable proportion of your net worth; for many people, it's their largest single asset. So it's worth some time to plan ahead and to consider what will happen to that money when you die. You need to consider beneficiary designations for your retirement accounts in the context of your overall financial and estate planning.

Money left in tax-sheltered retirement plans at death can be hit by a double whammy of taxes. *Income tax* is always due on retirement plan balances at death. *Federal estate tax* may also be due if your taxable estate exceeds specified amounts (see Table 12.2 on p. 238). Fortunately, a former triple hit has been eliminated. Until it was repealed by the Taxpayer Relief Act of 1997, there was a federal excise tax on large retirement accounts. When the excise tax was combined with income and estate taxes, as much as 85 percent of inherited retirement money was in danger of being eroded.

Assuming that you have other assets to cover your living expenses, you may want to take the smallest distributions allowed during your lifetime and let your heirs spread payments over as many years as possible. Doing so maximizes the tax deferment possibilities built into a tax-sheltered retirement plan. But, until recently, doing both—taking small distributions and letting your heirs stretch out payments—required specific action on your part, under the complex regulations governing distributions. Under regulations proposed in 1987 and in effect for 13 years (although never formally adopted), you had to choose both a distribution method and a beneficiary. To make matters worse, you were locked into your choices as soon as you reached your required beginning date (RBD) and had to start taking distributions. The RBD was, and is, April 1 of the year following the year in which you reach age 70½. The exception: Participants in an employer-sponsored plan can wait until April 1 after their retirement.

Now, thanks to proposed regulations introduced in January 2001 and scheduled to take formal effect in January 2002, life has become much simpler. Amazing taxpayers and retirement advisers alike, the Treasury Department introduced the new regulations by stating: "In general, the need to make decisions at age 70½, which under the 1987 proposed regulations would bind the employee in future years during which financial circumstances could change significantly, was perceived as unreasonably restrictive. In addition, the determination of life expectancy and designated beneficiary and the resulting required minimum distribution calculation for individual accounts were viewed as too complex."

"Complex" is putting it mildly. The previous regulations were nothing short of a nightmare; their intricacies kept legions of lawyers and accountants busy. The new taxpayer-friendly regulations apply, across the board, to 401(k) plans, 403(b) plans, and Individual Retirement Accounts. (Application to 457 plans is anticipated as well.) Note, though, that federal regulations provide outside limits. Plan documents for employer-sponsored plans may be more restrictive.

Some things have not changed: How much you can contribute to a tax-sheltered plan, income limitations on deductible contributions, and the required beginning date for distributions all remain the same. But the new rules let you extend tax deferral by taking smaller distributions over a longer period of time. The RBD continues to be a critical date, but the new rules make it almost impossible to make the kind of mistake that sometimes sent 75 percent of a retirement account straight to the tax collector.

Estate taxes still apply—only Congress can change those rules—but income tax should no longer be an issue.

The trade-off for simplification is more stringent tax reporting. The banks, brokerage firms, and mutual funds holding retirement accounts will have to report account balances and distributions to the IRS and to account holders, just as they now report interest and dividends. The exact method of reporting is yet to be determined, pending final adoption of the proposed regulations, but will not change the fact that you may take required IRA distributions from just one IRA, even if you hold more than one. The proposed regulations stipulate that the custodian must report the amount of the required minimum distribution, but would indicate that the distribution may be taken from a different IRA.

There has always been a 50 percent penalty for taking less than the required minimum distribution, but enforcement was rare. It was just too difficult to track who was getting what, when everybody had a different distribution schedule. In fact, this may have been one reason for the change. In the words of CPA Ed Slott, editor of *Ed Slott's IRA Advisor*, "Trillions of dollars are being built up in these accounts, just waiting to be taxed." With a new uniform system, it will be easy for the IRS to check up on individuals through cross-matching information returns. The result will be better tax compliance.

Better tax reporting may be worthwhile because the proposed regulations, in brief:

- Provide a simple uniform table (Table 12.1) to determine lifetime distributions based solely on the account holder's age (except where a spousal beneficiary is more than 10 years younger; a more favorable joint life expectancy table then applies).
- Eliminate the need to decide whether to recalculate distributions each year.
- Allow a change of beneficiaries at any time, without affecting required distributions.
- Provide that the beneficiary designation is not final until the end of the year following the date of death, thereby permitting a named beneficiary to relinquish claims to the account in favor of another beneficiary.

For the 2001 tax year, IRA owners can choose the old system or the new—although there seems to be very little reason for anyone to stick to the old system. The new proposal is so much better. Furthermore,

TABLE 12.1 Determining the Distribution Period for Lifetime Distributions

AGE	DISTRIBUTION PERIOD	AGE	DISTRIBUTION PERIOD
70	26.2	93	8.8
71	25.3	94	8.3
72	24.4	95	7.8
73	23.5	96	7.3
74	22.7	97	6.9
75	21.8	98	6.5
76	20.9	99	6.1
77	20.1	100	5.7
78	19.2	101	5.3
79	18.4	102	5.0
80	17.6	103	4.7
81	16.8	104	4.4
82	16.0	105	4.1
83	15.3	106	3.8
84	14.5	107	3.6
85	13.8	108	3.3
86	13.1	109	3.1
87	12.4	110	2.8
88	11.8	111	2.6
89	11.1	112	2.4
90	10.5	113	2.2
91	9.9	114	2.0
92	9.4	115 and older	1.8

if the final regulations differ from the proposed regulations when adopted, the Treasury Department has promised that they will not be applied retroactively.

With respect to employer-sponsored plans, however, the new regulations are not quite so simple. First, unless the plans adopt an interim amendment outlined in the new regulations, they can postpone adoption until 2002. Second, employer-sponsored plans can be more restrictive than the law allows. If your plan requires total distribution of plan assets within five years, as an example, you may want to move the account to a rollover IRA when you leave your job or retire.

NOTE

The new regulations have widespread impact:

- **Because beneficiary designations are not final until December 31 of the year after the year in which the account owner dies, some analysts believe that the new regulations may be applied to deaths in the year 2000.**
- **Required minimum distributions are smaller than they were under the old rules and can be adjusted going forward, even if you are already taking distributions under a prior schedule.**
- **If you adjust distributions going forward, be sure to talk to your tax adviser about reducing your estimated tax payments to reflect the lower distributions.**

Beneficiary Choices

If you fail to name a beneficiary, Uncle Sam could wind up with much of the money meant for your family. Don't wait. Although you aren't required to name a beneficiary until April 1 of the calendar year after you reach age 70½, you never know what may happen. It's always best to have the beneficiary designation in place. In fact, it's more important than ever under the new regulations because naming a beneficiary guarantees that distributions—and the income tax on those distributions—can be stretched out over your beneficiary's life expectancy. Without a beneficiary in place (read on, for more details), the distribution period is your remaining life expectancy.

With respect to your company plan, you probably picked a beneficiary when you first became eligible to participate. If you were married at the time, that beneficiary was your spouse. Have you changed the beneficiary designation if you divorced and remarried? Or if you divorced and have remained stubbornly single? (Division of plan assets at the time of divorce is another issue; review Chapter 10 for the ins and outs.)

If you rolled over your 401(k) into an IRA, don't assume that your beneficiary designation rolled right along with the money. You have to fill out a new form to designate the beneficiary to your IRA. That beneficiary can be anyone you like; it does not have to be your spouse.

With respect to your IRA, don't assume that the forms you filled out to open your account did the job right. First of all, the personnel at financial institutions are not necessarily trained to provide tax and legal advice. They probably couldn't fill you in on the ramifications of primary and contingent beneficiaries and the tax implications of your choice. What's more, with the pace of mergers and acquisitions in the financial services industry, many beneficiary designation forms are simply missing.

If you're rolling over a qualified plan now, read the rest of this chapter and think carefully about your beneficiary designation. If you opened an IRA a while back, ask to see the form you filled out. If it doesn't meet your current wishes or address the issue of successor beneficiaries, fill out a new form and keep a copy for your records. And if the form provided by your IRA custodian doesn't meet your needs—some, for example, don't allow naming co-beneficiaries—send a separate letter that spells out your wishes. Ask that a signed copy be returned to you for your files. If your IRA custodian balks at fulfilling your wishes, consider moving your account to another institution that will be more accommodating.

Remember: You do not technically need a beneficiary until you die or distributions begin. But, because no one knows when death will occur, you should be sure your beneficiary designation is in place. You can always change the beneficiary later, if circumstances change. Under the new regulations, a change of beneficiary will have no impact on your lifetime distributions; they will continue to be based on your own life expectancy. If you designate a beneficiary, that person will be able to continue distributions after your death, based on his or her own life expectancy. If you fail to name a beneficiary and die after your required beginning date for distributions, the person who winds up with the money will have to continue taking distributions based on your life expectancy. And if you fail to name a beneficiary and die before your required beginning date, the money will have to be completely distributed within five years.

Some people never get around to naming beneficiaries because they assume that their retirement account, like their other assets, will be distributed in accordance with the terms of their will. Not so. The plan documents override a will.

If there is no designated beneficiary on a retirement account, some custodians will direct it to a surviving spouse. That may be okay. But many custodians take the course of least resistance; they let the money wind up in your estate. If you die before your required beginning date, this is the worst possible outcome. Because an estate has no life expectancy, the money must usually be distributed—and income taxes paid—within five years of your death. This provision is the same under the old *and* the new regulations.

A second potentially costly mistake is naming your spouse as beneficiary but not naming a secondary or contingent beneficiary. Your spouse will have maximum flexibility in dealing with your account only if you think ahead and name successor beneficiaries. Let's say your spouse does not need the income and your children are secondary beneficiaries. If your spouse files a "disclaimer" within nine months of your death, the money can go to your children and be paid out over their longer life expectancies.

Try to think through all the "what if" scenarios before you designate your beneficiary. Although a spouse is automatically assumed to be the beneficiary on an employer-sponsored plan (you must both sign a waiver to name a different beneficiary or to switch from the joint-and-survivor form of payment), this is not true of an Individual Retirement Account. You may name anyone you choose as an IRA beneficiary.

There are advantages to naming your spouse as beneficiary. First, there will be no estate tax because unlimited amounts can pass to a spouse (so long as that spouse is a U.S. citizen) without estate tax. And, equally important, only a spouse can roll an inherited IRA into his or her own account and name a new beneficiary, thereby extending tax-deferred accumulations.

If you are widowed—or if you are certain that your spouse will have adequate income without tapping the IRA—you may want to name children or grandchildren as beneficiaries, to stretch out the distributions and the income tax deferral. As an example, if you are age 70 and you name your 12-year-old granddaughter as beneficiary, the balance left at your death can be paid out over the child's real life expectancy, possibly extending the distribution period by another 70 years.

If you name minor children or grandchildren as beneficiaries, you may want to set up a trust to hold the assets for them. Consult an attorney, because a boilerplate trust won't do. Complex IRS rules must be met, although things have recently gotten a tad better. Until recently, trusts had to be irrevocable by the required beginning date for distributions. This provision invalidated living trusts and credit shelter trusts that became effective at death. Now, however, the IRS has ruled that existing trusts are okay so long as they become irrevocable at the IRA owner's death. (Later in this chapter, we'll discuss leaving retirement plans to minors through trusts or through the Uniform Gifts to Minors Act or the Uniform Transfers to Minors Act of your state.)

Two other points. First, if you are naming more than one beneficiary to share in the proceeds, be sure that the institution's form confirms that they are *co-beneficiaries*, not primary and successor beneficiaries. Specify the percentage of the proceeds that each is to receive, and state what is to happen when one of them dies. Does the survivor get all of the balance? Or do the heirs of the deceased beneficiary receive his or her share? In other words, if your two married daughters are your beneficiaries and one of them dies, does the surviving sister or the children of the deceased sister get her share? Spell out your specific intent on the beneficiary designation form. If your custodian's form doesn't have room for such fine-tuning, file a detailed letter with the custodian and ask for a signed copy, acknowledging your request, for your files.

You may be able to avoid a lot of grief for your beneficiaries by splitting the IRA into equivalent parts—especially if there is a significant age difference between the beneficiaries. The oldest beneficiary's age governs distributions, and a younger beneficiary is generally forced to take the money—and pay the tax on it—faster than would otherwise be necessary.

Under the proposed regulations issued in January 2001, it is no longer technically necessary to split the IRA before your death. Because beneficiary designations are not final until the end of the year following the year of death, your beneficiaries should have ample time to split the account themselves and thereby take advantage of their individual life expectancies in calculating the distributions. If you do it beforehand, however, there will be one less paperwork chore after you are gone.

The IRS recently issued a Private Letter Ruling allowing several beneficiaries to split an inherited account and use their own ages for purposes of taking distributions. But even if it's OK (Private Letter Rulings technically apply only to the specific case in which they are issued) multiple beneficiaries on a single IRA can be an administrative headache. Your beneficiaries might prefer to manage their own money, so that they can choose investments that suit their own objectives. In any case, Seymour Goldberg, author of *J.K. Lasser's How to Protect Your Retirement Savings from the IRS*, notes that the ruling is a liberal interpretation pertaining to a single case. Until more rulings are issued, it's safer to split the IRA into separate accounts, each of which has its own beneficiary. As noted above, however, your beneficiaries can now do it themselves after you are gone.

BENEFICIARY DESIGNATIONS

Some IRA custodians offer additional choices in beneficiary designations. As an example, the Vanguard Group recently added these five choices to its beneficiary menu:

1. *Per Stirpes* divides your account equally among your children. If one of your children dies before you, that child's share is divided equally among his or her own children.
2. *Per Capita* distribution divides the IRA assets equally among your children and the offspring of any child who dies before you. If one of your three daughters dies before you, each of her children will receive a share equal to that of your other two children—effectively splitting your account not into three shares but into four shares if she had two children, five shares if she had three children, and so on.
3. *"All My Children"* is an option that divides your retirement account proceeds equally among your *surviving* children. The share that otherwise would have belonged to any sons and/or daughters who predeceased you will be divided among the surviving siblings. Nothing will go to your children's offspring.
4. *Designation with Disclaimer* has you name a primary beneficiary, an alternate beneficiary, and a secondary beneficiary. The primary beneficiary has first rights to your retirement account. The alternate beneficiary receives the money if the primary beneficiary disclaims (turns down) any or all of the proceeds. This flexible approach lets your primary beneficiary decide whether to accept the money; if it isn't needed, it might go to the next generation or to a trust you've named as the alternate beneficiary. The secondary beneficiary receives the assets only if the primary beneficiary dies before the account owner.
5. *Designation with 30-Day Contingency* means that your primary beneficiary receives the assets only if he or she survives you by at least 30 days. If not, your secondary beneficiary receives the assets—and an immediate second round of estate taxes on the same money is eliminated.

Ask the custodian of your retirement assets about beneficiary options, and keep up-to-date because the options may change over time.

The new regulations institute another significant improvement. Under the old system, I would have told you to never name a charity and a human being as co-beneficiaries to your IRA. Because a charity has no life expectancy, your human beneficiary would have had to withdraw the money and pay taxes much more quickly. Now, because the designated beneficiary is not official until the end of the year following the date of death, the charity can cash out its share before then, and the individual can then take distributions based on his or her own life expectancy.

Charitable inclinations are commendable. Strategies for donating IRAs to charity are discussed later in this chapter.

Who Gets What, When

Distributions used to be tied to beneficiary designations. Spouses were in one special category and everyone else was in another. Now, a single life expectancy table governs distributions, with one exception: spouses who are at least 10 years apart in age. If a spousal beneficiary is more than 10 years younger than the plan participant, a more favorable joint life expectancy table may be used. In every other case—no matter who your beneficiary is or when you name the beneficiary—a uniform table allows smaller minimum required distributions, over a longer period, than were heretofore possible.

The new life expectancy table accounts for longer life expectancies since the earlier tables were developed. And, as the Treasury Department states, "[It] generally eliminates the need to fix the amount of the distribution during the employee's lifetime based on the beneficiary designated on the required beginning date and eliminates the need to elect recalculation or no recalculation of life expectancies at the required beginning date."

The new table (formerly used only when a nonspouse beneficiary was 10 or more years younger than the IRA owner) makes a significant difference. An example has been provided by CPA Robert Keebler, of Green Bay, Wisconsin.

Example

Charles and his wife Helen were recalculating IRA distributions prior to Helen's death. Under the old rules, at age 75, Charles had to take distributions based on a life expectancy of 12.5 years. Under the new rules and with the new table, he can adjust his distributions—and reduce them by 40 percent—by using a life expectancy of 21.8 years.

To take the example a step further, Charles named his children as beneficiaries after Helen's death. Charles died at age 76. Under the old rules, Keebler points out, because the change in beneficiary took place after the RBD and therefore could not affect the distribution schedule, the children would have had to withdraw the entire account balance by December 31 of the year following the year of death. Under the new rules, the beneficiaries can take distributions over their life expectancies.

Under-Age Beneficiaries

When you have named a beneficiary who is not yet of legal age, you may want to have distributions after your death payable to either a trust or a custodial account, under the Uniform Gifts to Minors Act (UGMA) or Uniform Transfers to Minors Act (UTMA) of your state. UGMA and UTMA accounts are essentially the same, although the newer UTMA accounts are more flexible.

Many parents customarily use UGMA or UTMA accounts to hold money intended for minor children, but these may not be the best vehicles for future distributions from a tax-sheltered retirement plan. As Seymour Goldberg explains, you must first find out whether your state permits a custodian to receive IRA distributions.

Because money in a custodial account legally belongs to the child when he or she becomes an adult (typically either 18 or 21, depending on state law), a trust may be preferable where sizable sums of money are involved. The trust must be irrevocable—or, under a recent IRS ruling, must become irrevocable at the date of the IRA owner's death. But even though the trust is irrevocable, you are still able to change the beneficiary designation on your IRA.

When you establish a trust, you select the trustee or trustees who will manage the trust assets. The trust document can include specific instructions to the trustees, but it is generally better to choose trustees carefully and then let them exercise their best judgment in investing and distributing trust proceeds to the beneficiaries. Elizabeth Mathieu, president and CEO of Neuberger Berman Trust Company, cautions against "inflexible trusts, documents that do not allow trustees to administer the trust in light of the beneficiary's current situation."

You might want to name co-trustees—a corporate trustee to handle the administrative chores associated with a trust, and a family member or close friend to carry out your wishes. The beneficiaries can become trustees when they are of legal age, or, if you choose, at a later date. A grandparent might decide, as an example, that a grandchild can become a trustee at the age of 35. You can also incorporate, in the trust document, language that makes it easy to change trustees.

The new regulations incorporate one change concerning trusts as IRA beneficiaries: Trust documents or a complete list of the trust's beneficiaries must still be filed with the IRS—but not until the end of the year following the year in which the IRA owner dies. This is the date for final determination of designated beneficiaries.

If You Are the Beneficiary

Everything said so far also applies when you are the beneficiary. However, because 401(k) plans may be more restrictive than federal law permits, you must look at the plan itself to determine what rules apply in your situation. If the money has already been rolled into an IRA by the owner, you may have other options. But, because the clerks at banks, mutual funds, and brokerage houses are generally not thoroughly trained in the legal intricacies of IRA distributions, you may receive bad advice. To put it mildly, there are some minefields along the way. Be alert for these situations:

- You inherit your spouse's 401(k) plan and would like to leave the account intact, delaying the taxes that will be due. Although federal regulations permit this arrangement, the plan document may say otherwise. The plan document governs. If you do have to take the money, there is one saving grace: The money will be subject to federal, state, and local income tax where applicable, but, even if you are under age 59½, it will not be subject to the 10 percent tax penalty for early withdrawal.
- You inherit your father's IRA and are told that you should open a rollover IRA in your name. Big mistake. Only a surviving spouse can roll an inherited IRA into his or her own name. If you put your name on this IRA, you will convert it into a taxable distribution. You can open a rollover IRA but the account must be in your father's name, with some version of this label: "IRA of [name of original owner], deceased [date of death], for the benefit of [your name] as beneficiary." There has been some discussion among legal eagles as to whether the account should then bear your Social Security number or your father's. Some say you

should retain the original owner's Social Security number, to clearly identify the account as inherited. Other suggest using your own number because using a deceased individual's Social Security number may set off alarms at the IRS and trigger an audit. Rotenberg has an additional reason for using your own number: "If you don't use the new beneficiary's Social Security number, the IRS has no way of matching it up. The deceased's Social Security number will disappear, so using it will give you grief."

- You inherit your husband's IRA. Now you can open a rollover IRA in your own name, and you may want to do so in order to name your own beneficiary. However, if you are not yet age 59½ and you need the money, a better idea might be to leave the account in your husband's name. You can then take withdrawals at any time, as a beneficiary, and avoid the 10 percent tax penalty on withdrawals from your own account before age 59½.
- You inherit a sizable IRA from your father, and an accountant says you must take all the money within five years after his death. Not necessarily. If you were designated as the beneficiary, you can spread the distributions over your own life expectancy, no matter when your father died. However, if you were not designated as beneficiary and your father died before his required beginning date, the five-year rule applies.
- You inherit your mother's $1.1 million IRA. Her estate paid $450,000 in federal estate taxes, and no one told you that the entire amount could be deducted from your income taxes. This is a common error because the tax break known as "income in respect of decedent" (IRD) is not well known even among professional advisers. (More on this important deduction later in this chapter.)

Donating an IRA to Charity

If you're charitably inclined—and, of course, if you don't need the money for your retirement—you and your heirs can come out way ahead if you leave your IRA to charity.

Unfortunately, the gift must be linked to your death. There's no way to give away tax-qualified retirement money during life without triggering a tax hit. (Legislative proposals, if enacted, may make it possible in the future.) There's no way to make a direct transfer, so you would first have to withdraw the money and pay income tax on the full amount (plus tax penalties if you are not yet age 59½), and then make the gift.

After death, however, a charitable bequest can be a perfect way to save on taxes. Remember that all the money in your IRA is subject to income tax. It also counts toward calculating your estate for federal estate tax purposes. The combination of income taxes (at rates ranging from 15 percent to 39.6 percent) and estate taxes (at rates ranging from 37 percent to 55 percent) can eat up three-quarters of the money that would otherwise go to your family.

Any assets you leave to your family are potentially subject to estate tax. The amount excluded from your taxable estate, pending possible repeal of the federal estate tax or change in the amounts excluded, ranges from $675,000 in 2000 to $1 million in 2006 and thereafter. With many people holding accumulated tax-qualified retirement funds in the high six figures, more and more estates are subject to estate tax.

A possible tax-saving strategy entails leaving money in retirement plans to charity, and assets other than tax-sheltered retirement accounts to your family. There are two good reasons for doing so:

1. There will be no income tax or estate tax on IRA assets left to charity, so, potentially, your family could save considerable sums.
2. Assets other than retirement accounts receive a "step-up in basis" at death. This means that the assets are valued as of the date of death for capital gains purposes; subsequent sales are taxed only on any appreciation in value between the date of death and the date of sale.

Assets within tax-qualified retirement accounts don't receive a step-up in basis and are not taxed at the lower capital gains rate; instead, they are fully taxable at ordinary income tax rates.

But don't use your will to fund a charitable bequest with the IRA. Because your will is irrelevant where the disposal of your IRA is concerned, that's the exact equivalent of taking the money out, paying the tax on it, and then making the bequest. The only governing document is the beneficiary designation form on file with the IRA custodian. In the absence of a designation (or if the form is missing), your IRA will go to the default beneficiary—either your estate or your spouse—designated by the custodian. As noted above, your estate is the worst possible beneficiary. Don't let this happen.

If you decide to leave an IRA to charity, you have more than one option:

- Leave it outright, by naming the charity as beneficiary. The downside of this approach under the old rules was that, because a charity is not a person and therefore has no life expectancy, you would have had to take larger distributions during your lifetime based on your individual life expectancy. You would also have owed income tax on those distributions, so that, in the end, not much was left for the charity. Under the new regulations, smaller lifetime distributions are based on your own life expectancy, regardless of who or what is named as beneficiary.
- Name your spouse as the primary beneficiary; name the charity as the contingent beneficiary. Then ask your spouse to disclaim the IRA at your death so that it goes directly to the charity when you die. (A disclaimer has the same effect as the death of the primary beneficiary; the bequest goes to the named contingent or secondary beneficiary.) This approach preserves flexibility. If circumstances should change so that your spouse needs the money, failing to exercise the disclaimer will keep the money in the family.
- Establish a charitable remainder trust so that income from the trust goes to your family and the remaining principal goes to the charity you've designated. You may want to consider this approach with an IRA you inherit from your spouse because, as Boston attorney Natalie Choate points out, "The critical time in terms of taxes is when a surviving spouse dies." There is, as noted earlier, no federal estate tax on assets passing from one spouse to the other. But all the assets (less the amount excluded under federal law) are then subject to estate tax when the second spouse dies.
- Establish a charitable remainder trust with employer stock from your retirement plan. If you hold such stock, as discussed in Chapter 11, you can pay income tax only on the cost basis (and not on the full appreciated value) if you take the stock out of the plan when you leave a job, instead of rolling it over into an IRA. Marvin Rotenberg, national director of retirement services for

> Fleet Bank's Private Clients Group in Boston, notes that "if the basis is low enough, the tax deduction for putting the stock into the trust will offset the income tax. You can take the stock out of the 401(k) plan and put it into a charitable remainder trust with no economic detriment."

When you designate a charity as a direct beneficiary of your IRA, there is a deduction for the entire amount. When you place the account in a charitable remainder trust, the deduction is limited to the actuarial value based on the age of the income beneficiary. Because this area of tax law is so complex, and laws and regulations change so frequently, this is definitely an area to check with a knowledgeable adviser.

Estate Planning: Wills and Trusts

Although this book focuses on 401(k) plans, I hope I've made clear by now that you should never look at your tax-qualified retirement plans in isolation. They are very much a part of your overall financial planning and investment planning, and they must be considered an integral part of your estate planning as well. In fact, because required withdrawals are smaller under the new regulations, more money can be left to your heirs. Estate planning therefore becomes all the more important.

With the new regulations, you can preserve tax deferral and—if you don't need the money—leave more of your retirement savings for your children. But I'm sure you've seen the tongue-in-cheek bumper sticker, "I'm spending my children's inheritance." It's meant to be humorous, but folks who want to avoid the double hit of income and estate taxes on retirement accounts often try to spend the money while they're alive, and to leave other assets for their children and grandchildren. If you have the luxury of deciding which funds to spend first, you may want to consult a financial adviser about the approach that best fits your personal circumstances.

The only retirement account that doesn't fit the standard pattern is the Roth IRA. The Roth (described in Chapter 3) is like other IRAs in many respects, but has some distinct advantages for estate planning. First, because contributions are after-tax, no income tax is due on distributions. Second, there is no required beginning date. You can leave an entire Roth IRA, with its tax-free growth, in place for your grandchildren.

With respect to other qualified plans and your other assets, there is one significant difference. Most assets can be disposed of in your will. But jointly owned assets, which have a right of survivorship, go to the survivor. And qualified plans (along with life insurance and annuities) go to the designated beneficiary. Name that beneficiary!

Many people of means jump through hoops to keep assets out of their will, in an effort to avoid the cost and nuisance of probate. I have two brief comments on this practice:

1. Probate, in most states, is not the demon it's made out to be. Even where it's a chore, avoiding probate does not save either estate taxes or the cost of administering an estate.
2. Under some circumstances, probate may actually be desirable. As attorney Jason Goldberg writes, in *Ed Slott's IRA Advisor*, "If there are no assets to go through probate, who pays the estate tax?" Without a probate estate—the normal source of any estate tax that is due—the IRS will go after the beneficiaries and/or the money in the IRA. If the beneficiaries squabble over paying the tax, there may be extra legal fees and there will certainly be hard feelings. If the money must be withdrawn from the IRA, it will immediately be subject to tax, and the family loses out in the long run.

So, even if you arrange your affairs so that many assets do pass outside of a will, you may want to leave enough in your probate estate to pay estate taxes, professionals' fees, and other final expenses. Remember, even with designated beneficiaries to some assets and joint ownership of others, you still need a will to dispose of personal property and, for that matter, an accident settlement that might be due your estate after your death.

An Integrated Tax

The federal estate tax is actually an integrated gift and estate tax. In 2001, each taxpayer may exclude $675,000 from this integrated tax, and, under current law, the excluded amount will rise gradually (see Table 12.2) to $1 million in 2006 and thereafter. For a married couple, the current exclusion is $1,350,000. While these may be sizable sums, many Americans are worth more dead than alive. Add up the value of your home, life insurance, and retirement benefits, and you may be surprised at just how much you're worth.

TABLE 12.2 Amounts Excluded from the Integrated Gift and Estate Tax

YEAR	EXCLUDED AMOUNT
2000	$ 675,000
2001	675,000
2002	700,000
2003	700,000
2004	850,000
2005	950,000
2006 and later	1,000,000

There is no estate tax on assets left to a surviving spouse, so long as that spouse is a United States citizen. Assets left to noncitizens are subject to the same estate tax exclusions as assets left to nonspouses. But the fact that no estate tax is due on the first spouse's death doesn't mean that it's wise to simply leave everything to your spouse in what lawyers call a "sweetheart will." Doing so, if you have assets above the estate tax exclusion, will subject the combined estate to estate tax when the second spouse dies. The tax will then hit earnings on the assets in the intervening years.

One tried-and-true strategy to reduce the estate tax is giving money away during life. You are allowed to give up to $10,000 per year to each of as many people as you like and no gift tax is required. If your spouse consents, you can jointly give up to $20,000 per year. A couple with two children can effectively remove $200,000 from their taxable estates over a 10-year period. Add in daughters- and sons-in-law, along with grandchildren, and you can give away much more. Two caveats here:

1. Don't give away money you may need. Minimizing taxes should never be your overriding concern.
2. Keep annual gifts to slightly under the $10,000 ceiling, to make room for birthday and holiday gifts.

In addition to these gifts, you may give unlimited amounts by writing checks directly to educational or medical institutions. This can be a good way to pay a grandchild's college tuition or cover the cost of straightening teeth, while simultaneously removing the cash from your taxable estate.

Giving larger sums brings gift tax into play. The tax doesn't have to be paid until the total of all your lifetime gifts exceeds the integrated gift and estate tax exclusion, but a gift tax return will have to be filed so that the IRS can start keeping a running tally of your gifts. Giving larger sums may still be a sensible move, if you don't need the money, because even though the gift and estate tax is "integrated," a quirk in the law makes it less expensive to pay the tax during life than after death.

This is confusing, so bear with me. Estate and trusts attorneys explain that the gift tax is "exclusive" and the estate tax is "inclusive." In plain English: the gift tax is paid out of the amount you give; the estate tax is levied on top of the amount you leave. In a classic example involving $1 million, a lifetime gift of this amount, taxed at 50 percent, leaves about $667,000 for the objects of your generosity because the tax is half that amount or about $333,000. Leave the same amount in your will and Uncle Sam gets half—$500,000—while your heirs receive the same amount. Your children get more if you give them the money during life. And there's a double bonus: You not only remove the gift itself (and future appreciation on the gift) from your taxable estate, but you may get to see how they put the money to good use—and enjoy their thanks—while you're still around.

Trusts

Another tried-and-true way for married couples to reduce the eventual estate tax on their combined estates is through the use of a credit shelter or bypass trust. A trust—any trust—is simply a three-party agreement in which the owner of property (the donor, settlor, or grantor) transfers ownership to someone else (the trustee) for the benefit of one or more third parties (the beneficiary or beneficiaries).

Bypass or credit-shelter trusts let a married couple shelter twice the amount excluded from federal estate tax. You simply set up a trust to receive up to the excluded amount when the first partner dies. The survivor can receive the income from the trust and can invade the principal up to a limited amount, but the remaining principal goes directly to the children when he or she dies, without being subject to estate tax. You can set up a bypass or credit-shelter trust in your will; it does not require a separate trust document. You should consider using this form of trust if your combined assets exceed twice the current federal estate tax exclusion. (In 2001, that amount is $1,350,000.)

A bypass trust won't work, however, if all of your assets are jointly owned or if most of them are owned by one of you. For the trusts to be effective, you should each separately own assets in the amount excluded from federal estate tax. This poses a significant problem where the bulk of the assets are in a tax-qualified retirement plan. Ownership of those assets cannot be transferred without creating a distribution and an income tax liability. Seymour Goldberg suggests that, if your spouse will have enough money to live on, you can establish two IRAs with one payable to her and one to your children. That would at least remove, from your spouse's taxable estate, the amounts paid to your children.

Be cautious about using assets in a qualified plan to fund a bypass trust under your will. Although technically possible, this tactic calls for advice from someone knowledgeable about the intricacies of both trust law and qualified plans. Otherwise, you run the serious risk of disqualifying the plan or losing sizable sums to income tax.

Life insurance is often used to cover estate taxes that may be due—especially if it would otherwise be necessary for your heirs to tap an IRA to pay the estate tax, thereby triggering income tax. Now that the new regulations make it possible to leave more retirement money to your family, in fact, you may want to increase the amount of life insurance you carry. You can keep life insurance proceeds out of your taxable estate by having the life insurance policy owned by either a responsible adult child or an irrevocable trust. There's just one trick element here: You must live at least three years after a new policy is taken out or an existing policy is transferred, or the proceeds will be back in your taxable estate.

Because transferring ownership of an existing cash value policy may trigger a gift tax, most advisers suggest taking out a new policy. You can give the money to cover the annual premium to your child or to the trust. But be sure that you don't retain any "incidents of ownership," such as the right to change the beneficiary, or the policy will still be in your taxable estate. Also stay away from what insurance expert Lee Slavutin calls the "unholy trio" of a three-part arrangement. If your spouse owns a policy on your life, with your child as beneficiary, the death benefit will be a taxable gift from your surviving spouse to your child.

Cutting the Tax Bill

If, despite your best efforts, your retirement funds wind up subject to both income tax and estate tax, there is one ray of light. As "income in respect of a decedent" (IRD), an income tax deduction can be claimed for the amount of estate tax attributable to the IRA. Again thanks to Seymour Goldberg, here is an example: If a federal estate tax of 40 percent is due, a beneficiary who withdraws $30,000 from a $100,000 IRA to pay the tax is entitled to an itemized income tax deduction of 40 percent of the distribution, or $12,000. The deduction can be carried forward to subsequent years, until the total of $40,000 is reached. Then the estate tax on the IRA will be completely offset and no further deduction may be claimed. (Note, though, that the deduction is lost unless an itemized federal income tax return is filed.)

Two points with respect to this deduction:

1. It may be taken only by beneficiaries other than spouses because surviving spouses do not owe estate tax.
2. Although the deduction is designed to avoid double taxation on the same money, many accountants and attorneys are not familiar with the concept of IRD. You may have to be on your toes to be sure that you don't miss out on this valuable deduction.

CHAPTER 13

Finding Help

After reading this book and consulting additional resources in Appendix B, you may not have all the answers when it comes to planning your retirement income, but you will definitely know the right questions to ask. That means that you can save time, and therefore money, when dealing with a financial adviser. It also means that you can stay in the driver's seat in making decisions—as you should, because no one, ever, cares as much about your money as you do.

Many retirement issues, as we've seen, are very complex. Which investments are right for you? How can you best integrate your investment portfolio, inside and outside your tax-sheltered plans, to suit your personal goals? What method of distribution should you elect when it is time to take the money out? How can you, if appropriate, pass the money on to your children and grandchildren with a minimum tax bite?

Professional advice may be essential. If it is, the best time to seek that advice is before you reach your required beginning date under any employer-sponsored or individual tax-qualified plans. You may want to consult an accountant, a financial planner, an investment manager, and/or an attorney who specializes in estate planning.

Choosing a competent knowledgeable professional is key to getting the right answers. Despite recent simplification, the laws surrounding distributions from tax-qualified plans are as complicated as any legislation ever drafted by Congress. This means that many accountants, financial planners, and attorneys, while skilled in their areas of specialization, can make critical mistakes when it comes to taking money out of retirement plans. Those mistakes can cost you and your beneficiaries sizable sums in the form of taxes and tax penalties.

Financial Advisers Come in All Sizes and Shapes

You may want an accountant to help you with the financial decisions accompanying retirement as well as preparing income tax returns. You may want an attorney to help you with estate planning, especially when it comes to the actual drafting of wills and trusts. You may need an insurance agent to tailor the life insurance that can complement your estate plan or provide ongoing income for surviving loved ones. You may want to use an investment adviser to manage your investment portfolio. And you may want the advice of a financial planner to coordinate the separate pieces of advice and pull the whole team together.

Financial Planners

Often working as part of a team with your accountant, attorney, and insurance agent, a financial planner can make suggestions and help you develop and implement a comprehensive financial plan. A good financial planner understands the role of your qualified retirement plans in your overall financial life. A better financial planner knows the complex rules governing retirement plan distributions and beneficiaries or will bring in a specialist to help you with making decisions in this critical area.

Some financial planners work on commission, charging you little or nothing directly but earning their compensation in the form of commissions on the products they sell you to implement the plan they recommend. Commission-based planners can serve you well but they also have a built-in potential for conflict of interest, since the financial products paying the highest commission may not be the products that are most appropriate for you. In addition, when a planner also manages investments for you, commissions may be an incentive for more frequent trades than might be prudent.

Fee-only planners do not earn commissions. Instead they charge flat fees either for an entire plan or on an hourly basis. While a flat fee is often fairly steep, running to several thousand dollars, it may cost less in the long run than commission-based services.

Some planners, confusingly called fee-based, use a combination of commissions and fees. These planners may charge a nominal fee for the plan itself and then charge commissions on the products they sell.

According to the Certified Financial Planner Board of Standards—the organization that confers the CFP designation—there are several critical steps involved in the financial planning process, including:

1. Establishing and defining your relationship. After an introductory meeting, which is often free of charge, the planner should clearly explain the services to be provided and make his or her compensation clear.
2. Gathering data, including goals. The planner should ask for detailed information or have you fill out a questionnaire with

FINANCIAL PLANNERS

Financial planners are unregulated. Anyone can hang out a shingle. To find a reputable planner, contact one of these organizations:

- **National Association of Personal Financial Advisors (NAPFA), representing fee-only planners, at 888-FEE-ONLY (1-888-333-6659) or www.napfa.org.**
- **American Institute of Certified Public Accountants, for CPAs who are Personal Financial Specialists, at 1-888-999-9256 or www.aicpa.org.**
- **The Financial Planning Association, formed by the recent merger of the Institute of Certified Financial Planners and the International Association for Financial Planning, confers the Certified Financial Planner designation for planners who have passed a series of rigorous exams. Referrals to planners in your area may be obtained by calling 1-800-282-7526 or www.fpanet.org.**
- **The Society of Financial Service Professionals, formerly the American Society of CLUs and ChFCs, represents financial professionals specializing in insurance and may be reached at 1-888-243-2258 or www.financialpro.org.**

details of your assets, liabilities, and—as important—your short-term and long-term financial goals. After reviewing relevant information, the planner should help you to define and prioritize your goals and assess your risk tolerance and time horizon.

3. Analyzing and evaluating your financial status. The planner should analyze and evaluate the information you've provided to determine whether or not your goals are realistic.
4. Developing and presenting specific recommendations. You should receive suggestions in line with your situation and tailored to meet your specific goals. The recommendations should be clearly communicated to you so that you can make informed decisions.
5. Implementing the recommendations. Once you agree on which recommendations to follow, will the planner provide the products and services to implement the recommendations? Or will the planner refer you to other professionals, such as attorneys, insurance agents, and stockbrokers?
6. Monitoring the recommendations. If you've agreed to an ongoing relationship, the planner should review and evaluate changing circumstances and make new recommendations as appropriate.

Investment Managers

Some financial planners, stockbrokers, and accountants run investment portfolios for their clients. If you have substantial assets, however, you may want an independent investment manager who will work closely with your other advisers. Many require a minimum level of investment dollars before taking on a client. The minimum might be $100,000 or it might be $1 million. In selecting an investment manager, find out where you would fit in his or her client base. If most clients have smaller portfolios, expertise might be limited in areas where you need advice. If most have much larger portfolios, you may not get much attention.

If you delegate asset management, you can expect to pay a percentage of the assets under management. The idea behind this payment arrangement is that it puts you and the asset manager on the same team by linking compensation to performance. As you make more money in the market, so does the manager. That's good—but watch those percentages. You may pay as little as 0.65 percent ($650 per $100,000 under management) or as much as 3 percent ($3,000 per $100,000). Most asset-based fees average about 1 percent, a bit more on small portfolios and a bit less on large ones. This may not sound like much, but be sure to translate it into dollars. On a $500,000 portfolio, a 1 percent fee will cost you $5,000 a year.

This arrangement contrasts with the typical compensation received by stockbrokers, who make money only when you buy and sell securities. While most stockbrokers are honest, there is a conflict of interest in this scenario between your objectives (to make money on performance while keeping transaction costs down) and the broker's self interest (to boost his or her own compensation through more trades).

When using an investment manager, however, the percentage of assets under management is not the only cost. In addition, you will pay commissions on transactions if you purchase individual securities and annual management fees if you invest through mutual funds. Always ask exactly what costs to expect before you link up with any financial adviser.

Anyone who manages money must be a Registered Investment Adviser. The RIA designation does not mean that the individual possesses any special credentials or has received any special education. All it means is that he or she has registered with the Securities and Exchange Commission and filed an information form called the ADV. When you sign up with an investment manager, you should be given a copy of the ADV form. It will indicate the manager's training, affiliations, and compensation arrangements.

Part One of the ADV provides detailed information about the applicant's background, including any disciplinary actions by federal and state regulatory agencies, self-regulatory organizations such as the AICPA or FPA, and civil or criminal sanctions. Part Two describes the applicant's education, types of service offered, and method of compensation.

Most investment managers want discretionary authority over your portfolio so that they can buy and sell securities without consulting you on each transaction. Be very careful before granting discretionary authority to anyone. If you decide to do so, discuss your objectives and tolerance for risk with the adviser. Set forth exactly what you want, then monitor your statements very carefully. If you see excessive trading, or purchases of securities too risky for your taste, cancel the arrangement.

Before you select a money manager, you'll want to review performance of current accounts. Be careful here. There are a number of ways performance can be presented, but so-called "model" accounts may not reflect an accurate picture. Ask to see actual accounts, without client names. And ask to see performance over a complete market cycle, including periods when the market as a whole has been in decline. Anyone can make money in a bull market, and many advisers will be happy to show you bull-market performance records, but it takes real skill to hold steady in a prolonged bear market. As of this writing, it's been so long since a sustained downturn that many of today's money managers have never seen one.

Questions to ask a money manager (in addition to those you should ask of any financial adviser; see pages 249–251):

- Do you report portfolio returns after excluding fees and expenses?
- Are transaction commissions included in your management fee? If not, do you offer clients a discounted rate?
- Do you make the trading decisions? If not, who else is involved?
- Do you tailor a portfolio to each individual client? Or do you use essentially the same portfolio for all your clients?
- Do you tend to develop an appropriate asset allocation for each client, then buy and hold securities for the long term? Or do you frequently adjust portfolios based on current conditions?
- How many securities do you hold in a typical account? How often do you trade those securities? The frequency of trades is called turnover; a high level of turnover is expensive.
- Do you consider the tax consequences of selling securities? What proportion of your capital gains are long term?
- What is your goal for investment returns? How do you adjust that goal when the broad market is flat or down?

NOTE

Professional advisers may bill for their services in a variety of ways, including

- **By the hour or day, typical of accountants, attorneys, and fee-based financial planners.**
- **By commissions, as is the case with stockbrokers and some financial planners.**
- **By the project; a financial planner might charge a set fee for a comprehensive financial plan.**
- **As a percentage of assets under management, typical of investment managers.**

- What was your biggest investment mistake? What would you do in the same situation today?
- Do you send confirmations of each transaction, monthly statements, and quarterly reports? Are the reports easily read and understood (ask for samples)? How often will you sit down with me to review my account? Will you respond to telephone queries without delay?

Making Your Choice

As you select your advisers, bear in mind that many financial advisers develop a special area of expertise. If you want an accountant to do more than prepare tax returns, to help you with retirement and estate planning, you may want to select a CPA who is designated as a Personal Financial Specialist. If you want an attorney to prepare a comprehensive estate plan or advise you on the tax consequences of withdrawing money from a tax-sheltered retirement plan, don't go to a divorce lawyer or one who specializes in corporate bankruptcy.

Start your search by securing referrals from friends and colleagues, but be aware that they may not be able to adequately evaluate professional competence. As Harold Evensky, a noted financial planner and wealth manager in Coral Gables, Florida, has stated, con artists are very good at persuading people of their financial skill; the persuasion sometimes lasts until the money is gone. So get personal suggestions but check them out with your other professional advisers. Be careful here, too, because financial advisers may refer clients to each other in the hope of building their own client list. There's nothing wrong with this, especially if the referrals are of competent people, but you should be told if anything else is involved. Be aware of possible conflicts of interest.

Then interview several people, asking each:

- What is your professional training? How do you stay up-to-date with new tax laws and other developments in your field? (Appropriate answers include seminars, continuing education, in-service training, reading professional literature, belonging to professional organizations.)
- What licenses, certifications, and/or registrations do you have? (The appropriate answer will vary with the specialty but most professionals, with the exception of financial planners, have

some sort of license to practice. Financial planners are not licensed but the best have passed stiff exams qualifying them as Certified Financial Planners or Personal Financial Specialists.)

- Have you ever been censured, suspended, or reprimanded for your business practices? (Understandably, advisers may be reluctant to reveal this information. Before finalizing your choice, you should contact the regulatory agency in the specific field for information.)
- How long have you been offering financial advice? How many clients do you currently have? Are those clients similar to me in income, assets, and life situation? (If you own a small business, as an example, you may want an adviser familiar with the nuances of a business owner's financial, retirement, and estate planning needs.)
- Will you provide me with names of current and past clients I can talk to? (An adviser may wish to check with clients before releasing their names—indeed, should do so—but should be able to get back to you with the names of several people willing to be interviewed.)
- Can you tell me about a tough problem you solved for another client? (The adviser's approach to the problem should let you see his or her thought processes and help you determine your comfort level in working with this adviser.)
- May I see a sample of work you've done for other clients? (Names and identifying details should be concealed, to protect client confidentiality—you would never want to deal with an adviser who would make your affairs public—but you should be able to see a sample financial plan, investment report, or estate plan.)
- Do you sell financial products as well as financial services? If I buy a particular product that you recommend, will you tell me exactly how you will be compensated for that purchase? (You may not object if your adviser sells products, but full disclosure is always a good idea.)
- If you recommend financial products or services from other providers, do you have a business affiliation with any of those providers? Do you receive a referral fee or commission for your recommendations?

- Will you tell me if you disagree with something other advisers have recommended? Or if you find errors in any of their work? (A reluctance to do so may indicate a reliance on referrals—or, worse yet, fees—from the other advisers and a reluctance to antagonize them.)
- Will you be the only person working with me? (If not, you may want to meet other staff members and find out about their experience and areas of expertise. You may also want to know if the same hourly fee—if your arrangement is on an hourly basis—is charged for every staff member.)
- Will you put our fee arrangement in writing, including exactly what services are provided for the specified fee, what extras I can reasonably expect, and when fees are to be paid? Will your bills be itemized, so that they can be clearly understood? (Stay away from anyone who won't answer these questions or doesn't give satisfactory answers.)
- What is your attitude toward risk? (Will an investment manager take more risk than you are comfortable with? Will an accountant chance an audit by taking an aggressive position that you'd rather not take? It's reasonable to argue that you can reap more rewards by taking more risk, but you also need to be able to sleep at night.)
- Do your clients earn an income similar to mine? Have similar concerns? (A financial adviser may pay little attention to you if most other clients have far more to spend. And an adviser may not have the right answers to your questions if no one has asked similar questions before.)
- What happens if either of us severs the relationship? How much notice is required? Will there be fees? Will assets be transferred promptly?
- Do you belong to professional organizations in your field? (Most such organizations—including the AICPA, the American Bar Association, and the financial planning associations—have codes of ethics and disciplinary procedures. They also require continuing education for their members.)

Be sure to ask the same questions of every adviser you interview. It's the only way to make a valid comparison. You'll find a useful set of worksheets for evaluating advisers in a free booklet from the

CHECKING DISCIPLINARY HISTORY

Check the disciplinary history of financial advisers by contacting:

- The Certified Financial Planner Board of Standards (CFP Board), at 1-888-CFP-MARK or www.CFP-Board.org, to find out whether any disciplinary action has been taken against a CFP or to lodge a complaint if you believe a CFP has acted unethically.
- The National Association of Insurance Commissioners (NAIC), at 1-816-842-3600 or www.naic.org, for direction to state insurance commissioners who can check to see if an insurance agent has any violations or if a financial planner is licensed to sell insurance.
- The North American Securities Administrators Association (NASAA), 1-888-84-NASAA (888-846-2722), for referrals to state securities regulators who keep disciplinary records of advisers licensed to sell securities.
- The National Association of Securities Dealers (NASD), 1-800-289-9999, www.nasdr.com, for the disciplinary history of registered representatives and broker-dealers in your area.
- The Securities and Exchange Commission, 1-800-732-0330 or www.sec.gov, to find information about a particular individual or firm providing securities and investment services, or to lodge a complaint against a financial adviser.
- The Financial Planning Association, 1-888-237-6275, www.fpanet.org.
- The National Fraud Exchange (NAFEX), 1-800-822-0416, X33, for a "one-stop" background check on securities brokers, financial planners, real estate agents, trust advisers, mortgage officers, and financial advisers of all kinds. The other services are free but NAFEX charges a fee of $39 for the first individual checked and $20 per additional person.

Vanguard Group; call 1-800-414-5546 and ask for "How to Select a Financial Adviser."

A Cautionary Note

One thing you want from a professional adviser, above all else, is objective advice. Yet more and more professional advisers are urging products and services on their unsuspecting clients. The advisers are lured by the promise of big fees, but you may find yourself caught by a serious conflict of interest. Can an adviser objectively represent your best interests while earning referral fees and commissions?

Ralph Engel, a partner with the law firm of Rosen & Reade in New York, doesn't think so. "How is it possible," he asks, "for a person supposed to be an independent financial adviser to be independent if in fact he is selling a product at a profit?"

Engel is disturbed by a flurry of e-mails directed at his law firm, soliciting client referrals for asset management services. One such message offers the opportunity for "attorneys to simply leverage existing client relationships into more fee revenue." Another offers "a generous, ongoing percentage of the portfolio management fee of all accounts that would be referred to us."

Not all advisers are following this practice. About half of the midsized accounting firms surveyed by Neuwirth Research in 2000 have a policy against receiving compensation for referrals, believing it to be unethical or a conflict of interest. Yet a growing number of accountants see no problem in accepting referral fees from brokerage firms and insurance agents. Others are taking a giant step toward generating even more revenue by becoming registered investment advisers so that they can earn commissions by selling mutual funds and variable annuities. This direct product selling is expected to become even more prevalent in the next few years.

Commissions for accountants used to be prohibited by state law but, in a rapid turnaround, at least 40 states now permit commissions. The American Institute of Certified Public Accountants (AICPA) reversed its prohibition in 1991 in an effort to help accountants remain competitive with other financial advisers. To overcome concerns among some CPAs about potential liability, the professional insurance offered to accountants through the AICPA now covers claims arising out of the promotion, sale, or solicitation for the sale of securities. Optional endorsements provide coverage for acts as a broker/dealer or insurance agent.

So the adviser may be protected. But what about the client? Codes of ethics promulgated by the professional organizations can lead to loss of accreditation if violated. But it's still up to you to protect yourself by choosing advisers carefully and monitoring their performance.

Accountants are only one among many professions when it comes to potential conflicts of interest. Commission-based financial planners have always sold products and services to their clients. But the trend toward planners becoming asset managers in return for a percentage of the assets under management is relatively new and—in some circles—disturbing. The questions is, will a planner who is concentrating on running an investment portfolio devote enough time to a comprehensive financial plan?

On the legal eagle side, the American Bar Association (ABA) has a rule expressly prohibiting any division of fees between lawyers and nonlawyers. A spokesman for the ABA says such a system divides the allegiance of lawyers between the client and the partner and is "unacceptable." But the ABA position does not deter Web-based pushers of referral fees. And it does not ensure that you'll know what's going on. Disclosure is recommended, but you should ask.

Across the board, with every financial professional, the issue is disclosure. Whether commissions and referral fees are right or wrong, you have a right to know how your adviser is paid and whether there is a potential conflict of interest. You may find it convenient to do one-stop shopping for all your financial needs through a trusted accountant, attorney, or financial planner. But you should be told, and you should ask, if your adviser is being compensated for referring you to a provider or if he or she is receiving a commission on the sale of a product.

Appendix A
Glossary

Active management. Portfolio management that seeks to exceed the returns of the financial markets by using research and individual judgment in making investment decisions.

After-tax contributions. 401(k) contributions made from salary on which taxes have already been paid. Unlike before-tax contributions made through salary deferral, after-tax contributions are not taxable when they are withdrawn.

Alternate payee. Someone other than the plan participant, often a spouse, who has the right under a Qualified Domestic Relations Order to receive all or some of the participant's plan benefits.

Annuitant. An individual receiving regular periodic payments from an annuity.

Annuity. A stream of regular payments, typically from a retirement plan or an annuity policy issued by an insurance company.

Asset allocation. An investment strategy involving a balance among different types of investment vehicles.

Automatic enrollment. The practice of automatically including employees in an employer-sponsored retirement plan. The size of the contribution and how it is invested are initially determined by the plan sponsor but can be changed by the participant.

Basis points. One percentage point is divided into 100 basis points. For example, 25 basis points equals one-quarter of a percentage point.

Benchmark. Another term for an index; an unmanaged group of securities whose performance is used as a standard to measure investment performance.

Beneficiary. The person named to receive the proceeds from a financial instrument such as a retirement plan or life insurance contract.

Bequest. Property left to an heir under the terms of a will.

Bond. A debt instrument issued by a corporation or government agency; the issuer typically pays periodic interest and promises to return the principal at maturity.

Bond fund. A mutual fund with holdings that consist primarily of bonds.

Capital gain/loss. Profits or losses from the sale of invested assets, based on the difference between the purchase price (cost basis) and the sale price.

Capital gain distribution. Profits distributed by mutual funds to shareholders, based on sales of assets within the fund. Capital gains are distributed after subtracting any capital losses for the year.

Cash equivalents. Liquid investments, such as money market mutual funds or certificates of deposit, that can be quickly converted to cash.

Cash-out. The distribution of assets from a plan, prior to retirement. A cash-out typically occurs when a participant has a balance under $5,000 and leaves the company. Cash-outs are subject to federal income tax and, if the participant is under age 59½ and the money is not rolled over into an IRA or a new employer plan, to a 10 percent tax penalty as well.

Closed-end fund. A professionally managed fund with a fixed number of shares that are publicly traded on a stock exchange.

Commission. A fee paid for buying and selling securities.

Conduit IRA. Also called a Rollover IRA. An IRA established to receive a lump-sum distribution from an employer-sponsored retirement plan

Contingent deferred sales charge. A sales commission ("load") paid when mutual fund shares are sold. Sometimes called a redemption fee, these charges may be phased out over several years.

Cost basis. The original purchase price of an investment, including any commissions or loads, reinvested dividends, or capital gains distributions. The cost basis is subtracted from the sales price to determine any capital gain or loss at the time of sale.

Credit risk. The possibility that a bond issuer may not be able to make periodic interest payments or repay the debt at maturity.

Custodian. The financial institution—typically, a bank, mutual fund, or stockbroker—responsible for safeguarding financial assets. You must choose a custodian for an Individual Retirement Account.

Daily valuation. A method of determining the value of your 401(k) account balance (or any investment) on a daily basis.

Default. Failure to pay principal or interest when due.

Defined benefit plan. A traditional pension plan in which fixed lifetime benefits are based on salary and years of service.

Disclaimer. The rejection of a bequest in favor of a secondary or contingent beneficiary.

Distribution. A payment made from a tax-sheltered retirement plan.

Diversification. The strategy of investing in a variety of asset classes in order to minimize the risk of loss on any one investment.

Dividend reinvestment plan (DRP). A method for automatically reinvesting cash dividends in additional shares. Many DRPs allow additional cash purchases at little or no cost.

Dollar cost averaging. The strategy of making regular fixed investments, thereby buying more shares when prices are down and fewer shares when prices are up and reducing the average cost of shares over time.

Dow Jones Industrial Average (DJIA). The Dow is the oldest and most widely quoted measure of stock market performance, although it represents the average of just 30 actively traded stocks on the New York Stock Exchange.

Duration. A measure of the sensitivity of bonds or bond funds to changing interest rates.

ERISA. The Employee Retirement Income Security Act of 1974, governing employee benefit plans.

ESOP. An employee stock ownership plan is a defined contribution plan in which plan assets are invested in the employer's stock.

Expense ratio. The amount paid for mutual fund operating expenses and management fees, expressed as a percentage of each shareholder's total investment.

Face value. The amount, stated on the face of the security, that a bond's issuer must repay at the maturity date.

Fiduciary. An individual or corporation entrusted with the management, investment, or disposition of property. Fiduciaries are required, under ERISA (see above), to make decisions based solely on the best interests of the plan participants.

Fixed-income investments. Securities, such as bonds and bond funds, that pay a regular stream of interest.

401(k) plan. An employer-sponsored retirement plan that permits plan participants to make tax-deferred contributions from their salaries to the plan.

403(b) plan. An employer-sponsored retirement plan, permitting employees of universities, public schools, and nonprofit organizations to make tax-deferred payroll contributions. Also called a tax-sheltered annuity (TSA).

457 plan. An employer-sponsored retirement plan, permitting employees of state and local governments and other tax-exempt employers to make tax-deferred contributions from their salary.

Growth stocks. Shares issued by companies with a strong likelihood of improved earnings. Growth stocks, unlike value stocks, typically generate much of their total return in the form of appreciation instead of ordinary income.

Guaranteed investment contract (GIC). An investment backed by an insurance company and available through defined contribution plans. Returns are guaranteed for a specific period of time.

Hardship withdrawal. Distributions permitted from some employer-sponsored retirement plans under specific conditions. Despite the hardship requirement, these distributions are subject to income tax and, if the participant is under age 59½, to the 10 percent tax penalty as well.

Highly compensated employee. An employee who owns 5 percent or more of the business or who is paid $85,000 or more (in 2000, indexed for inflation). As a measure to prevent discrimination in favor of highly paid employees, contributions to 401(k) plans by highly compensated employees may be limited if adequate numbers of rank-and-file employees do not participate.

Income in respect of decedent. A provision permitting an income tax deduction for the portion of estate tax attributable to an IRA, thereby avoiding double taxation on the same money.

Index. A measure of market performance, such as the Dow Jones Industrial Average or the Standard & Poor's 500 Composite Index.

Index fund. A mutual fund that holds the securities in a particular stock market index, thereby mirroring the performance of the index.

Keogh plan. A tax-sheltered retirement plan for the self-employed.

Large-cap stocks. Stocks of companies with large capitalization, generally defined as companies with total outstanding shares valued at $2 billion or more.

Liquidity. The ability to quickly and easily draw cash from invested assets.

Load. A fee or commission paid when buying or selling shares in some mutual funds.

Lump-sum distribution. A single payment from a retirement plan, made within a single tax year on the occasion of retirement (or other separation from service), death, disability, or attainment of age 59½.

Management fee. Charge paid to an investment adviser for running a mutual fund.

Maturity date. The date on which the principal amount of a bond is scheduled to be repaid to investors.

Municipal bond. A debt obligation issued by a state or local government. Interest on "munis" is generally free from federal income tax and may also be free from state and local income taxes.

Net asset value. The market value of mutual fund shares, calculated by subtracting the fund's liabilities from its assets and then dividing by the number of shares outstanding.

Net unrealized appreciation (NUA). The gain in company stock held in a retirement plan, from the date of initial purchase to the date of distribution.

Ordinary income. Any income taxed at ordinary tax rates instead of preferential capital gains tax rates. Ordinary income includes both earned income (wages, salaries, self-employment income) and unearned income (interest and dividends).

Passive investing. A strategy that seeks to mimic market performance, typically through investing in an index fund.

Pension Benefit Guaranty Corporation (PBGC). The federal agency that guarantees benefits from traditional defined benefit pension plans, up to specific limits, if the company goes into bankruptcy or closes its plan.

Portfolio. A collection of securities owned by an individual or an institution. It may include stocks, bonds, and cash equivalents.

Price/earnings ratio (P/E). Shows the "multiple" of earnings at which a stock sells. Determined by dividing the current share price by current earnings per share.

Principal. The amount of money originally put into an investment.

Profit-sharing plan. A flexible arrangement that lets corporate employees share in corporate profits, with defined contributions typically based on compensation and corporate earnings.

Prospectus. The legal document that sets forth information about a mutual fund. The prospectus is required to include the fund's investment objectives and policies, risks, costs, and past performance.

Qualified Domestic Relations Order (QDRO). A court order that recognizes someone other than the plan participant (typically, a former spouse) to receive some or all of the participant's retirement benefits.

Qualified retirement plan. A plan approved by the IRS and therefore eligible for favorable tax treatment.

Realized. When an asset is sold, the resulting gain or loss has been realized; until then, profits or losses are unrealized because they are only on paper.

Rebalancing. Periodically adjusting an asset allocation to keep it in line with the original allocation.

Recalculation. A method of determining the minimum required distributions from a qualified retirement plan, based on the life expectancies of the beneficiaries in each successive year. Recalculation was often the default method applied by plan administrators in the absence of another election by the participant.

Required beginning date (RBD). April 1 of the calendar year after the year in which 70½ is reached: the date on which IRA owners must begin taking required minimum distributions.

Required minimum distribution (RMD). The amount, based on life expectancy tables, that you must withdraw each year from tax-sheltered retirement plans. Withdrawals must start on April 1 of the year following the calendar year in which age 70½ is reached.

Rollover. A tax-free transfer from one retirement plan to another.

Roth IRA. An Individual Retirement Account in which contributions are not tax-deductible but withdrawals are not subject to income tax.

Rule of 72. A rule of thumb showing how long it will take money to double at various rates of interest. Divide the quoted rate of return into 72 for the answer. As an example, assuming that interest is compounded annually, money will double in nine years if invested at 8 percent.

SEP-IRA. A Simplified Employee Pension plan, often established by small businesses, in which the employer makes contributions for the employees.

SEPP. Substantially Equal Periodic Payments. Not to be confused with the SEP-IRA, SEPP is an arrangement whereby regular distributions from a tax-sheltered retirement plan avoid the 10 percent penalty on premature distributions.

SIMPLE. The Savings Incentive Match Plan for Employees can be used in companies with 100 or fewer employees.

Sector fund. A mutual fund concentrating on a specific industry group, such as health care or technology.

S&P 500. A performance index of the 500 largest stocks in the United States. Widely recognized as a measure for the entire stock market.

Spread. The difference between what an investor pays for a bond and what the bond dealer pays for it; the spread is the bond dealer's profit.

Surrender charge. A fee imposed on some investments when they are sold. An example would be a back-end charge or a contingent deferred sales charge on a mutual fund.

Tax-deferred. Descriptive of a vehicle, such as a retirement plan, in which interest, dividends, and capital gains are not taxed until the money is withdrawn.

Tax-exempt (tax-free). An investment, such as certain municipal bonds, for which the income is never subject to income tax.

Tax-sheltered annuity (TSA). Also known as a 403(b) plan, a TSA is a tax-sheltered retirement plan for employees of tax-exempt entities such as public schools.

Top-heavy plan. A defined contribution plan in which 60 percent of the total account balance is held by highly compensated employees.

Total return. The change in value of an investment over a given period of time, assuming reinvestment of all income; expressed as a percentage of the original investment.

Trust. A three-party arrangement under which a donor or grantor gives assets into management by a trustee or trustees for the eventual benefit of one or more beneficiaries.

12(b)1 fee. An annual fee imposed by some mutual funds and designed to cover the costs of marketing and distribution.

Unified credit. The federal tax credit applied to gifts and estates and therefore not subject to the unified gift and estate tax. At this writing, the credit is $675,000 per person. It is scheduled to rise to $1 million in 2006 and thereafter.

Unit Investment Trust (UIT). Similar to a mutual fund, but with an unmanaged portfolio in which shares are initially bought and then held until the trust is dissolved at its maturity date and proceeds are paid to shareholders.

Value stocks. Shares in companies with good long-term prospects that are currently undervalued, given the companies' potential for profit. These stocks, unlike growth stocks, tend to produce much of their return in the form of dividends (taxed as ordinary income) instead of capital gains (taxed at the lower capital gains rate).

Variable annuity. A tax-deferred insurance-based investment in which returns are based on an underlying portfolio of "subaccounts" similar to mutual funds.

Vested. Having rights to money in a retirement plan, typically after a specified period of service.

Volatility. Fluctuation in the values of securities. The greater the volatility, the wider the gap between high and low prices.

Yield. Earnings on an investment, typically expressed as a percentage

Yield to maturity. The amount earned on a bond over its lifetime when each interest payment is reinvested at the same rate of interest

Zero coupon bond. A bond sold at a deep discount from its face value, with no periodic payments of interest.

Appendix B
For More Information

Apostolou, Barbara, and Nicholas G. Apostolou, *Keys to Investing in Common Stocks* (Hauppauge, NY: Barron's Educational Series, Inc., 2000)

Apostolou, Nicholas G., and D. Larry Crumbley, *Keys to Understanding the Financial News* (Hauppauge, NY: Barron's Educational Series, Inc., 1994)

Apostolou, Nicholas G., *Keys to Conservative Investments* (Hauppauge, NY: Barron's Educational Series, Inc., 1996)

Berg, Stacie Zoe, *The Unofficial Guide to Investing in Mutual Funds* (New York: Macmillan, 1999)

Bogle, John C., *Bogle on Mutual Funds* (Burr Ridge, IL: Irwin Professional Publishing, 1994)

Boroson, Warren, *Keys to Investing in Mutual Funds* (Hauppauge, NY: Barron's Educational Series, 1997)

Brenner, George D., Stephen Abramson, Barry L. Rabinovich, Stanfield Hill, and Steven K. Rabinaw, *Plan Smart, Retire Rich* (New York: McGraw-Hill, 1999)

Chilton, David, *The Wealthy Barber* (Rocklin, CA: Prima Publishing, 1993)

Choate, Natalie B., *Life and Death Planning for Retirement Benefits* (Boston, MA: Ataxplan Publications, 1999). Designed for professionals in estate planning, this somewhat technical guide is worth a look.

Clements, Jonathan, *15 Myths You've Got to Avoid if You Want to Manage Your Money Right* (New York: Simon & Schuster, 1998)

Davis, Rod, *What You Need to Know Before You Invest* (Hauppauge, NY: Barron's Educational Series, 1999)

DeJong, David S., and Ann Gray Jakabcin, *J.K. Lasser's Year-Round Tax Strategies* (New York: Wiley, 2001)

Ernst & Young's Retirement Planning Guide (New York: Wiley, 2000)

Ernst & Young Tax Guide, The (New York: Wiley, issued annually)

Friedlob, George Thomas, and Ralph E. Welton, *Keys to Reading an Annual Report* (Hauppauge, NY: Barron's Educational Series, 1995)

Gardner, David, and Tom Gardner, *The Motley Fool Investment Guide* (New York: Simon & Schuster, 1996)

Godin, Seth, *If You're Clueless About Retirement Planning and Want to Know More* (Chicago: Dearborn, 1997)

Goldberg, Seymour, *J.K. Lasser's How to Protect Your Retirement Savings from the IRS* (New York: Wiley, 1999)

Hoffman, Ellen, *The Retirement Catch-Up Guide* (New York: Newmark Press, 2000)

Jacobs, Sheldon, *Sheldon Jacobs' Guide to Successful No-Load Investing* (Irvington-on-Hudson, NY: The No-Load Fund Investor, 1998)

Kess, Sidney, and Barbara E. Weltman, *CCH Retirement Planning Guide* (Chicago: CCH Incorporated, 2000)

Koch, Edward T., and Debra DeSalvo, *The Complete Idiot's Guide to Investing Like a Pro* (New York: Alpha Books, 1999)

J.K. Lasser's Your Income Tax (New York: Wiley, issued annually)

Lavine, Alan, Gail Liberman, and Jonathan D. Pond, *The Complete Idiot's Guide to Making Money with Mutual Funds* (New York: Alpha Books, second edition, 2000)

Lemke, Thomas P., and Gerald T. Lins, *How to Read a Mutual Fund Prospectus* (Great Falls, VA: Mercer Point Press, 1999)

Malaspina, Margaret A., *Don't Die Broke: How to Turn Your Retirement Savings into Lasting Income* (Princeton, NJ: Bloomberg Press, 1999)

Malkiel, Burton G., *A Random Walk Down Wall Street* (New York: W.W. Norton & Company, 1999)

Mamis, Justin, *The Nature of Risk* (Reading, MA: Addison-Wesley, 1991)

Maranjian, Selena, and Roy A. Lewis, *The Motley Fool's Investment Tax Guide 2000* (Alexandria, VA: The Motley Fool, 1999)

Morris, Kenneth M., and Alan M. Siegel, *The Wall Street Journal Guide to Understanding Personal Finance* (New York: Lightbulb Press, 1992)

Morris, Kenneth M., Alan M. Siegel, and Virginia B. Morris, *The Wall Street Journal Guide to Planning Your Financial Future* (New York: Lightbulb Press, 1995)

Morris, Virginia B., *Creating Retirement Income* (New York: Lightbulb Press, 1998)

O'Shaughnessy, Lynn, *The Unofficial Guide to Investing* (New York: Macmillan, 1999)

PriceWaterhouse, *Secure Your Future* (Burr Ridge, IL: Irwin Professional Publishing, 1996)

Rowland, Mary, *The New Commonsense Guide to Mutual Funds* (Princeton, NJ: Bloomberg Press, 1998)

Sease, Douglas, and John Prestbo, *Barron's Guide to Making Investment Decisions* (Englewood Cliffs, NJ: Prentice-Hall, 1994)

Slesnick, Twila, and John C. Suttle, *IRAs, 401(k)s & Other Retirement Plans: Taking Your Money Out* (Berkeley, CA: Nolo Press, 1998)

Strumeyer, Gary M., *Keys to Investing in Municipal Bonds* (Hauppauge, NY: Barron's Educational Series, Inc., 1996)

Tobias, Andrew, *The Only Investment Guide You'll Ever Need* (San Diego: Harcourt Brace, 1998)

The Vanguard Group, *Investing During Retirement* (Burr Ridge, IL: Irwin Professional Publishing, 1996)

Wasik, John F., *The Late-Start Investor* (New York: Owl Books, 1998)

Wasik, John F., *Retire Early and Live the Life You Want Now* (New York: Henry Holt, 2000)

Weinstein, Grace W., *The Complete Idiot's Guide to Tax-Free Investing* (New York: Alpha Books, 2000)

Web sites

www.aarp.org—information for retirees

www.ebri.org—research and surveys from the Employee Benefit Research Institute

www.fairmark.com—tax information and other useful stuff on traditional and Roth IRAs

www.financenter.com—calculators for number-crunching

www.fool.com—check out these tax strategies from The Motley Fool

www.401kafe.com—very useful features and retirement calculators

www.investinginbonds.com—step-by-step bond investing

www.investorama.com—wide-ranging financial news

www.irs.gov—for tax forms and information; for the latter, click onto "Tax Info For You"

www.mfea.com—the Mutual Fund Education Association, representing low-cost mutual funds, offers educational information

www.moneycentral.com—wide-ranging financial news, including retirement planning and tax information

www.morningstar.com—lots of information, including calculators for IRA eligibility, comparisons between traditional and Roth IRAs, and Roth conversions

www.quicken.com—investing, financial planning, tax tools, and information

www.rothira.com—information specifically on Roth IRAs

www.savingsbond.gov—for information on Series EE bonds and other savings bonds

www.ssa.gov—information about Social Security and online filing for benefits

www.taxplanet.com—tax tables, forms, and information

www.teamvest.com—Quicken's 401(k) Advisor, with fund-specific recommendations for participants in more than 1,100 company plans

www.thestreet.com—stock market news

www.troweprice.com—retirement calculators and information from T. Rowe Price

Index